FINANCING STATE AND LOCAL GOVERNMENTS IN THE 1980S

Financing State and Local Governments in the 1980s

Issues and Trends

edited by
Norman Walzer

Western Illinois University

David L. Chicoine

*University of Illinois
Urbana-Champaign*

 Oelgeschlager, Gunn & Hain, Publishers, Inc.
Cambridge, Massachusetts

International Standard Book Number: 0-89946-109-3

Library of Congress Catalog Card Number: 81-11085

Printed in West Germany

Library of Congress Cataloging in Publication Data
Main entry under title:

Financing state and local governments in the 1980s.

  Includes index.
  1. Finance, Public—United States—States—Addresses, essays, lectures. 2. Local finance—United States—Addresses, essays, lectures. I. Walzer, Norman.
II. Chicoine, David L. JH275.F54   350.72'0973   81-11085
                                                            AACR2

ISBN 0-89946-109-3

Contents

v

List of Figures

List of Tables

Preface

The tax limitation movement of the late 1970s and the proposed cutbacks of intergovernmental aid to state and local governments by the Reagan administration have created a climate of uncertainty and confusion for policy makers regarding the future of state and local finance. Rampant inflation and a sluggish national economy have placed many governments in a serious fiscal squeeze. These conditions are aggravated further when residents seek to cut back revenue-raising powers at a time when public employees are becoming more adamant in their demands for wage increases.

In light of the importance of recent events for the future of state and local finance, we assembled a panel of experts in the various areas of state and local finance asking them to review the trends in the 1970s and to speculate about the implications for the first half of the next decade. This book is an outcome of that conference.

Many persons have assisted in the assembling of the conference at which most of these papers were presented, and it is not possible to thank each individually. However, several individuals deserve special recognition. Financial support was provided by Dr. Harvey J. Schweitzer, Cooperative Extension Division, University of Illinois; Walt Armbruster, Farm Foundation; George Dinges, Department of Commerce and Community Affairs, State of Illinois;

and Terrel E. Clarke, Local Government Finance Study Commission, State of Illinois. Special thanks go to Richard McClure and David A. Ward for their assistance. Gratitude also goes to Douglas and Virginia Norvell for their assistance in copy editing the papers. Without the assistance of these and many other persons this book would not have materialized.

N. W.
D. L. C.

Introduction

The 1970s represent an exciting decade for students of state and local finance. In 1972, the State and Local Fiscal Assistance Act brought a major new program of federal funds to 39,000 state and local governments. In addition to receiving more intergovernmental aid, local policy makers received greater discretion over the projects on which the money could be spent through the use of block grants.

During the early 1970s, however, inflation had become a serious problem for many local governments. The costs of providing services were rising, in some cases faster than the revenues available to provide services. For governments reliant on income and sales taxes, such as state governments, the picture was much brighter, though. States were able to increase spending to meet the needs of residents and in some instances accumulate substantial budgetary balances.

The latter 1970s brought a very different era, however. Citizen discontent with rising tax bills and increases in public sector spending culminated with the passage of Proposition 13 in California in June 1978. While Proposition 13 was by no means the first expression of taxpayer discontent, the wide publicity it received and the magnitude of tax reduction it provided triggered a series of tax and spending limitation movements across the nation. The attitude of taxpayers had become more adamant against tax increases, particularly of property taxes.

The tax limitation movement was not limited to state and local governments, however. Candidates for national office had promised attempts to balance the federal budget and other tax relief measures, but relatively little had been accomplished in this direction. A movement to call a constitutional convention to consider the issue of requiring a balanced federal budget was gaining the approval of many state legislatures, and such a convention seemed a possibility at the close of the decade.

The election of the Reagan administration on a platform of federal budget cuts and tax relief signaled a new era in public sector spending. Many of the liberal spending programs developed during the period of major income tax growth were threatened. Candidates, nationwide, who in earlier years had voted for large spending increases on social programs were not returned to office. Elected in their place were persons who had campaigned for smaller government, fewer regulations, and programs to stimulate private sector development. The tide had turned and liberals, who in the past had favored higher federal spending, were now supporting spending cutbacks and income tax relief.

This climate left many state and local officials confused. Surveys taken at the voting booths showed that voters favoring property tax relief also favored a continuation of most public programs, although they apparently did not favor increases in welfare spending. Voters were convinced that there was fat in the budgets and that taxes could be lowered without cutting essential services. In the wake of the tax reduction programs, local officials were left to determine which programs should be eliminated and whether they could obtain additional revenues from non-property tax sources.

State and local officials, in 1980, also faced the possible loss of General Revenue Sharing, the highly popular program begun in 1972. Although the program was finally renewed at the eleventh hour, the funding level was less than hoped for and state governments were eliminated from the program for at least one year. The attitude in Washington was shifting away from support for state and local governments, at least on as broad a scale as in the past.

Thus, public officials had to accept the facts that revenue growth was going to be less than in the past and that an era of fiscal constraint had begun. While they perhaps could recoup some of the lost revenues from user charges or fees from services, the opportunities for raising significant revenues from these sources are limited, especially when residents have been pushing for reduced taxes and controls on government spending.

After the November election and during the early months of 1981, it was quite clear that state and local governments, in many states, were going to have to make do with less. Tax referendums were defeated and, in many instances, local officials had to work to keep the revenue sources they had. The role of the federal government was a big question, and rumors were that significant cutbacks in specific programs were coming. The real questions were, how much and in what areas?

PURPOSE OF THIS BOOK

The challenges facing state and local policy makers during the next several years and the events that occured during the latter half of the 1970s make it imperative for policy makers to take stock of recent events and to examine what lies ahead for state and local public finance. A panel of state and local finance scholars was assembled to assess the impact of taxing and spending limitations on the ability of state and local governments to finance public services in the next decade. The contributors were also asked to examine the proposed policies of the Reagan administration and speculate on their impact on state and local public finance.

Students, practitioners, and policy makers will find the chapters in this volume informative and thought provoking. The authors have placed recent events in perspective and have attempted to illustrate some of the long-range effects of the programs under consideration. While some of the implications for state and local finance are not bright, the issues that policy makers must face are nonetheless considered.

The following chapters are arranged by topic. The discussion begins with chapters on the trends in fiscal condition of large cities and the nationwide effects of the tax limitation movements. Each major revenue source is then examined in detail to identify trends and develop a prognosis for the immediate future.

Attention is turned next to shifts, nationwide, in fiscal capacity and tax burden with an effort made to evaluate the potential of the currently proposed programs to stimulate economic development in central cities. The discussion concludes with thought given to the types of issues that must be faced in the 1980s if attempts continue to balance the federal budget.

Fiscal Condition and Tax Limitations

The tax limitation movements have left many policy makers uncertain about the future. On the one hand, policy makers hear requests for a particular program or service. On the other hand, taxpayers are voting to limit the amount of taxes that can be imposed or total government spending. Some supporters of tax limitations say that more should be provided with less, while others think the government is providing the appropriate amount of most public services.

There have been many explanations offered for tax limitation support. Are citizens frustrated by high inflation and attempting to reduce outlays for public services so that they can spend more on private goods? Do voters think that only programs affecting other residents will be cut and therefore the savings in taxes will represent a net gain? Do residents believe that governments tend to waste money and that a tax cut can be accomplished without any real cut in services? Finally, is it possible that voters do not understand enough about public finance to make an intelligent voting decision and, if they had more information, might they vote differently?

Clark describes a method of assessing the fiscal strain facing a government so that insight into financial problems besetting a city in the future can be obtained. Particular attention is paid to the partnerships between public and private agencies that may be needed to make the city financially sound. The options available for local officials to rebuild the economic base of the city in the present climate of tax resistance are then considered. It is quite clear that local officials must carefully assess their current fiscal condition before embarking on new programs or getting involved in major new developments. Priority must be given to long-term development of the economic base in the community if a long-range solution to the fiscal problems is to be found.

Brazer examines the tax limitation movements that have occurred across the nation in the context of theories about size of government and taxpayers' preferences for services. Using evidence from the recent tax limitation movements in California, Massachusetts, and Michigan, he examines motives for supporting tax limitation movements, and speculates on the impact of these limitations for financing local services in the future.

Much concern following the fiscal crises in New York City has been given to determining the fiscal condition of large central cities. Many of these cities have experienced an exodus of wealth and economic activity while, at the same time, experienced an immigration of minorities and economically disadvantaged populations. Shrinking tax bases and increasing costs of public services have created considerable fiscal strain to the point that cities such as New York have been on the edge of bankruptcy.

The tax limitations imposed have seriously affected the ability of some large cities to provide services. Following the passage of Proposition 2 ½ in Massachusetts, for example, the school system in Boston ran out of funds and the mass transit system was on the verge of shutting down. Of course, the tax limitations are not the only, and probably not even the most significant cause of the fiscal problems facing these cities, where a process of economic decline has been underway for decades. The populations in these cities need high-cost services. The capital stock is depleted. The relatively high tax rates needed to finance the city accelerate the outmigration of business activity.

Property Tax Trends

For many years the property tax has been the mainstay of local governments nationwide. The tax was relatively easy to collect, it provided a stable revenue source, and it could be administered locally. However, property taxes, in recent years, have not been popular. Residents must pay one or two large installments, and property tax increases are not directly related to increases in income.

The majority of the tax limitation controversy in the 1970s centered on the property tax. Rising housing values in California brought unprecedented increases in property tax payments by residents. These increases met with major opposition that culminated in the passage of Proposition 13. The rest is history.

The growing resistance against the property tax came at a time when property taxes represent a declining share of state and local tax collections. Fisher examines the changing role that property taxes play in the financing of state and local services and speculates about the future for this revenue source. In particular, he asks whether the property tax has not been instrumental in the stability of the structure of local governments. If many of the local governments, as they now exist, had to finance services from another revenue source, could they survive? If not, what other governmental arrangements would be forthcoming?

One reason for the declining importance of property taxes has been the property tax relief programs across the country, instituted because of mandates from voters or because of a state budgetary surplus. These programs include homestead exemptions, circuit breakers, and outright property tax reductions. In other instances, public officials, fearful of taxpayer opposition, simply did not raise taxes and chose to cut back services instead.

Gold describes the property tax relief programs instituted in twelve Midwestern states. These states have been leaders in providing property tax relief and provide an excellent laboratory for studying the effects of a number of such programs.

Property tax relief in the 1980s is difficult to predict. Certainly pressures for such relief will continue. However, most state governments, at least in the very near future, will not be in a financial position to provide such programs. Thus, any relief provided may come from state-imposed programs. If this is true, local governments will face even greater pressures in financing services and will search for other revenue sources.

Non-Property Tax Revenues

The decline in relative importance of property taxes was also accommodated by a significant increase in federal support to state and local governments. In 1950, for instance, federal aid was 10.4 percent of state and local expenditures; but by 1979 it had increased to 25.4 percent.[1] Much of this growth came about as a result of the categorical grants initiated during the 1960s with a recognition that state and local governments were facing growing demands that were outstripping their resources for providing services. A large infusion of funds was provided with General Revenue Sharing and block grants in the 1970s.

Dommel examines trends in intergovernmental aid, traces the growth in the various elements, and speculates about the outlook for these programs in the immediate future. The prospects for continued federal intergovernmental assistance at existing levels are not bright. A decline in constant and current dollars is expected as these programs compete with other demands for federal revenues.

The impact of the reductions in federal support will depend on the specific programs affected and the dependence by recipient governments on this support. Cutbacks in the state portion of General Revenue Sharing, for example, will probably mean reduced intergovernmental aid for local governments. Those governments that have come to rely heavily on federal support will have to find alternative revenue sources.

With increased resistance to property tax increases and the prognosis for intergovernmental assistance not being bright, how are state and local services going to be financed in the future? Spain and Wooldridge indicate that nonproperty tax revenues will assume a growing importance. Growth in nonproperty tax revenues during the 1970s appears to have been in the user charges and "other taxes" categories, including taxes on amusements and similar activities. Part of the growth in user charges resulted from pressures caused by property tax limits. The slow growth in the relative importance of sales and income taxes may have resulted because of a reluctance by state legislatures to increase local government authority in these areas.

There is little doubt but that governments will place increased emphasis on user charges in the future as pressures on the property tax increase. However, the opportunities for pricing public services are limited and it is hard to imagine user charges ever becoming a major revenue source, with the exception of enterprise funds such as sewer and water or parking. In a time of fiscal restraint, however, the benefits of finding public services that can be shifted to the private sector or financed by fees are obvious.

While revenues from taxes, user charges, and intergovernmental aid provide the main support for local services, in some instances borrowing represents a reasonable method for financing services. Construction of a major new facility will usually be financed by municipal borrowing so that future generations benefiting from the service pay a share of the cost.

The market for municipal debt has undergone marked changes during the past decade. Prior to 1970, general obligation bonds, sometimes known as full faith and credit debt, constituted a majority of debt issued by local governments. By the end of the decade, however, another type of debt—revenue bonds, which are retired with the proceeds of the project being financed—had replaced general obligation debt as the dominant form and increased to nearly 70 percent of the market.

Petersen explores changes during the 1970s in the capital markets in which state and local governments obtain credit with special attention paid to changes by class of borrower and projects financed. He concludes with a brief glimpse of capital markets in the future.

Changes in Fiscal Capacity and Tax Burden

In the 1970s much attention was paid to population shifts from the Northeast and Midwest to the South and West. The regions losing population and economic resources encounter declining tax bases and experience greater difficulty providing public services.

Major population shifts and shifts in the location of industry will require significant readjustments by public officials in the regions undergoing change. Growing areas presumably will have the resources needed to accommodate the population changes. Declining areas, on the other hand, will encounter substantial difficulty as they attempt to cut back the public sector.

Some of the difficulties that must be faced by public officials during the 1980s are outlined by Phares. Particular attention is paid to a possible need for realignment of responsibility for services and powers to raise revenues. Governments that will be called upon to provide more services are not necessarily the ones with the authority to raise revenues. The past several years of tax and expenditure limitations and the current thrust to slow the increase in federal spending requires a re-examination of the abilities of governments to provide services for which they are responsible. Any realignment will certainly involve a careful review of intrastate revenue sharing. During the 1980s state governments will be in a position to assume a greater role in financing services.

The Reagan administration has proposed a series of economic development programs and block grants to alleviate the fiscal problems facing aging central cities. A key component of the proposed approach is the use of enterprise zones. Depressed or blighted areas within a city would be designated as enterprise zones. Businesses locating in these areas and hiring a certain proportion of their work force from the zone would qualify for tax subsidies. These businesses would benefit from accelerated depreciation of assets, reductions in capital gains taxes, reduced corporate tax rates, reductions in property taxes, and wage subsidies.

Jacobs and Wasylenko examine the enterprise zone concept as a tool for urban development to assess its appropriateness for large U.S. cities. Their study makes quite clear that certain types of firms stand to benefit from these subsidies. In particular, firms with a high proportion of costs in labor and capital will be the large gainers as compared with firms employing large amounts of materials and energy. The effectiveness of the enterprise zone concept may be limited by attempting to combine the objectives of urban revitalization and employment stimulation into a single program. Jacobs and Wasylenko ask whether these two objectives might not be more effectively accomplished with two separate strategies. In their essay, Jacobs and Wasylenko offer several suggestions for changing the proposed approach to enhance the chances of the enterprise zone concept to succeed. Since the key to any long-term solution to the financial problems facing large central cities involves a rebuilding of the economic base, the proposed development policies need to receive careful attention.

Issues for the 1980s

The 1980s began with high inflation, a lagging economy, pressures for cutbacks in government spending, and demands for tax relief. The notion that a balanced federal budget might hold the key to controlling inflation has gained considerable support. The idea of a balanced federal budget is certainly not a novel idea, having been promised by both Presidents Ford and Carter, but the concept took on new meaning with the large support obtained by President Reagan. One interpretation of the election results was that voters had sent a message to Washington that the federal government had become too large and actions must be taken to at least reduce its rate of growth, if not its absolute size.

The first several months of 1981 gave notice that difficult times lie ahead for many groups and institutions. State and local governments are going to have to make do with less federal assistance. With the exception of the military, the federal cuts are to be across the board with some programs being completely phased out.

Haider examines the political processes involved in attempting to balance the federal budget and traces the reasons behind the ever growing deficit. In particular, he examines the budgeting process per se to illustrate the way in which factors operate to increase budgets and complicate the balancing effort.

It is virtually certain that in the federal cut backs intergovernmental aid will be a casualty. The loss of federal aid will occur for several reasons. As has already been noted, the military sector will assume a larger share of the total federal budget. Underspending in the past has created a need to strengthen the military capabilities of the United States in the near future. Second, the largest growth in federal spending in recent years has been in transfer payments and programs tied to inflation or other formula components. One might expect that assistance to the aged, Social Security, and payments for health care for the needy will continue to increase as long as inflation runs rampant. Thus, at the very least, the future of federal support for state and local services looks bleak.

The tax limitations and reductions in intergovernmental support will be manifested in reduced expenditures by state and local governments. In fact, since 1977 this slowdown has been apparent. According to Shannon, it was triggered by four major events: the 1974-1975 recession, the New York fiscal crisis, Proposition 13, and the election of a new administration with a conservative attitude toward government spending. In his essay, Shannon examines the events during the late 1970s that will bring several significant adjustments in state and local finance. The role of the federal government will definitely decrease. This may be evidenced not only by reductions in support but also by a shifting of the financing of services to state and local governments. Second, it seems likely that, with access to sales and income taxes, state governments will assume a greater role in financing services. This increased importance may also be brought about by the federal government's reformulation of grant programs giving state government greater responsibilities.

While much of the above discussion has presented a somewhat bleak picture for state and local governments, there certainly are regions in the United States that will escape many of these problems. States with growing tax bases, and particularly those with energy resources, will be in a much better position than their counterparts in other areas of the country. States such as Alaska, for example, will find their treasuries swelling at unprecedented rates. Cochran and Prestidge explore the growing disparity among states in revenues obtained from royalty and severance taxes. They indicate that the 1980s will bring a new era of competition among states and will create an even greater need for a study of the way in which public services are financed. The widening differences in fiscal capacity will surely be an important item on the agenda for the 1980s.

The 1970s, particularly the latter half, brought many significant changes in the structure of state and local government finance. State and local policy makers are facing taxpayer resistance at the same time that inflation is driving the costs of public services higher. The 1980s may represent one of the most important decades in this century as we struggle to bring responsibility for providing services in line with the fiscal capacity to provide them. A careful examination of the issues covered in this volume will assist in broadening the perspective of state and local officials who face these increasingly complex issues daily.

NOTE

1. *Significant Features of Fiscal Federalism,* 1979, (Washington, D.C.: Advisory Commission on Intergovernmental Relations, 1980), Table 52.

PART I

Background and Overview

Chapter 1

Urban Fiscal Strain: Trends and Policy Options

Terry Nichols Clark*

Three trends important for cities in the 1980s are movement of population and jobs, a slowdown in federal aid, and state and local fiscal retrenchment. The three trends combine to force a questioning of many current urban policies. For some cities the three have already generated considerable fiscal strain, which is likely to increase further in many instances. But while the three trends all have national and regional linkages, they are translated into policies that may or may not generate fiscal strain at the local level. It is reasonable for analysts to consider what local officials both can and cannot affect. This paper stresses what they can affect, thus concentrating on trends and policy options most directly important for local officials and their friends. But it stresses that a critical part of leadership is to recognize what one can and cannot change, and to allocate resources appropriately.

This paper was prepared with partial support from USPHS HD13121-01. Portions of it draw on material for a presentation to the Convocation on Status of the Cities, sponsored by the Department of Housing and Urban Development, U.S. Conference of Mayors, and National League of Cities, Washington, D.C., April–May 1979 and an editorial introduction to a special issue on "Community Development: Decision-Making and Public Performance," of *Urban Affairs Papers,* 1981, in press.

*Associate Professor of Sociology, University of Chicago

THREE BASIC TRENDS

Relocation of population and jobs in the 1980s is likely to continue following the broad trends of the last decades, including growth of many smaller suburban and nonmetropolitan areas, especially in the South and West. Many larger central cities of the Northeast and Midwest are likely to continue to decline in jobs and population. These trends are driven largely by national, private sector forces over which individual cities have limited control during the short terms to which most public officials are elected. Many observers have suggested that such trends bring fiscal strain to cities. I suggest below that this need not be so. But there is still no doubt as to the importance of the general trend for cities. My concern below is with the policy options appropriate for addressing the trend.

One national policy option has been federal aid to cities. Cities declining in jobs and population were baptized "distressed" in the 1970s, and given special treatment in a variety of urban administrative procedures as part of the Carter National Urban Policy. New programs such as Urban Development Action Grants were devised, and efforts made to "target" federal funds to distressed cities. But efforts to target funds toward specific problems ran counter to stronger pressures from local officials to decategorize and deregulate aid to cities. Ever since the multiplication of categorical grants in the 1960s, local officials have pressed for more general assistance, and the success they achieved in creating General Revenue Sharing and in consolidating individual categoricals into broader block grants seems to have a more responsive ear in Washington in the early 1980s than just a few years earlier. Nevertheless, if deregulation and more autonomy in federal grants seem likely, so is a decline in dollar volume. The implication is that local officials probably can and will be asked to think more for themselves about how to use more limited federal funds to achieve more locally defined goals. This presents a challenge in that it is sometimes easy to blame the Feds when things go wrong; harder choices seem in store for local officials themselves.

The third trend makes choices all the more focused: fiscal retrenchment is likely to continue at state and local levels. The taxpayers' revolts receiving most publicity were aimed at state spending, as in Propositions 13 and 2½. A majority of the states now have adopted some form of tax cap or spending limitation. Since about 40 percent of "state" aid to cities has been "pass-through" monies of the federal government, neither this portion nor state-generated revenue is likely to grow at past rates. Both may continue to grow in absolute dollars in selected states with expansive economies, but the growth rate relative to the population and private sector is likely to decline for cities in all parts of the country.

These three trends are important as background for this paper, but they are taken here as givens. The questions I ask are, What kinds of policy options are reasonable for local officials and their friends to consider to help adapt to such trends? What in particular can we say about "public-private partnerships" and adapting to fiscal strain? The remainder of the paper addresses these questions.

PUBLIC-PRIVATE PARTNERSHIPS

Discussions of urban or community development often imply a public-private partnership to encourage growth in jobs, population, and local government revenues, with the federal government cast in a key role via intergovernmental grants, like Community Development Block Grants (CDBGs) or Urban Development Action Grants (UDAGs). But how valid is this view? Consider the logic of some basic relationships in Figure 1.1, which

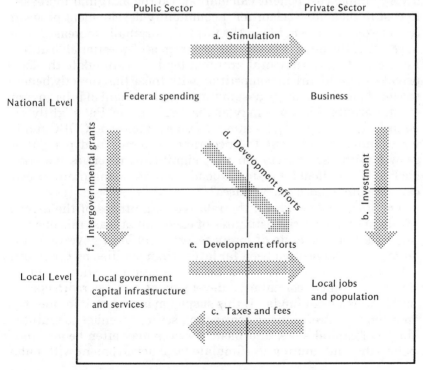

Figure 1.1. Major flows of funds affecting local governments.

distinguishes private from public sectors, and national from local
levels, thus indicating four separate actors. Arrows portray the
major resource flows among the actors. Arrow *a* suggests that the
national government can stimulate private sector growth, which in
turn shifts the flow of jobs (arrow *b*) in different local areas. Increases in jobs and population result for some; others decline.

A key policy question is how large are the impacts of different
arrows linking the local jobs and population box to the three others.
Increases in jobs and population can add revenues to local government (arrow *c*); indeed the absence of such growth often leads local
public officials to search for policies to strengthen the economic
base. Resulting policies of federal and local governments (arrows *d*
and *e*) are often designed to enhance growth or curtail decline (in
population and jobs). But the hard question for local officials and
their friends is how much is it in their interest to press for programs
like those of arrows *d* or *e*? This question has two parts: (1) How
much impact do arrows *d* and *e* have on changing the location of
population and jobs? and (2) if there is some such development,
how much revenue does it return to the city government? Consider
a very simple cost-benefit calculation. Do the marginal increases,
in cost to the public sector for a community development program
($d + e$) exceed the benefits in the form of marginally increased revenues (c)? If the answer is yes, the program is of questionable utility.
Further, intergovernmental grants intended to stimulate the local
private sector (d) are in competition with those that directly benefit
the local public sector (f), assuming a constant total of intergovernmental grants. Thus one may ask is $c + f \geq d + e$? Put slightly differently, is it in a local government's interest to spend CDBG funds,
for example, to attempt to encourage economic and population
growth with the expectation that significant revenues will flow
back to it? Or should it instead spend the funds to maintain its own
capital plant and basic services?

The answer depends on the relative magnitudes of the arrows.
We do not have precise estimates of each, but at least this observer
suspects that the costs of many federal and local government efforts ($d + e$) have often been far larger than justified by the returns
(c). They have been founded on unrealistic expectations of the
degree to which community development can be redirected by
small infusions of funds.[1] If this suspicion is correct, it implies that
in a time of retrenchment, redirecting scarce revenues to maintain
the local capital stock and basic services may often be a sounder
policy than attempting to stimulate local development with public

funds. Of course such calculations depend on the relative importance assigned to different goals, and development has long been an almost sacred goal in itself for many Americans. But we are at a point where one must ask how much it is reasonable to spend if the goal is not growth per se, but rather maintaining a viable local government.

These ideological issues are especially complex for many recently elected Republicans. The normal expectation of Republicans (and many Democrats) is that the private sector works better when unfettered by government. This is consistent with our analysis of local growth dynamics. But in choosing among government programs, should one favor those oriented toward private sector growth or government itself? A Republican response here may be less clear, but my suggestion is that if government spending is going to be decreased anyway, it might be best to cut those programs that attempt to stimulate the private sector. Their benefits are questionable and largely undemonstrated, while basic municipal services are essential and faltering in many cities.

Calculations may be particularly unrealistic if arrow *f* is ignored. That is, in the past, local officials have often treated their likely level of UDAG funds, for example, as unrelated to those from General Revenue Sharing. For selected cities there may be enough "slack" that intergovernmental revenues could be increased through more concerted grantsmanship. But this strategy has definite limits. If plausible for a few cities, it is unreasonable for many others, and especially for cities in the aggregate.[2] If a city were given all intergovernmental revenues as part of a single grant, and it had the option of spending funds either to attempt to stimulate local development, or to maintain its own capital infrastructure and public services, it might well spend more on the latter. This by no means implies that local officials should not seek to encourage local development efforts, help coordinate projects, and contribute some local funds. It suggests only that they consider carefully if what they are spending is justified compared to alternative uses of the funds, especially "self-development" of the city government.[3] A local government with a good physical plant, basic services, and low taxes may encourage more development over time than if it neglects these concerns to raise development funds. "Self-investment" in a city's capital infrastructure and basic services generates public goods shared by many firms as well as individual citizens. Subsidies, by contrast, are separable or semiprivate goods usually available only to a single firm. As long as the public goods are such basics as bridges, streets, and water, they are essential for most firms and probably should be given higher priority than subsidies to individual firms.[4]

If cities followed such "self-development" policies, they would also alleviate their fiscal strain, the subject of the remainder of this chapter. But to address questions of fiscal strain more precisely, it is useful to consider alternative conceptions of fiscal strain, next causes of fiscal strain, and then turn to policy implications.

ALTERNATIVE CONCEPTIONS OF FISCAL STRAIN

What is urban fiscal strain? Many policy discussions in this area have been troubled by a lack of focus. The approach I have developed with co-workers in Chicago differs from two others. One is that fiscal strain may be gauged by performance of a city in the bond market, bond ratings, and related indicators. This is reasonable for the investor, but less useful for city officials and others concerned with what it is that causes performance in the bond market. A second conception defines fiscal strain using measures of the private sector resources in the city, such as gains or losses in jobs and population. I feel that this is important, but only half the story.

My definition of fiscal strain by contrast is *the degree to which municipal expenditures and debt are adapted to the city's private sector resources.* Fiscal strain can thus be measured by computing ratios of municipal expenditure and debt to such resources as the level and change in population, median family income, and equalized property tax base. I have computed and analyzed many such indicators for a national sample of 62 cities.[5]

A related approach uses funds flows, such as revenues minus expenditures in a city's general fund, or totals of these for all state and local governments. The problem with these is less conceptual than methodological. They are often misleading due to differences in accounting practices across local governments, such as cash or accrual basis, differences as to what is included in the general fund across cities or over time, etc.[6] And if aggregated across state and local governments, they ignore all differences across cities.

Causes of Fiscal Strain

Consider next the causes of fiscal strain. These are of two general sorts: (1) those affecting what the city government does in terms of

expenditure and debt, and (2) those affecting private sector resources. These basic ideas may be shown in the following simple
equation:

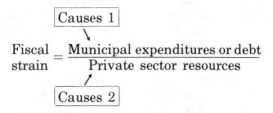

The separate boxes and arrows suggest separate and distinct
causes for the numerator and the denominator. Changes in either
one can generate fiscal strain. In particular, cities losing jobs and
population do not inevitably have fiscal strain. They become fiscally strained only if their spending and borrowing policies get out
of balance with these private sector changes. This general point
was made in *How Many New Yorks?* and it has gradually become
more accepted, such as in reports by Treasury, CBO, and Touche
Ross/First Boston.[7] Nevertheless, it has not yet been recognized
by everyone. And it does imply a serious rethinking of many still
widely accepted views. This issue can be illustrated using three
examples. All three document the basic point concerning the relative independence of municipal fiscal policy from private sector
resources. *Private sector resources do not automatically determine
city fiscal policies.*

Example 1 appears in Figure 1.2, a simple cross tabulation of
cities on the two basic dimensions of fiscal strain. It shows that
cities may be high or low independently on each. Pittsburgh and
Schenectady are low on such private sector resources as taxable

		Municipal Expenditures[a]	
		Low	High
Private-Sector Resources[b]	Low	Pittsburgh 1 Schenectady	Newark 2 Atlanta
	High	San Diego 3 Houston	New York City 4 San Francisco

[a]Especially common functions per capita, debt, and total expenditures
[b]Taxable property value and median family income

Figure 1.2. The two basic dimensions of fiscal strain.

property value and median family income, but also in city government expenditures. Expenditures are adjusted for the range of functions performed using a new method.[8] Although not wealthy cities, they have kept expenditures reasonably consistent with their private sector resources in such a manner that their fiscal strain ratios are not high. Newark and Atlanta also are low in terms of private sector resources, but spend at higher levels than Pittsburgh and Schenectady, and thus are high on fiscal strain. San Diego and Houston have strong economic bases, and low spending, and thus very low fiscal strain ratios. New York and San Francisco are reasonably wealthy cities, but also spend at high levels, so they have medium to high fiscal strain scores, depending on the specific indicators considered (see Figure 1.3).[9]

If fiscal strain were solely determined by private sector resources, all the cities would be in boxes 2 and 3. The fact that cities are found in all four boxes illustrates the independence of the two dimensions. In passing, note that Figure 1.2 suggests another point: the Northeast-Sunbelt characterization is too simplistic. Cities in the Northeast like Pittsburgh and Schenectady may be in reasonably good fiscal health, while Southern and Western cities like Atlanta or San Francisco may be fiscally strained.

Still, one may ask if these eight are representative of U.S. cities. Hence our second example to document the same basic point is shown in Table 1.1. These are simple correlations between several measures of private sector resources and municipal expenditure and debt. These are based on the Permanent Community Sample, a randomly selected national sample of 62 cities. All correlations are low, the population and economic base measures explaining no more than 31 percent of the variance in the expenditure and debt measures (that is, 0.56 squared). This, like the other findings reported here, is excerpted from technical reports that provide further

Municipal
Expenditures

		Low	High
Private-Sector Resources	Low	M	H
	High	L	M

Figure 1.3. Fiscal strain ratios for four types of cities in Figure 1.2.

Table 1.1. Relationships Between Economic and Demographic Indicators and Fiscal Indicators

	LPOP[a] 6070	LPOP 7075	LPOP 6075	CITY AGE	N.E.	N.E. and N. Central	LPOP 75T	CITY DE70	PC70 LOCL	PC70 NONW	PC70 OLDH
FS27072	−.09	−.2284	−.14	.2279	.2029	.0826	.1793	.5629	−.2865	−.0837	.2486
FS01Y76	−.006	−.2038	−.066	.4819	.0326	−.1559	.5829	.2107	.3109	.3424	.0693
FS08Y76	−.3410	−.397	−.3924	.5111	.1691	−.0031	.3899	.5283	.2272	.3706	.4061

Note: Correlations are Pearson rs. Those above .21 are significant at the .10 level; above .32 they are significant at the .01 level.

[a]Key to acronymns

FS27072:   Total local tax burden per capita, 1972
FS01Y76:   Long-term debt per capita, 1976
FS08Y76:   Expenditures per capita on nine common functions, 1976
LPOP6070:   Log of percent change in population 1960–1970
LPOP7075:   Log of percent change in population 1970–1975
LPOP6075:   Log of percent change in population 1960–1975
CITY AGE: Decade when city reached 20,000 population
N.E.:   1 if Northeastern Region, 0 if not
N.E. and N. Central: 1 if Northeastern or North Central Region, 0 if not
LPOP75T: Log of population in 1975
CITYDE70:   Population per square mile, 1970
PC70LOCL: Percentage of families with income under $3,000, 1970
PC70NONW: Percentage of families nonwhite, 1970
PC700LDH: Percentage of housing constructed before 1950

Similar analyses have been completed for sixteen measures of long-term debt, general expenditure, common functions, and own-source revenues using changes from 1960–1970, 1970–1974, and 1974–1977, and 1977 levels of each. The results are similar to those here: most correlations are weak or insignificant.

11

detail. But for bottom-line statisticians, this suggests simply that these private sector resource measures are only weak determinants of municipal fiscal policy. This is the same story told in Figure 1.2 for the eight cities.

Example 3 is a case study of an individual city, documenting the specific procedures by which expenditures and debt have changed in recent years.[10] The same pattern could be seen if several individual cities were studied carefully. Space permits only a very quick overview of one, Pittsburgh, which achieved its present fiscal position in good part due to the dramatic efforts of Mayor Peter Flaherty from 1970 to 1977. Pittsburgh was declining in jobs and population, losing its tax base, increasing in its percentage of minority and poverty residents, and facing problems common to many other older Northeastern cities. But in Pittsburgh these problems were recognized earlier than elsewhere, and from 1970 to 1974, when most city governments were still growing rapidly, Flaherty trimmed the municipal work force by 18 percent and reduced property taxes. Critics looked for corresponding service reductions, but found almost none; this seems to have been achieved through a dramatic productivity program, spearheaded by the mayor and his top staff, who would personally arrive on worksites and help formulate improvements in working conditions. There may have been a lot of room for improvement in Pittsburgh, but one top aide commented: "We could do the same thing in most big cities east of the Mississippi."

Through these three examples we have seen that government fiscal policy and private sector resources vary quite independently. Cities may be high or low on either one, separately of their position on the other.

If we move back further, however, what can be said of the respective causes of the two components of fiscal strain—private sector resources and government fiscal policy? Let me try to summarize what we know about these matters, inevitably very briefly.

More detailed analyses suggest that the causes of change in private sector resources often involve national economic trends such as recession, inflation, labor and land costs across the country, changes in production technology, and transportation costs. Local officials can intervene in these to some degree, but usually only a modest degree, especially in the short term.[11]

By contrast, causes of the second component of fiscal strain— that is, municipal expenditure and debt—are much more locally determined and much more political and administrative in their dynamics. These dynamics include: preferences of voters concerning spending, political activity by organized groups, preferences of and policies pursued by elected officials, and legal authority of public officials. Analyses currently underway show the importance of all these political and administrative factors in some cities, some of the time.[12] Organized group pressures were often critical in the late 1960s; by contrast the late 1970s are characterized by a taxpayers' revolt that had been mounting for years. This revolt is broad and deep, and has brought new public officials to office. Many have pursued policies of fiscal retrenchment of the sort that Peter Flaherty initiated early in the decade. And this can happen in cities that are either poor or wealthy in terms of private sector resources.

Policy Implications

What policy implications follow from this?

There are many causes of urban fiscal strain; hence there are many points where policy intervention is feasible. But these are of two general classes: those that seek to change the level of private sector resources, and those that concern city government spending. Given the national workings of private sector forces, government programs in this area probably have to commit huge sums of money before they are likely to have enduring impacts. This is not to suggest zero effects, but only that the forces affecting the location of jobs and people in places like the South Bronx versus San Diego are such that while they may be rechanneled somewhat, they cannot be reversed without enormous efforts. And even if programs do increase somewhat the number of jobs and population, these do not automatically generate revenues for the city government. This suggests that Urban Development Action Grants or similar efforts are blunt instruments by which to affect urban fiscal strain.[13]

Like it or not, we are in a period of fiscal austerity, such that new commitments of public funds from federal and most state governments are likely to be limited. More than ever, this demands asking hard questions about how far limited dollars can go in alternative programs. How can state and federal grants be improved?

Most funds for cities from federal and state grants remain highly constraining. Many categorical grants instituted in the past are very narrow in focus. Priorities of the groups that helped create these programs have often changed, but the old priorities remain frozen in federal regulations. Even though block grants for community development and other programs were created to permit more local autonomy, this flexibility has been eroded by expanded federal regulations.

Federally mandated costs for environmental protection, and responsiveness to special user groups like the disabled, increase the costs of some projects to the point that basic services must be cut. Many grants are funded on a year-to-year basis, so that even cities like San Diego, with sophisticated revenue-forecasting procedures, are forced to leave out most federal grants altogether. Such grant administration policies were bad in a period of general growth. In time of retrenchment, they can create fiscal chaos for cities.

Things could change by consolidating many highly specific grants and drastically simplifying administrative procedures. If at least some funds—in the manner of revenue sharing—could be budgeted for several years in advance, this would also help.

Targeting formulas and other grant allocation procedures should be more explicit as to their goals. Grants aimed at city governments rather than the private sector should incorporate more adequate measures of the functional responsibilities of city governments.[14] Currently cities equal in poverty levels or population, for example, would receive equal amounts in grants using these two targeting elements. But if one city was responsible for public education, health, and hospitals, and the second for none of these, the two would still receive equal grants. This could be changed by including a measure of the range of functional responsibilities of the city.

Federal and state grants could be targeted to productivity or fiscal management areas; but most mayors would probably agree that this would create administrative complications of just the sort we should try to avoid.

Still, federal and state agencies can help in supporting research on fiscal policy-making, productivity, and related matters. They can produce manuals and offer technical assistance. They can support conferences and self-study efforts. But all these will be used *only when and if* local officials *want* to use them.

How do these issues look from a local policy-making perspective?

Policies oriented toward helping cities do more with what they have, adjusting their revenues and debt to declining or growing private sector resources, may well deserve further emphasis.

Four critical areas for all cities are *collective bargaining, improving productivity, careful capital spending,* and *better fiscal management.* And virtually all cities can improve in each. But which specific areas might a local official look to improve most? One answer is areas where the city is lagging compared to others.

One way to find this out is by comparing a city with others on a range of different activities. To this end, consider indicators for such matters as wage levels, numbers of municipal employees in various departments, types of capital maintenance and new construction programs, and, where possible, productivity indicators. City finance departments are increasingly including such indicators for past years as part of the budgetary process. Still, few cities are aware of how they compare to others in these and other detailed aspects of finance and administration. In recent years several groups of city officials have been meeting to compare notes using such fiscal indicators—in Minnesota, Massachusetts, and in conjunction with HUD and the U.S. Conference of Mayors.

Comparative indicators of this sort can suggest that a city like Pittsburgh may be a good candidate for so-called "deviant case analysis." Several mayors have been very curious as to just how Flaherty succeeded in cutting back on the number of municipal employees at all, given the strong union situation. And how were worksites reorganized to maintain service levels? How was political support for such programs maintained? How was Flaherty reelected? Answers to questions like these can be discussed at roundtables, or summarized in manuals and case studies of particularly interesting policies.[15]

Of course, cities differ enough that very different policies are appropriate in different cities. Those like San Diego and Houston are booming in terms of their private sector resources. But they too suffer many fiscal problems in handling such rapid development. They also have citizens who are demanding that public officials justify public spending.

San Diego, like Pittsburgh, offers many lessons for other cities. Productivity has been dramatically improved recently, even though San Diego started from a very different position from Pittsburgh.[16] Creative procedures for handling new capital construction to support housing developments in outlying areas have been devised. Fiscal management in San Diego is very efficient already, but special task forces have been created to study pensions and Proposition 13-related issues. They have developed new procedures for estimating revenues and for organizing their budgets and financial statements, using such methods as consolidated reporting.

Many other policies also follow from this perspective on urban fiscal strain: more careful analysis of fiscal conditions by local, state, and federal agencies; and studies in depth of such pressing issues as capital stock deterioration, municipal employee incentives, use of new accounting systems, cash management, measuring and improving service delivery, and the like.[17] HUD's Financial Management Capacity Sharing Program has been particularly important in encouraging work on these issues. A number of lessons are emerging from such policy-oriented studies.

At the mayoral level, however, it is perhaps still more important to stress the fundamental decisions that lead to such specifics. How big should our city government be? Are the tax burden and service levels consistent with our changing resource base? Should we try to spend city funds more efficiently? How should one deal with the voters and organized groups that stand to gain or lose from new policies? These are the big decisions that, in the final analysis, each official has to make. Then he can turn for advice from others in reaching specific solutions.

Most cities have strengths as well as weaknesses, and thus can both learn from and teach others in different policy areas. Policy analysts working together with city officials can document some of the most urgent problems, and the more suggestive solutions emerging across the country. The huge diversity of American cities is one of the great strengths of our nation in that many, many policies can be and are being tried to address widespread urban problems.

NOTES

1. Most reports of economic development projects are success stories. They tend to document individual cities or specific programs such that answering the sort of cost-benefit question posed here is difficult in general terms, although still clearly amenable to systematic investigation. Examples of cities that have probably overinvested in urban development include several cities in the South that have offered extensive tax abatements, free land, and other subsidies to attract new industry. Cities elsewhere complained that when they sought to cost out possible development subsidies, they were outbid. Public officials in the cities in the South, discussing these issues, admitted that they did not even attempt to compute costs and benefits because they were so intensely concerned to attract industry at almost any cost. These examples come from roundtables organized by the U.S. Conference of Mayors in the late 1970s; city names are omitted because the phenomena seem quite general. Similar results are reported in a study of small municipalities in Missouri: "Tax exemptions and subsidies ... were ... given greater emphasis in the least urbanized areas and were not correlated with economic development success." See the review of related results in Roger J. Vaughan, *The Urban Impacts of Federal Policies: Volume 2, Economic Development* (Santa Monica: Rand, 1977), p. 73.

   A detailed study concluding that government development funds were not cost effective was Martin Anderson, *The Federal Bulldozer* (Cambridge, Mass.: MIT Press, 1964). Jerome Rothenberg, *Economic Evaluation of Urban Renewal*

(Washington, D.C.: Brookings, 1967) similarly found few specific benefits, although an update of these studies in a 1980 Ph.D. dissertation at the University of Chicago by Michael J. White found some neighborhood specific growth apparently stimulated by Urban Renewal. Such criticisms as Anderson's helped lead the Community Development Block Grant program to replace Urban Renewal. See also footnotes 6 and 8 below.

2. Cities in the national context (via the U.S. Conference of Mayors, National League of Cities, etc.) confront the choice of what programs to press for in Washington. Here, perhaps even more than for the individual city, it seems in their interests to press for aid not tied to development, but available for a range of activities. If such decategorization seems consistent with the Washington climate of the early 1980s, so is the assumption that $c + f$ is governed by a budget constraint.

3. Specific suggestions as to how to complete cost-benefit analyses of urban development projects are in Leonard Vignola, "Economic Development," in George J. Washnis, ed., *Productivity Improvement Handbook for State and Local Government* (New York: Wiley, 1980), pp. 135–138; Public Technology, Inc., *Multi-Year Revenue and Expenditure Forecasting,* HUD–PDR–602 (Washington, D.C.: Department of Housing and Urban Development, 1980), pp. 81–85; and Robert W. Burchell and David Listokin, *The Fiscal Impact Guidebook,* HUD–PDR–566 (Washington, D.C.: Department of Housing and Urban Development, 1980).

4. I discuss here mainly firms as a source of jobs. But city officials are often concerned with jobs as a means to expand the tax base. They should be aware of recent research that suggests that recently jobs have often been following people instead of just people following jobs. Simultaneous equation studies suggest the significance of the arrows from both jobs to people and from people to jobs. Cf. Michael J. Greenwood, "Research on Internal Migration in the United States: A Survey," *Journal of Economic Literature* 13 (June 1975): 397–433. For example, people may move to San Diego and once there create new businesses for themselves. This implies that local policies designed to maintain a tax base should be focused on attracting residents as well as firms.

5. Terry Nichols Clark, Irene S. Rubin, Lynne C. Pettler, and Erwin Zimmermann, *How Many New Yorks?— The New York Fiscal Crisis in Comparative Perspective* (Chicago: Comparative Study of Community Decision-Making, University of Chicago, Research Report 72, 1976). A nontechnical version appeared in *New York Affairs* 3, no. 4 (Summer/Fall, 1976): pp. 18–27 and was reprinted (with one page missing) in *Congressional Record—Senate,* 95th Congress, Second Session, vol. 124 (Thursday, March 16, 1978), pp. S–3801–3803.

6. Terry Nichols Clark, "Fiscal Management of American Cities: Funds Flow Indicators," *Journal of Accounting Research* 15 (Supplement 1977): 54–106.

7. U.S. Department of the Treasury, Office of State and Local Finance, *Report on the Fiscal Impact of the Economic Stimulus Package on Urban Governments.* (Washington, D.C.: U.S. Treasury, 1978); Peggy Cuciti, *City Need and the Responsiveness of Federal Grant Programs* (Washington, D.C.: Congressional Budget Office, 1978); Touche Ross and First National Bank of Boston, *Urban Fiscal Stress* (New York: Touche Ross, 1979). See also Larry E. Huckins and George S. Tolley, "Investments in Local Capital Infrastructure," in Terry Nichols Clark, ed., *Urban Policy Analysis: Directions for Future Research,* Urban Affairs Annual Reviews, vol. 21 (Beverly Hills: Sage 1981).

8. Terry Nichols Clark and Lorna Crowley Ferguson, *Political Processes and Urban Fiscal Strain,* book manuscript, University of Chicago, 1981.

9. Clark and Ferguson, *Political Processes and Urban Fiscal Strain.*
10. U.S. Conference of Mayors, *Issues in Financial Management of Local Governments* (Washington, D.C.: U.S. Conference of Mayors, Final Report to Department of Housing and Urban Development, 1978).
11. The power of these essentially private sector forces has been stressed, among others, by Vaughan, *The Urban Impacts of Federal Policies: Vol. 2;* George S. Tolley, Philip E. Graves, and John L. Gardiner, *Urban Growth Policy in a Market Economy* (New York: Academic Press, 1979); John D. Kasarda, "The Implications of Contemporary Redistribution Trends for National Urban Policy," *Social Science Quarterly* (December, 1980); and Barry M. Moriarty, *Industrial Location and Community Development* (Chapel Hill: The University of North Carolina Press, 1980).
12. Clark and Ferguson, *Political Processes and Urban Fiscal Strain.*
13. Others who have come to similar conclusions are Kasarda, "The Implications of Contemporary Redistribution Trends for National Urban Policy," and Roy Bahl: "Neighborhood Commercial Reinvestment programs and expanded UDAG funding all seemed to lean toward renovating a deteriorated economic base in distressed cities. At least the rhetoric of Federal policy would imply a belief that the declining economies can be revitalized. Yet there is little evidence that such programs work or have any effect on the employment base of declining cities." "Prepared Statement," in *Hearing Before the Special Study on Economic Change,* Joint Economic Committee, Congress of the United States, *State and Local Government Finances and the Changing National Economy,* 96th Congress, Second Session, July 28, 1980 (Washington, D.C.: U.S. Government Printing Office, 1980), pp. 6–15. Roger Vaughan concurs: "UDAG was...one of the most popular federal development programs ever, it was also one of the most wasteful.... The government has an established track record in economic development unmatched since the Edsel." "Some Thoughts on Federal Development Policy," draft paper, 1981.
14. Several past measures are reviewed, and a more adequate one proposed in Terry Nichols Clark, Lorna Crowley Ferguson, and Robert Y. Shapiro, "Functional Performance Analysis: A New Approach to the Study of Municipal Expenditures," *Political Methodology,* in press.
15. See U.S. Conference of Mayors, *Issues in Financial Management of Local Governments.*
16. U.S. Conference of Mayors, *Issues in Financial Management of Local Governments.*
17. See Office of Evaluation, Community Planning and Development and Evaluation Division, Office of Policy Development and Research, Department of Housing and Urban Development, *Conference on Methodology for Studying Implementation of the Community Development Block Grant Program (CDBG)* (Washington, D.C.: Department of Housing and Urban Development, 1980).

Chapter 2

On Tax Limitation

*Harvey E. Brazer**

If we define taxes as compulsory charges levied by government without a quid pro quo, then it is easy to understand why the tax protest movement in this country is at least as old as the Boston Tea Party. Each individual's tax liability may be viewed as "too high," in the sense that he can easily imagine himself better off with a lower tax liability unaccompanied by a reduced flow of benefits from public goods or transfers. Thus it is not surprising that tax protest movements appear periodically, whenever an individual or a group succeeds in channeling the self-seeking interests of individuals into political action.

Various aspects of these movements are examined in this chapter. First I look at the models of excessively large government that provide their intellectual underpinning. Then the empirical evidence on voter dissatisfaction is examined. The third part of the chapter provides an analysis of the California Proposition 13 phenomenon. This is followed by discussion of experience with similar types of proposals in other states during the years 1978–1980. The chapter concludes with an evaluation of that experience and of the tax limitation movement.

The author is indebted to Paul N. Courant for many helpful suggestions, to Mary Walz for research assistance, and to Colleen Smeekens for making sense of an earlier draft.

*Professor of Economics, University of Michigan

ALTERNATIVE REASONS FOR PROPOSALS

Historically tax or expenditure limitations have been used either to restrict or prohibit public support for essentially private enterprise, or to alleviate hardships imposed by the Depression of the 1930s. The movement of the 1970s, however, gains no support from either of these earlier motivations. In fact in the United States today people have substantial access to the decision processes governing state and local levels of taxes and expenditures, and one would expect that the majority is getting pretty much what it wants. The question then is, What is behind the current support for tax limitations, and why has this support emerged so prominently only in recent years?[1]

A number of observers have claimed that government is too large and out of hand; that representative democracy is not working in a manner leading effectively to the expression of voter preferences in the budgetary sphere. Proponents of this view specifically deny the existence of efficient outcomes of the Lindahl–Samuelson–Musgrave genre or the Hotelling–Bowen–Downs median voter model. The former model provides a general equilibrium analytical framework for efficient allocation of resources between the public and the private sectors of the economy and within the public sector. The latter demonstrates that, under a carefully specified set of assumptions, it may be possible to achieve similarly efficient outcomes.

The most extreme form of this position is presented by Brennan and Buchanan, who posit a "Leviathan" model of nonbenevolent despotic government.[2] Government is held to use its coercive power for its own purposes, the principal one of which is to maximize the "income" of Leviathan. Thus the objective function is to maximize the difference between tax revenues and expenditures on public goods, or $Y = R - G$, with Y as income to Leviathan, R as total tax revenue, and G as expenditures on public goods. In this model electoral constraints are held to be "utterly ineffective." The seeking of tax limitation amendments by voters is seen by Brennan and Buchanan as a means through which the individual citizen can avoid "exposing himself to gross exploitation by government— exploitation in the form of disastrously excessive tax burdens...."

A missing link in the Brennan–Buchanan model is the definition of "government." The suggestion is that there may be "leakages" into the pockets of "politicians/bureaucrats," but this does not seem to be the driving mechanism in the model. Actually, it appears that the alleged failure of the political system to obtain results desired by the electorate is simply assumed. No empirical evidence is offered in its support, and the appeal to Hobbes and John Stuart Mill is very much less than convincing.

Another line of reasoning has been proposed by Niskanen, who argues that government is "too large" because self-seeking bureaucrats are able to expand their own status and influence by enlarging the size of their budgets in an atmosphere of intense interbureau competition.[3] Niskanen's bureaucrats function in a world in which they are not required to justify their budgetary requests before responsible elected representatives. Somehow they are permitted, with little or no constraint other than with respect, perhaps, to the total size of the budget, to move well beyond the limits preferred by the voters. This view of government has the virtue of having been developed with the aid of many years of inside experience gained by the author in the federal bureaucracy. At best, however, Niskanen has a testable hypothesis, one that he himself does not test. Still, it is conceivable that self-seeking bureaucrats are responsible for government's being "too large." They may, therefore have been responsible, in part, for the widespread emergence of proposals for tax and expenditure limitations.

A third set of hypotheses emanates from a number of academic sources.[4] In this line of analysis voters pursue private, divisible benefits through the public sector. Consequently, the public sector inevitably grows "too large." This hypothesis can be placed in historical perspective by observing the increasing shift, particularly in the postwar period, from government provision of general benefits to expenditures benefiting identifiable minority groups, as in welfare programs, higher education, or health. This view of the world has much appeal. A source of dissatisfaction with the public sector, for a disaffected set of middle-class voters, may be that they see themselves as being harshly put upon by the tax system while they realize few of the fruits of government largesse.

Michael Boskin and others have suggested as a basis for limitation proposals the continuing growth of government expenditures since 1973 while real income increases have held close to zero.[5] The combination of these circumstances with what appears to be a general political movement toward the right may provide the source of much support for tax and expenditure limitations designed to relieve what are seen as excessive burdens arbitrarily imposed by unresponsive government.

A contributing factor behind the tax limitation movement may be the fact that its leaders enjoy vast amounts of publicity, including innumerable invitations to speak before dinner meetings, radio and television audiences, and to a wide range of groups concerned with the objective of improving their economic lots through constraining overblown government. The notoriety enjoyed by a minor officeholder in a rural county or by an otherwise unknown insurance executive of suburban Detroit must be a source of enormous satisfaction, sufficiently important to put him back on stage in election after election.

Tax limitations will always have considerable support even if none of these phenomena is occurring. When government is responsive to the median voter, a substantial proportion of the electorate may believe that levels of taxes and/or expenditures are too high. When this fact is coupled with the willingness of people to take a leadership position in the quest for tax limits, we have the assurance that proposals for tax limitation will appear with considerable frequency and regularity. This phenomenon then provides an opportunity for the emergence of something approaching the "tyranny of the few." This is the case when campaign funds are available and the issues are put before the electorate in statements that appear on the ballot as very brief summaries of the substantive proposals, summaries that may be drafted by their proponents. For example, the Michigan rule requires that all proposals appearing on the ballot must be stated in not more than 100 words. Once constitutional amendment proposals such as Tisch (1978 and 1980) and Headlee (1978) have been condensed to 100 words from a length of 500 to 1000 words or more, it is clear that what appears on the ballot—all that most voters ever see—bears little resemblance to the actual proposal in its substantive detail. It follows therefore that an intelligent, rational voter response is not possible. Those initiating, drafting, and gathering support for the proposals are commonly in a position to exercise a kind of tyranny in the realm of political choice that poses real dangers for free and efficient public choice in a democratic setting.

ARE VOTERS DISSATISFIED?

The proposition that voters recognize a condition in which government expenditures and/or revenues are "too large," and that they would prefer to curtail them, is a refutable hypothesis. In Michigan, immediately following the election of November 1978, Courant, Gramlich, and Rubinfeld surveyed a representative sample of the Michigan population.[6] Respondents were asked to express their preferences regarding levels of public spending for police and fire protection, welfare, elementary and secondary education, higher education, highway maintenance, and parks and recreation. Respondents were also asked whether they preferred spending, by function, to be less than existing levels, about the same, or higher. If higher, respondents were asked whether they would be willing to pay higher taxes to finance the expansion in outlays. The authors conclude that "The most striking empirical result from the survey concerning taste for public expenditures is that by and large citizens of Michigan are satisfied with current levels of output at both the State and local levels. Indeed, with the exception of spending on welfare programs, there is a decided sentiment for expansion (and a stated willingness to pay for expansion) in all the program areas for which responses were elicited."

A similar poll conducted in California in June 1978, just prior to the Proposition 13 vote, led Citrin to conclude that "people tend to favor more rather than less spending on police, fire departments, mental health programs and education while demanding cuts in spending on welfare, public housing, and the government's own administrative services."[7]

These and other surveys conducted in recent years indicate that, in general and with respect to overall expenditure levels, most people prefer current or even higher outlays. At the same time, however, a substantial majority of respondents to these surveys make it clear that they believe that governments have gone further than is desirable in spending for welfare and related programs such as health and housing. Moreover, it seems apparent that a substantial proportion of the population believes government to be wasteful and inefficient, as was brought out emphatically in Citrin's poll in 1978.

In California, Massachusetts, Michigan, and many other states the tax limitation movement has had as its primary target curtailment of the property tax. Given what we have learned about preferences with respect to government expenditures, this seems strange indeed, for in most states the share of welfare and income support programs of other kinds paid from property tax receipts is either small or nonexistent. On the other hand, such services as police and fire protection, which seem to enjoy wide popular support, are mainly or even entirely financed with property tax receipts. And yet we find the property tax a very unpopular levy.[8] Thus it is not clear whether people voting on property tax limitations in California, Massachusetts, Michigan, Idaho, Arizona, Nevada, Oregon, and several other states are expressing a distaste for the property tax, regardless of the kinds, qualities, or quantities of public services supported by it, or are expressing a preference for lower levels of government expenditures.

Focus on the property tax as the primary target is not difficult to understand in the circumstances of the past seven or eight years. To most people it is a highly visible tax, one which, unlike the sales tax, is paid in a large single installment or, at most, monthly installments. It does not lend itself to the convenience of periodic withholding as do federal and state income taxes. Thus property taxes are seen as a burdensome levy and a major irritant.

The property tax as levied by local authorities is commonly regarded as being more controllable than taxes imposed by federal and state governments. Inflation in residential real estate values, particularly in states where conscientious efforts are made by assessors to keep assessments current, has typically brought sharp annual increases in tax liabilities. The effect of such increases in the face of declining school enrollments and few, if any, local manifestations of improved or additional public services, has been a rising level of annoyance on the part of some taxpayers. Others fear that rising property taxes might make it impossible for people on fixed nominal incomes to continue living in their homes. The outcome has been a growing determination to "do something about it."

Nevertheless, in the national picture we find that overall levels of property taxation, while having gone up from $152 per capita in 1968–1969 to $295 in 1978–1979, actually declined during the past decade as a proportion of income from 4.5 percent to 3.8 percent. Of course not all states experienced such a decline. In fact the proportion of income collected in property taxes rose during the decade in Massachusetts from 5.8 percent to 7.2 percent in 1977–1978 and 6.8 percent in 1978–1979. In California the ratio of property taxes to income remained constant throughout the period. On the other hand, in many of the states the property tax declined sharply as a proportion of income. For example, the proportion of income taken in property taxes in North Dakota fell from 5.9 to 3.6 percent, in Kansas from 5.5 to 4.6 percent, in Iowa from 5.4 to 4.2 percent, and in Ohio from 4.2 to 3.3 percent.[9] Not surprisingly, what one finds is that the appearance of tax limitation amendments tends to be most prevalent in those states in which the property tax relative to income was high throughout the decade, or even both high and rising.

Some insights into the issues involved may be found by taking a closer look at experience with tax limitation proposals in several of the states. I begin with California's Proposition 13.

PROPOSITION 13

For several years prior to 1978 the efforts of the people promoting tax and expenditure limitations were largely unsuccessful. Limitation proposals had been turned down several times in California, Michigan, and other states. The sweeping victory of Proposition 13 in California in June 1978 was widely heralded as the harbinger of the taxpayers' revolution. Proposition 13 placed a maximum on the property tax rate of 1 percent of assessed value, rolled back assessments to their 1976 levels, and permitted a maximum 2 percent per year increase in assessments after 1976. It also imposed the requirement that any new tax or tax increase had to receive approval of two-thirds of the legislature or of the electorate.

The immediate question is, Why did Proposition 13 pass by an overwhelmingly large majority? Did the results contradict the survey findings suggesting that the electorate did not strongly favor cutting public services? There is strong reason to believe that the passage of Proposition 13 did not signify a demand on the part of the public for reduction in expenditures or a widespread view that government is too large. In fact the impression that drastic reduction in property tax rates would in fact not result in major curtailment of expenditures seems to have prevailed. This view was inspired in part by publicity with respect to the state's large and growing surplus, a surplus estimated to have approached $7 billion by June 1978. The vote appears to have been essentially a vote to do precisely what the proposal offered, namely, reduce sharply the property tax rate. Clearly there is a strong demand on the part of the public to do that. This demand is easily understood when it is recognized that in 1978 and for well over a decade property taxes in California were at close to 6.5 percent of personal income, compared with an average of about 4 percent in the United States as a whole during the decade of the 1970s. In per capita terms Californians consistently found themselves among the top three states for high property taxes.

Absolutely and relatively high property tax rates were not enough in themselves to sell the tax limitation proposal, as earlier defeat of propositions similar to 13 at the polls indicated. A combination of other factors gave rise to the overwhelming support for 13 by 1978. To a greater degree, perhaps, than anywhere else in the country, Californians in the 1970s experienced an extremely high rate of inflation in housing values. And, in contrast to many states, California has developed an excellent system of property tax assessment. This system served to capture inflation in assessed valuations about as rapidly as it occurred. Thus Californians faced rapidly rising residential tax bills. The situation was exacerbated by the fact that nonresidential property values lagged substantially behind the increases in residential values. Consequently, owner-occupiers of single-family homes found themselves having to meet a sharply rising share of the total property tax levy and a rising tax price for local goods and services. Over the decade prior to 1978 the share of property tax represented by residential property rose from approximately 33 to 43 percent.

In a sense, perhaps somewhat paradoxically, the inflation that seemed to bring increasingly heavy tax burdens to owners of residential property was simultaneously instrumental in producing an increasingly huge state surplus. Inflation, therefore, contributed on two fronts to the sentiment in favor of Proposition 13. As has been noted, this surplus, coupled with a widespread view that there was a great deal of waste and inefficiency in government that could be eliminated before services needed to be cut, led many who were not in favor of reducing public services to vote, nevertheless, in favor of 13.

Adding further to resentment and contributing to support for the proposition was the failure on the part of local governments to reduce tax rates as school enrollments fell while tax bases were rising very rapidly. Nor was it apparent in nonschool areas that the quantity or quality of public services was increasing as tax bills rose sharply.

Further compounding the problem was the existence of a foundation grant program in support of elementary and secondary education. As local assessments rose, the amount of school aid automatically dropped, thus increasing the local (reducing the state) share of the cost of education. This fact also increased the average tax price paid locally for education and at the same time increased the state surplus. Finally, along with taxpayers throughout the country who observe that their tax bills rise with increased assessments, Californians felt strong resentment against what many people perceive to be taxation of unrealized capital gains.

Some of these factors enumerated as contributing to the massive victory of Proposition 13 can be found in most, if not all, states. Others, however, are more or less peculiar to the circumstances in California as of 1978 and the immediately preceding years. Inflation, of course, has been rampant everywhere, but housing values have not skyrocketed at anything like the California rate in the rest of the country, with some rather isolated exceptions. The existence of a very large and well-publicized state surplus is a phenomenon known only in California and perhaps two or three other states. At least half of the states operate under foundation grant programs of school aid, but prompt adjustments in the basic grant or in the level of deductible millage has probably gone further in other states to reduce the impact on the local share of school costs imposed by rapidly rising assessed values. Perhaps most important of all is the fact that only in the Western states of Montana and Wyoming, in New Jersey and New York, and in the New England states of Massachusetts, New Hampshire, and Vermont does the level of the property tax approach or exceed the pre-1979 California level (Alaska may now be regarded as a special case).

Thus it seems that the elements of the California case were sufficiently peculiar that predictions based upon the California sentiment expressed at the polls in June 1978 regarding the likely outcome of referenda on tax limitations in other states were bound to be mistaken. There simply is no other state in which the combination of an enormous state surplus, an extremely heavy reliance on property taxation, and rapidly escalating prices of single-family residential housing may be found.

LIMITATION REFERENDA ELSEWHERE— 1978-1980

In 1978 three states, Idaho, Nevada, and Oregon, held referenda on Proposition 13-like proposals.[10] The Idaho proposal, which passed by a substantial 58 to 42 percent margin, provides for the reduction of property tax rates to a maximum of 1 percent of market value and permits tax increases or the introduction of any new tax only upon approval by two-thirds of the electorate. The Idaho provision, however, unlike the one in California, is subject to statutory action by the legislature.

The Nevada case is a particularly interesting one because constitutional amendments in that state must be approved in two successive elections before taking effect. In 1978 Proposition 6, bearing a very close resemblance to California's Proposition 13, was passed overwhelmingly, by a vote of 140,509 to 40,154. This action by the voters threw the Nevada legislature into a flurry of tax action. When the proposition was submitted a second time in 1980 it was defeated by a margin of 58 to 42 percent of the votes cast.

In the same year the electorate in Oregon voted on Measure 6, which would have required reduction of the tax rates on property to a maximum of 1 percent of market value and a margin of 2 to 1 in voter approval for any new taxation. The measure was narrowly defeated, 52 to 48 percent. The defeat may have been attributable to the fact that Oregon had earlier imposed a limit of 6 percent on the annual growth rate of the assessed value of property.

In 1980 voters in eight states were asked to cast their ballots on constitutional amendment proposals that offered severe cutbacks in tax rates. Amendments were offered in Arizona in both June and November. The amendment approved in June under the broad Proposition 100 heading provided for repeal of the sales tax on food for home consumption, limited spending of schools and other local jurisdictions, and imposed a limit of 2 percent per year on increases in property tax liabilities. In addition, the amendment limited the property tax rate applicable to residences to 1 percent of full cash value, and increased various property tax exemptions. In November of the same year, however, an extension of the property tax limitation to a universal maximum of 1 percent of full cash value, as in California's Proposition 13, was defeated by approximately 70 percent no to 30 percent yes.

By a similarly wide margin California voters disapproved a constitutional amendment that would have cut income tax rates in half; Michigan voters turned down a proposal to cut the maximum assessment to market value ratio from 50 to 25 percent by a vote of 44 percent for to 56 percent against; Nevada, as noted, reversed its earlier position on severe constitutional limitations on property taxation; Oregon voters turned down, by a margin of almost 2 to 1, the Measure 6 that had been narrowly defeated two years earlier. Voters in South Dakota defeated a constitutional amendment proposal almost identical to Proposition 13 by 63 percent no to 37 percent yes, as did voters in Utah, where the vote was 45 yes to 55 percent no. Thus we find that during the two years 1978 and 1980 only Idaho voters followed California's lead and even in that one state the limitation requires statutory approval rather than being mandated by the constitution.

The largest, most significant departure from this pattern of rejecting extremely narrow and restrictive constitutional constraints on taxation is the case of Massachusetts' Proposition 2½, which was accepted in 1980. A major difference between the Massachusetts provision and that approved in California is that the Massachusetts voters, in effect, approved a statute rather than a constitutional provision unequivocally tying the hands of the legislature. Moreover, Proposition 2½, supported by almost 60 percent of the electorate, provides for a transition to the new maximum tax rate over several years. It carried a number of other provisions, including a reduction in the motor vehicle excise tax from $66 to $25 per

$1000 in value, a provision allowing renters to deduct half of their annual rent from income tax liability, and abolition of binding arbitration for police and firemen.

Among the interesting points to observe concerning these tax limitation proposals considered during the past several years is the fact that there is a remarkable likeness in the terms of the amendment proposals offered on the ballots in many states. One might think that, given the wide variation among the states in the existing property tax levels, some variety might appear in the numbers contained in the proposals. Observe, for example, that among the five states that voted on propositions more or less identical to Proposition 13, the proportion of personal income taken in property tax in 1978–1979 was relatively high in Arizona, South Dakota, and Oregon, at between 4.6 and 5.0 percent of personal income; but that in Nevada and Utah at 4.0 and 3.6 percent, it was very close to the U.S. average of 3.8 percent. And yet, in all five states the backers of the tax limitation proposal called for reducing the rate relative to market value of property to 1 percent. One is left with the impression that the forces behind the tax limitation movement are not entirely indigenous to the individual states.

It is by no means coincidental that the state joining California in voter approval of a drastic reduction in property taxation was Massachusetts. Property taxes in Massachusetts as of 1977–1978 were at 7.2 percent of personal income, close to double the national average. By the following year that proportion had dropped to 6.9 percent, after the recently approved system of property tax classification began to take effect. Nevertheless, at that level property taxes in Massachusetts were substantially higher than in any state other than Alaska. Almost all the reasons offered in explanation of the favorable California vote on Proposition 13 may be said to be relevant for Massachusetts as well. There is one major exception, namely, that the state does not enjoy a surplus. It is still not clear how cities and towns in Massachusetts will find a way to live with Proposition 2½ after it takes effect on July 1, 1981.[11] One may expect that part of the answer lies in the fact that its constraining provisions are to take effect gradually over a period of some years, during which it may be hoped that property values will rise.

A full discussion of tax and expenditure limitations might be said to require inclusion of such provisions as have been accepted by voters in Michigan, Hawaii, and Texas and defeated in Colorado and Nebraska. These place limits not on particular tax rates but on the share of personal income that may be taken in taxes, either at the local level, the state level, or state–local combined.

This form of limitation has gained substantial support in a number of states. However, despite a widespread appeal, it does not appear to be an approach which, when applied at levels that have been approved, appears to be constraining. In Michigan, in earlier elections when the proportion included in the ballot proposal would have required reduction in state revenues or expenditures, the electorate turned it down. In the case of the Headlee Amendment, passed in 1978, however, the provision simply is not constraining—the present leeway amounts to over $600 million.

To those who were sure in 1978 that the tax revolution was well launched, the decisive losses in battles in 1980 in Michigan, Oregon, South Dakota, and Utah, plus the defeat of the income tax amendment in California, must have been a disheartening, if not a bewildering experience. In seeking reasons for these losses, in contrast with California's experience with Proposition 13, one may note, as I have, that several of the circumstances existing in California such as the large state surplus and an extraordinarily high property tax burden were not present in these other states. And yet it seems strange that many more people are anxious and willing to declare their opposition to existing levels of property tax than are willing to carry this position into the voting booth. Nevertheless, we may not be observing widespread inconsistency on the part of voters. Rather, it is quite conceivable that the individual sees himself outside of the voting booth as wishing for lower taxes, recognizing that if his tax bill were lower the impact on the amount of revenue involved and on the flow of public services would be negligible. But he also recognizes that when he enters the voting booth he is about to participate in collective action, the outcome of which can be expected to have major consequences for the quality and quantity of public services he or she can expect to enjoy. Thus it is perfectly consistent to say that I prefer a lower property tax liability and at the same time to cast a negative vote on a property tax limitation amendment as I recognize my role in a process of collective decision making.

EVALUATION

Despite the arguments of Brennan, Buchanan, Niskanen, Meltzer, and others, I remain unconvinced that government is too large. For their position to be convincing and at the same time universally appropriate, governments must be too large in all local jurisdictions in the relevant regions at any one time. Otherwise, those who prefer a smaller scale of government activity would, presumably, in Tiebout fashion, change their place of residence in order more closely to satisfy their preferences for public services.

Given imperfect mobility and that residential choices are not simply a function of fiscal conditions, a Proposition 13-type statewide tax constraint may be an inefficient method of forcing a local reduction in tax rates, revenues, and the quantity and quality of public services supplied. If it is not constraining—that is, if the preferred property tax rate is less than the imposed limit—then obviously the limit is ineffectual and serves no purpose. But if the limit is in fact effective, if it prohibits tax rates and public service levels that are preferred to those permitted under the limitation, then clearly preferences are being frustrated and the limitation is obviously inefficient in the sense that voters are being denied consumer surpluses that would otherwise be available to them.[12]

It seems obvious that measures such as California's Proposition 13 and Massachusetts' Proposition $2\frac{1}{2}$ impose extremely uneven impacts on local jurisdictions, largely ignoring differences in local preference patterns and in other local influences on demand for public services. Just as there were jurisdictions in California in which the tax rates imposed on property were less than 1 percent of 1976 market value, so there are in Massachusetts some cities and towns in which the rate is less than 2.5 percent. Thus in some jurisdictions the limitation is not binding at all, whereas in others it imposes severe curtailment on the public sector.

These uniform limitations imply that circumstances giving rise to wants for public goods and services are uniform throughout a state (the national leaders of the tax limitation movement seem to believe that they are uniform across the nation!), irrespective of the character of the jurisdiction—central city, bedroom suburb, industrial enclave, resort community, or rural agricultural township. This kind of meat-axe or shotgun approach to constraining local taxes and expenditures also denies differences in tastes among communities as well as differences in income and wealth. Thus one can conclude only that these tax rate limitations, as well as income share limits in a somewhat less rigid way, can only either be ineffectual or impose inefficiencies, unless the variety of stories that are told to "prove" that government is inevitably too large are true. But these claims can hold up only if preferences of voters are not reflected in public budgets. And even if that were so, surely there is no evidence whatsoever to suggest that we move closer to satisfying the preferences of more voters as we impose uniform statewide or even nationwide constraining tax rate limitations.

To the extent that tax rate limits are effective their equity effects can be unfortunate. Under most circumstances one may expect that curtailment of local revenues and expenditures will have the severest impact on low-income groups. Higher-income residents may opt for private rather than public schools; seek their recreation through golf and country clubs, tennis clubs, or other private facilities; arrange for the private disposal of garbage and trash; or reinforce private protection against fire and crime against their persons and property. Moreover, such equity consequences may be exacerbated to the extent that efforts are made to maintain services through alternative revenue sources such as user charges and selective excise taxes on goods and services with low-income elasticities of demand.

Perhaps the most unfortunate consequence of the alleged "tax revolt" may be to panic legislatures into poorly constructed property tax relief measures. Current pressures for such measures in Michigan, for example, are very strong, despite the fact that in Michigan between one-quarter and one-third of the property tax is levied under so-called extra-voted millage approved by local electorates for elementary and secondary education and a wide range of special purposes such as community college capital construction, police and fire pensions, and local mass transit. Thus it would seem that, if the property tax rate in any given community in Michigan is too high, one need only look to the voters for the placement of responsibility for this condition.

An important aspect of the tax limitation movement is its ability to convince people in positions of political responsibility that its backers will keep trying to achieve their goals time after time, and that the only way to frustrate their efforts is to beat them at their own game. Thus, to pursue the case of Michigan, Governor William G. Milliken, in his 1981 State of the State Message,[13] set forth as his first priority to be laid before the legislature a constitutional amendment proposal to provide about $800 million of property tax relief to homeowners and renters. This proposal is regarded as a matter of great urgency in a state in which homeowners and renters already realize property tax relief in the amount of close to $500 million per year through the nation's most generous, universal circuit breaker.

The governor's proposal calls for a reduction in property tax liabilities of 35 percent for homeowners in general, up to a maximum reduction of $1400. For the aged and other special groups in the population the first $1400 of property tax liability would be forgiven. Renters would enjoy an increase in the property tax credit

provided under the circuit breaker. The second part of the proposal
is an increase in the sales tax rate from 4 to 5 percent, to yield,
along with revenue saved under the existing circuit breaker, $250
million per year less than the cost of the property tax reduction.

Passage of this proposed constitutional amendment would mean
a substantial shift in tax liabilities from those with houses carrying
a high value relative to their income in high tax rate jurisdictions
to residents whose purchases of taxable goods and services are
high relative to the value of their homes and the tax rate imposed
in their communities. Whether one gains or loses as a consequence
of the shift will depend upon one's stage in the life cycle, with older
people tending to come out ahead of the young, and on one's preference function for goods and services. Clearly families and individuals whose tastes run heavily toward housing, exempted food
for home consumption, and exempted services will do very well,
while others will pick up the slack. If existing property tax liabilities are capitalized in current values of the taxed residences, the
windfall gains will tend to be proportionate or more than proportionate to income, and the net effect of the proposal is very likely to
be regressive.

Finally, two interesting facts should be noted. The first is that a
proposal very similar to the current Milliken proposal was defeated
at the polls by a margin of about 3 to 1 in the election of November
1980. The second is that, despite Governor Milliken's determined
efforts, Tisch is back campaigning for "Tisch III."

One might well wish that those manning the barricades of the
taxpayers' revolution would go away and allow representative
democracy to function as it will. State constitutions may and probably should provide for general rules of taxation and lay down the
framework of terms under which the game is to be played. Fundamental rights of individuals and other entities must not be in-
fringed, through either taxation or other means. But the selection
of reasonable tax bases that can be applied with uniformity and
universality and the level and structure of tax rates are policy
issues that belong within the proper purview of elected representatives. If representative democracy is to be effective, differences
and changes in preferences, income, and such other factors as may
influence the demand for public goods and services, including
income maintenance transfers, must be permitted to determine
policy. The power to tax involves the power to destroy only when it
is used in a discriminatory manner; severe constitutional constraints on that power to tax may frustrate the wishes of the majority and reflect the tyranny of the few.

NOTES

1. The nontechnical reader may find it profitable to skip the remainder of this section.
2. Geoffrey Brennan and James Buchanan, "The Logic of Tax Limits: Alternative Constitutional Constraints on the Power to Tax," *National Tax Journal* vol. XXXII, no. 2 (June 1979), direct quote p. 14.
3. William A. Niskanen, Jr., *Bureaucracy and Representative Government,* Aldine-Atherton: Chicago, 1971.
4. See, for example, Peter H. Aranson and Peter C. Ordeshook, "Alternative Theories of the Growth of Government and Their Implications for Constitutional Tax Spending Limits," in Helen F. Ladd, editor, *Tax and Expenditure Limitations,* COUPE Papers on Public Economics 5, Urban Institute, forthcoming, and sources cited there.
5. Michael J. Boskin, "Some Neglected Economic Factors Behind Recent Tax and Spending Limitation Movements," *National Tax Journal,* vol. xxxii, no. 2 (June 1979).
6. Paul N. Courant, Edward M. Gramlich, and Daniel L. Rubinfeld, "Why Voters Support Tax Limitation Amendments: The Michigan Case," *National Tax Journal* vol. xxxiii, no. 1 (March 1980), p. 3.
7. Jack Citrin, "Do People Want Something for Nothing: Public Opinion on Taxes and Government Spending," *National Tax Journal* vol. xxxii, no. 2 (June 1979): p. 118.
8. Advisory Commission on Intergovernmental Relations, *1979 Changing Public Attitudes on Governments and Taxes.*
9. U.S. Bureau of the Census, *Governmental Finances in 1968-69* (Washington, D.C.: Government Printing Office, 1970); *Governmental Finances in 1977-78* (1979); and *Governmental Finances in 1978-79* (1980).
10. Information in this section on election results and the provisions contained in amendment proposals has been drawn from several sources, including compilations of the Congressional Research Service; Richard L. Lucier, "Gauging the Strength and Meaning of the 1978 Tax Revolt," *Public Administration Review,* (Washington, D.C.: American Society for Public Administration, July/August 1979); Advisory Commission for Intergovernmental Relations, *Significant Features Federalism, 1979-80*; (Washington, D.C.: ACIR, 1981); and *Time,* November 17, 1980.
11. Drawing upon the opinions of unnamed "politicians," a reporter asserts that "Fountains won't be spouting water on Boston Common anymore.... Schools, parks and beaches will be closed, lights will be shut off at gyms, athletic fields and tennis courts. High school sports will become a thing of the past.... Potholes will remain unfilled," *Wall Street Journal* (February 24, 1981): 29.
12. For a rigorous development of the basic ideas expressed in this and the following paragraphs see Paul N. Courant and Daniel L. Rubinfeld, "On the Welfare Effects of Tax and Expenditure Limitations," *The Journal of Public Economics,* forthcoming.
13. Hon. William G. Milliken, *State of the State, 1981,* pp. 4-7. In revised form the Milliken proposal appeared as Proposal A on the ballot in a special election on May 19, 1981.

PART II

Property Taxes as a Revenue Source

Chapter 3

The Changing Role of Property Taxation

*Glenn W. Fisher**

Few "tax reforms" have been as widely adopted as those involving the general property tax. In the United States in the nineteenth century, the uniform universal taxation of all types of property was hailed as the ideal form of taxation. A great many state constitutions written or revised in the post–Civil War period included provisions intended to guarantee that the property tax be a uniform, ad valorem tax applying to all kinds of property. The property tax was also intended to be the major form of taxation for both the state and its local governments.

Evidences of the predominant role of this tax are still abundant. Many state constitutions contain some or all of the original wording, but most have been amended to permit exemption or classification of some types of property and to make it clear that other kinds of taxation are permissible. Local government budgeting and accounting procedures show unmistakable evidence of their "property tax fund" origins, and, in some city halls, the unmodified word "tax" still means "property tax."

Historically, much of the scholarly literature about the property tax has been written by economists. Much of it has been prescriptive. Many of the comments about the political aspects of the tax

*Regent's Professor of Urban Affairs, Wichita State University

have been complaints about politicians' failure to adopt the pre-scriptions put forth. More recently, however, there has been in-creased emphasis on understanding the political process that brings about particular tax policies.

This chapter is a broad political systems analysis of the chang-ing role of the property tax. Historical trends are examined, the relationships between the property tax and local government are analyzed, and an attempt is made to assess the meaning of these factors for the future of the property tax and local government.

POLITICAL SYSTEMS

Because of the great complexity of the political system and the large number of participants in the process, it is difficult to analyze scientifically the political decision-making process, and to predict future decisions. There is no accepted theory of political decision making, but rather a number of different approaches that are helpful in analyzing particular policy areas.

The political system approach developed by David Easton is especially useful as a framework for analyzing decisions that may result in modifications of the political system itself, or for empha-sizing the relationship between these decisions and the political structure.[1] Because this chapter focuses on the relationship be-tween the property tax and the structure of local government, it is an appropriate framework in which to conduct the analysis.

Basically, Easton attempts to develop the framework for a theory of how political systems persist whether the world be stable or changing. The analysis is built on four general premises:

1. It is useful to view political life as a system of behavior.
2. A political system is distinguishable from the environment in which it exists and is open to influence from it.
3. Variations in the structures and processes (responses) within a system may usefully be interpreted as constructive or posi-tive efforts by members of a system to regulate or cope with stress flowing from environmental as well as internal sources.
4. The capacity of a system to persist in the face of stress is a function of the presence and nature of the information and other influences that return to its actors and decision makers (feedback).[2]

The first and second premises are, at least implicitly, common to a great many studies of political behavior, but the third and fourth emphasize the fact that Easton's analysis is concerned not only with how decisions are made within a particular system at a particular moment, but also with how the system adapts itself so that it can continue to exist in spite of changing circumstances in the environment and within the system itself.

Easton emphasizes that a political system is not a constellation of human beings but rather a set of interactions that are distinguishable from other kinds of social interactions in that they are oriented toward the authoritive allocation of values (valued things) for a society. Interactions that fall outside the political system are considered to be part of the environment. Exchanges or transactions at the boundaries between the political system and its environment constitute the inputs and outputs of the system. Inputs may be in the form of demands or of support.

Demands are expressions of opinion that an authoritive allocation should or should not be made by those who have the responsibility for doing so. They may take the form of a request for a specific action, such as the construction of a new school building in a specific location, or a vague request for "better government" or "better education." Support can be roughly characterized as willingness to accept the system even if it does not meet particular demands. It may be generalized, as in a general declaration of patriotism and love of country, or it may be directed toward particular political objects such as "freedom of the press" or "the right to elect my assessor."

The output of the political system may be called "policy." It is the means by which the system acts back on its environment, but the output changes the environment, and often this creates or modifies the demands being made on the political system. The chain of events described as demand–output–environmental change–demand is a feedback loop that is a distinctive feature of the analysis. *This approach focuses concern, not just on the ouput of a political system, but also on the way the political system transforms itself to meet changing conditions and, thus, to persist through time.*

Easton points out that the system's capacity to endure is always under stress. By their very nature, political systems are called upon to deal with relationships among members of a system that involve the sharpest kind of antagonism. In words that will strike a responsive note among students of taxation, Easton points out that scarcity is probably the most significant phenomenon of every society, and that when differences over the distribution of scarce values cannot be adjusted privately (by the market mechanism?), a resort to some sort of political allocation is inevitable. That political systems rarely collapse under the stress to which they are subject would, Easton suggests, be something to gaze at in wonder if it were not so commonplace. On the other hand, political systems rarely maintain themselves unchanged for long. Instead, they persist because they constantly transform themselves in response to stress (Figure 3.1).

The inclusion of symbolic output in the figure reflects the contributions to my thinking of Murray Edelman's *Symbolic Uses of Politics*.[3] It is added because of my convictions that symbolic outputs are extremely important even though policy-oriented writers often neglect them. The importance of such outputs increases in times of rapid change, instability, and alienation and are therefore of more than normal interest to the student of the property tax.

The Eastonian model does not describe the process that occurs within the political system (the black box), but it is compatible with many different methods of describing or analyzing decision making as it occurs within legislative, executive, or judicial agencies. It focuses attention on the possibility that periods of high or rising stress in a particular policy area are apt to result in changes in the political system itself and that such changes are apt to be part of a system of structural evolution that can produce major changes in the political system.

THE HISTORY OF LOCAL GOVERNMENT FINANCE: AN EVOLUTIONARY INTERPRETATION

It is not unreasonable to interpret the early history of the general property tax as an evolutionary development strongly affected by the need to reduce the stress that arises from the taxing process. In the colonial period and in the early years of the United States; property taxes were levied on specific items of property at specified rates. Statutes spelled out the rate of the tax to be applied to specifically defined types of property. For example, land of a certain type might be taxed at 25 cents per acre and cattle of a certain type and age at 10 cents per head. Such a system of taxation invited ceaseless legislative jockeying for advantage. Charges of favoritism were common. This problem led reformers to advocate the adoption of a general property tax that would be applied to all kinds of property at a uniform, ad valorem rate.

The change from specific property taxes to the general, ad valorem property tax is an example of the way a political system deals with stress. The existence of many conflicting demands for changes in the tax rate or in the items to be taxed created much

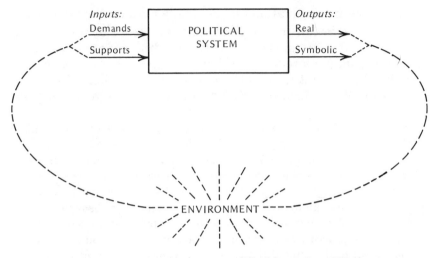

Figure 3.1. The Eastonian system, modified and simplified.

stress and may well have resulted in "demand overload" at the legislative level. The adoption of a *general* (uniform, ad valorem) property tax eliminated many demands at the legislative level by substituting a general rule of taxation and shifting to administrative agencies the problem of determining the amount of the tax to be paid on each type of property. Such a shift was most successful when the uniformity rule was imposed constitutionally, because this removed any possibility that the legislature might revoke or modify the rule. Adopting a general property tax also involved a significant amount of symbolic output. The words "general," "uniform," "universal," and "in proportion to value," which were often used in the constitutions and statutes, have connotations of fairness and equity.

Unfortunately, the reduction in stress was not permanent. Assessors found themselves under pressure to keep assessments low and unchanged. Certain types of property were easy to find and assess; others were not. Owners of some kinds of property were in a position to strongly influence the assessor, and others had much less influence. Assessors responded to this pressure, and the resultant tax differed, in practice, from the uniform universal property tax envisioned in theory and in state constitutions. There is a large literature documenting these developments. For example, in 1897 a special study by the Kansas Bureau of Labor declared that the annual conference of township officials "had become a school in which were taught the methods of releasing property from assessment, of lowering valuation and generally evading the tax laws."[4]

Critics also began to point out that the theory of the tax was defective. Different kinds of property have different economic characteristics and may represent different taxpaying abilities or obligations. At the First Annual Conference of the National Tax Association in 1907, a leading property tax scholar pointed out that:

> The general property tax is today the principal source of revenue in the great majority of states and localities in the American Union. It is a survival of the system of taxation universally adopted under more primitive economic conditions, when property was relatively homogeneous, consisting principally of land and agricultural capital, and constituted an approximately fair test of ability to bear the public burden. The conditions which rendered it tolerable have however long since passed away, and in the present stage of industrial development in the United States it has become utterly inadequate to afford a just and reasonable system of taxation. Ignorance, inertia, and ultra conservatism in the realm of state finance can alone explain its retention to the present day; and during the past thirty years constantly increasing evidences of dissatisfaction and protest have appeared on every hand.[5]

Almost twenty-five years later, a prominent student of property taxation began the concluding chapter of a book on property taxation with the following words:

> If any tax could have been eliminated by adverse criticism, the general property tax should have been eliminated long ago. One searches in vain for one of its friends to defend it intelligently. It is even difficult to find anyone who has given it careful study who can subsequently speak of its failure in temperate language.[6]

These words were written in the early days of the Great Depression of the 1930s. Within a few years, a major change in the property tax would occur as a result of the stress caused by that depression.

The Property Tax and Local Government

The development of the property tax in the United States paralleled the development of an unusual structure of local government. Both reflected the conditions of a vast, largely agricultural country populated by a diverse, independent-minded group of citizens. The states, as sovereign governments, chose to delegate many functions to local governments. Some, such as counties and townships, were created by the state and assigned specific responsibilities as agents of the state. Other units—such as school districts, municipalities, and special districts—were created on a local option basis.

The development and survival of both kinds of local governments were related to the development of property taxation. The legislatures reduced the pressures that converged on them by adopting a general uniform rule of property taxation and delegating to local officials the task of administering the tax. This delegation of power and responsibility involved a rather unusual set of circumstances:

1. The matters to be determined involved an unusual degree of potential conflict.
2. The state legislature was delegating responsibility, not to a salaried state bureauracy, but to locally elected officials who felt primary responsibility to the local electorate rather than to the state legislature.
3. The complexity of the task assigned was destined to grow as property rights became more diversified and society more mobile.
4. Because many local councils and boards levied taxes, there was an unusual degree of fragmentation of authority.

State constitutions often imposed the uniformity rule, but the state legislature provided detailed definitions and established the administrative procedures. These procedures involved a great many elected local officials. Typically, the county clerk was to prepare the tax rolls and provide the necessary blanks to local assessors, who were to list and value property. Local government boards or commissions were to levy the tax and certify that fact to the county clerk, who was to compute the tax bill. Taxes were collected by the county treasurer, a process that also involved the sheriff and state's attorney.

The legislative delegation of administrative authority to local officials, in an area of great policy importance, clearly violates the generally accepted conditions for effective administration. The state government charged local officials with carrying out specific, unpopular tasks, but at the same time provided little aid or supervision. In addition, the state had no weapons to force compliance except possibly the threat of removing the official from office or of bringing criminal charges. These were very blunt instruments, not likely to be used frequently.

As a result, local tax officials, especially assessors, were in a difficult position. Assessing property involves subjective judgment, and assessors soon found that their actions aroused much controversy. Elections were frequent, and assessors who wanted to be re-elected soon discovered that the rules that would maximize their chances for re-election were not the same rules that would provide uniform, ad valorem taxation. The "schools in which were taught the methods of releasing property from assessment, of lowering valuations and generally evading the tax laws" mentioned in the Kansas report could also be called "schools for survival." Assessors learned from each other various tricks that enabled them to minimize the pressures from taxpayers anxious for lower taxes and from local governing bodies and others interested in maintaining governmental services. The assessors who were successful were re-elected. The informal rules that they developed replaced the formal laws in constitutions and statutes. Of course, these rules varied greatly from place to place and, as conditions changed, from time to time. For example, homeowners were favored in some places and farmers in others. In localities seeking to attract or maintain an industrial base, industries were often favored. It was almost always found advantageous to change assessments as infrequently as possible, except, of course, in deflationary periods.

Many examples of the informal rules developed by assessors have been documented, but those of Cook County, Illinois, will serve. The de facto classification system in operation prior to 1970 apparently dated from depression years. The assessor exempted household goods and personal effects in Chicago simply by declaring that they had no value. The system of real estate classification in the assessment manuals resulted in the favorable treatment of residences and other small properties at the expense of large commercial, industrial, and apartment properties.[7] Superimposed on this well-known "almost formal" system there appears to have been a less-well-known system of providing relief to politically or economically important property owners or to those, important or not, who complained loudly enough. Kenneth Fisher and Gail Humphreys describe this mechanism, as it applied to personal property, in a remarkable article concerning the assessment of business personal property in Cook County.[8] Such property was, apparently, assessed rather arbitrarily, but large reductions were routinely obtained by clients of certain law firms who specialized in this practice. It was commonly supposed that these firms were sources of support for the dominant political party, but Fisher and Humphreys report that the same reductions were routinely available to all who appealed assessments, whether or not represented by legal counsel.

The picture of the property tax that emerges from the literature is one of a remarkably adaptive tax source. Each local assessor was free to take the course of action that permitted him to survive best in a hostile environment. Failure was punished by defeat in the next election. Success resulted in the development of a set of rules that superseded the legally established uniformity rule. Occasionally, reform-minded state supervisors attempted to enforce the law, but their weapons were ineffective and apt to be more dangerous to the governor and/or state legislators then to erring local assessors. Courts were sometimes forced to become involved, but after a careful look at the complexities they usually opted for a solution that would least disturb the status quo.

The remarkable survival of a tax system so widely condemned cannot be explained without reference of the unique role that the property tax played in financing the system of fragmented overlapping local governments. It is clear that the tax had one feature that was of great importance in explaining its development and growth: it was ideally suited to financing local government in a large, developing, diverse country populated by people with a very strong sense of independence and a very great distrust of centralized bureaucracy. Property was largely tangible, visible, and immobile. Its location and thus its taxable status was fixed and definite. Small overlapping units of government could be financed with little addition to administrative cost. Therefore, any county clerk who could add and divide could easily compute the tax due the several overlapping districts. The automatic lien and the *in rem* features of the tax also meant that the tax, especially on real estate, was easy to collect. Without payment of the tax, clear title to property could not be passed.

It is unlikely that any other revenue source could have supported the development and continuation of such a system of local governments. General sales and income taxation were not well developed at the time the local government system was being formed. Even today, there would be serious problems if we attempted to eliminate the property tax completely as a source of local government revenue.

There was therefore a symbiotic relationship between the property tax and the local government structure. Local government, as it developed in the United States, could not survive without the property tax. Local government provided many services, provided many jobs, provided officials and voters a sense of efficacy, and provided the community with a sense of identity. Attacks on the property tax were popular and attempts to shift the property tax to others were common, but in the end it was impossible to deny that property within a taxing unit was the major, if not the only, source of revenue to support that unit. This meant that attacks on the property tax and attempts to shift the burden to others must be limited if local units of government were to survive. Because these units had many local supporters and because local assessors had modified the tax so as to reduce the stress created in the local circumstances, both the tax and the local governments survived.

All this adds up to a perfect example of how a political system (or subsystem) is modified in response to stress. In this case the modifications were primarily made to the informal rules and procedures rather than to statutory or constitutional law. A number of historical developments support this interpretation. For example, the classes of property that were first or most frequently given favorable treatment (or eliminated) were those classes least useful for local government finance—i.e., intangible and easily movable personal property.

The changes in government structure that have occurred are also consistent with this thesis. The only major reorganization of local government structure has been the consolidation of school districts. This is significant because school districts were one type of government with an easily measured unit of need (the number of children to be educated), and the cost of providing a given level of service is relatively easy to compute. It is therefore much easier for the state to mandate consolidation and a given level of services and to allocate state funds than it is for smaller units of government to provide multiple or varied functions. It is also interesting that many states used their fiscal powers to encourage or force the development and adoption of consolidation plans.

Elimination of State Property Taxation

The depression years brought a major change in the formal structure of the property tax. One of the advantages of the property tax, from a government's viewpoint, is its stability; however, in periods of rapidly falling property values and income, such stability is also a source of stress. During the Great Depression, property owners often found it difficult, impossible, or unreasonable to pay taxes fixed at predepression levels. Default was widespread and political stress rose to such a level that some thought the entire political structure was threatened. The system persisted, however. The states largely abandoned the property tax and developed other sources of revenue—primarily general sales and income taxes.

These taxes probably would not have been a satisfactory form of taxation for states a hundred years earlier, but after some initial floundering both were adapted to state-level administration and soon became major sources of state revenue. These changes relieved the pressure on the property tax and allowed the local government structure to remain largely unchanged. The success of these state taxes did change the environment and had important long-run implications for local government.

DEVELOPMENTS SINCE WORLD WAR II

I have argued that the hundred years or so prior to the 1930s was a period in which the general property tax idea was adopted as a way of reducing political stress and demand overload on state legislatures. New stress soon arose, and local administrators, especially assessors, modified the tax by informal or extralegal practices that were well adapted to reducing stress in that locality. The tax, modified in these ways, proved to be a remarkably durable source of revenue. It remained unpopular both with the public and with scholarly critics, but the strong support enjoyed by local government helped the property tax to survive while it provided local governments with the revenue needed to operate and maintain a reasonable degree of independence from state control.

The post–World War II years constitute a new era. The property tax has remained unpopular, but there may be less willingness to tolerate the extralegal local adjustments. Certainly, the number of legal modifications has increased. Local units are imposing more nonproperty taxes and obtaining more aid from both state and federal governments.

Sources of Stress

In the post–World War II period, pressures against uniform property taxation seem to have increased. The factors involved, listed not necessarily in order of importance, include rapid changes in property values, widespread publicity concerning tax complaints, litigation and the Railroad Revitalization and Regulatory Reform Act, the movement of industrial development, and improved methods of assessment.

Rapid Changes in Property Values. Most taxes are levied at fixed rates so than an increase in the tax base results in an automatic increase in tax collections. The property tax is different. Theoretically, if not always in practice, the revenue required is first computed and then divided by total assessed value in the tax district to determine the rate of taxation. If strictly followed, this procedure would largely divorce tax levies from the value of the tax base so that increases in the latter would not necessarily result in higher taxes. If fact, tax rate limitation laws and local government policy often serve to focus attention on the stability of rates. To this extent, a time of rising property values will also be a time of rising taxes. If increases in the tax base represent increased ability to pay taxes or increased government benefits, the taxpayer should have no complaint; again, however, the property tax is different. The tax is levied on property that is not necessarily sold and that does not necessarily produce income that rises in proportion to value. Many owners of property find themselves taxed heavily as the result of unrealized capital gains on property that they have no wish to sell and that produces either no income or income rising more slowly than the value of the property. This is especially true when property values are rising as the result of inflationary expectations. Property may sell at prices that are not justified by current income.

The pressure that inflation places on the property tax is increased by the fact that two favorite inflation shelters are agricultural land and residential property. Both are large elements in the property tax base, and owners of both kinds of property are numerous enough to carry a great deal of weight in the political process.

Widespread Publicity Concerning Tax Complaints. It would certainly be inaccurate to say that dissatisfaction with the property tax is new. The quotations cited earlier are evidence of that. On the other hand, it appears likely that knowledge of property inequity and of taxpayer dissatisfaction with it have reached new levels in recent years. Accurate information regarding the property tax has been made available by the Governments Division of the U.S. Census Bureau, by the Advisory Commission on Intergovernmental Relations, and in a number of states by state agencies. In addition, the property tax has become a "hot" item in the popular press. This is well illustrated by the great amount of attention the national press gave to Proposition 13 in California. Property tax limitations of various types have had a long history. The only thing really new about Proposition 13 was the nationwide attention focused upon it as a result of media coverage. The information was not always entirely accurate and the analysis was superficial or nonexistent, but it certainly gave the impression that a major, nationwide revolt was in progress.

Litigation and the Four R Act. Litigation and threats of litigation have always been important in the property tax process. Historically, this means of making demands on the political system has been utilized by business or well-financed organized groups and often has been little publicized. In Illinois, for example, large taxpayers, especially railroads, followed the practice of paying taxes under protest and challenging the legality of levies on the basis of technicalities. The taxes paid under protest were placed in escrow, and eventually the taxes were quietly compromised.[9] In recent years, however, it appears that there has been an upsurge in the amount of litigation and the publicity that such litigation receives. Several factors may have contributed to this: the general tendency toward more litigation, the availability of better statistical evidence regarding assessment levels, and the courts' greater willingness to accept statistical evidence.

The passage of the Railroad Revitalization and Regulatory Reform Act (the Four R Act) in 1976 has given railroads access to federal courts and has made it clear that a level of railroad assessment that is higher than the level of other commercial and industrial property is illegal, even though the level of assessment is below the state-specified standard.

Litigation and threats of litigation are no longer used only on behalf of corporations and wealthy taxpayers. The success of the school finance cases has raised hopes that activities on behalf of low-income or minority groups will succeed. In an era of consumerism and concern for the poor and elderly, there has been no shortage of groups willing to make demands in the name of such groups. One author has argued cogently that the result has been of more benefit to the "haves" than to the "have-nots."[10] In any case, there has been little doubt that problems have been widely publicized and have been a source of stress.

Industrial Development Movement. Additional pressures have been brought upon the property tax by the growing importance of developmental tax concessions and the sophistication of business in seeking them. Local and state governments now have a wide array of tools available in the competition for industrial and commercial growth. A wide variety of tax-exempt bonds and tax exemption devices are available. Originally pioneered by the underdeveloped southern states, the practice has spread to the older industrial states as the battle to prevent loss of industry has intensified. Tax exemptions or reductions play a prominent part in the packages that are put together, and corporations have become very sophisticated in bargaining with local officials, who are often inexperienced in such bargaining and desperate to attract industry or to avoid the loss of existing industry.

A recent article in the *Public Administration Times,* headlined "Industrial Blackmail in the Cities?," detailed how General Motors has used the threats of plant closing to obtain large property tax abatements.[11] Such tactics succeed even though numerous studies have shown that taxes are far down on the list of the factors that determine plant location. Interestingly, the quality of local government services sometimes ranks above taxes in making location decisions.

Improved Assessment Methods. Also interesting is the fact that improvements in assessment administration may have contributed to the pressure on the tax. The use of computer-assisted appraisal has made it relatively easy to update accurately the assessment of certain types of property—especially single-family residences. Because these properties have also been subject to rapid inflationary increases in value, taxes have been shifted to more numerous, politically active groups of taxpayers. Many observers have identified this combination of events as the major cause of the overwhelming acceptance of Proposition 13 in California.

Changing Composition of the Tax Base

The stress that has been placed upon the property tax by the factors just discussed has, as would be expected, resulted in changes in the property tax system.[12] There have been changes both in the composition of the tax base and in the importance of the tax in government finance. Unfortunately, despite the very large literature on the subject of property taxation, detailed nationwide statistics on the composition of the tax base are not available. Broad trends are clear, and they support the idea that administrative feasibility and the ability to support fragmented local governments are important elements in the evolutionary development of the property tax. The types of property that are easiest to hide or move are those most likely to be exempted from taxation or given favorable treatment. Intangible property has largely disappeared from the tax base. Certain classes of tangible personal property have also been eliminated or given favorable treatment in many places. For example, household goods and personal effects generally have been eliminated because the administrative costs and taxpayer irritation were high in relation to taxes collected. Some kinds of business personal property, such as inventories and machinery, have been eliminated in many states because they are mobile. The "location of industry" argument often supports such a move.

Agricultural property has been given preferential treatment in many states by the adoption of use-value assessment. It also appears that much industrial real estate has been exempted or given favorable treatment in an effort to attract and hold industrial development. Evidence of the magnitude of these exemptions is difficult to obtain because many of the actions have been on a case-by-case basis, and a variety of relief methods have been used. Sometimes property is exempted, in accordance with statutory authority, as part of a package of inducements. Sometimes industrial areas are incorporated into districts that have tax advantages, and sometimes tax advantage results from "understandings" beween the assessor and the taxpayer.

An indication of the changes that have occurred in the relative importance of broad classes of property is clear from Tables 3.1 and 3.2. Table 3.1 shows net (subject to taxation) assessed value in three broad classes—locally assessed real property, locally assessed personal property, and state-assessed property. Locally assessed real property has risen from 74.5 percent to 80.6 percent of the total. Locally assessed personal property has declined substantially in importance—from 17.2 percent of the total to 12.2 percent twenty years later. State-assessed property, as defined by the Census Bureau, is largely utility and railroad property. This

Table 3.1. Net Assessed Value, by Type of Property, 1956–1976

	Amount (Billions)		Percent of Total		Percent Change
	1956	1976	1956	1976	1956–1976
Totals[a]	$272.2	$1189.4	100.0%	100.0%	337.0%
State assessed	22.5	84.7	8.3	7.1	276.4
Locally assessed	249.7	1104.7	91.7	92.9	342.4
Real property	202.8	959.1	74.5	80.6	372.9
Personal property	46.9	145.6	17.2	12.2	210.4

Source: U.S. Bureau of the Census, *Taxable Property Values and Assessment/Sales Price Ratios* (Washington, D.C.: Government Printing Office, 1978), p. 5.
[a]Details may not add to total because of rounding.

Table 3.2. Gross Assessed Value of Real Estate, by Type of Property, 1956–1976

	Amount ($ billions)		Percent of Total		Percent Change
	1956	1976	1956	1976	1956–1976
Totals	$209.2	$993.4	100.0%	100.0%	374.9%
Acreage and farms	29.1	117.7	13.9	11.9	304.5
Vacant plotted lots	4.8	38.0	2.3	3.8	691.7
Residential (nonfarm)	113.5	587.9	54.3	59.2	418.0
Single-family only	95.1	495.7	45.5	49.9	421.2
Commercial	34.8	166.2	16.6	16.7	377.6
Industrial	22.6	73.8	10.8	7.4	226.5
Other and unallocable	4.4	9.8	2.1	1.0	122.7

Source: U.S. Bureau of the Census, Taxable Property Values and Assessment/Sales Price Ratios (Washington, D.C.: Government Printing Office, 1978), p. 6.

type of property has declined from 8.3 percent of the total in 1956 to 7.1 percent in 1976.

Table 3.2 provides more detail for locally assessed real estate. The figures are for gross rather than for net assessed value and thus not strictly comparable with the date in Table 3.1. These data show that vacant lots are the most rapidly growing component of the real estate tax base, but of course this type of property is still a minor and often underassessed component of the base.

Unsurprisingly, the second most rapidly growing component is single-family houses. This is consistent with the theory that the Proposition 13-type "revolts" were fueled by the shift of property taxes to homeowners. The growth and assessments of commercial property were very close to the growth in total assessed value, but the growth of industrial property assessments have been almost as slow as the growth in personal property, as shown in Table 3.1. This slow growth is consistent with the theory that industrial development policies have resulted in property tax relief for industrial properties.

The Property Tax in Local Finance

Somewhat surprisingly, there has not been a clear and substantial decline in the percentage of federal, state, and local government revenue received from the property tax in the postwar years. Table 3.3 shows that 9.0 percent of 1946 revenue came from the property tax, as compared with 10.1 percent in the 1978–1979 fiscal year.

Table 3.3. The Changing Importance of Property Taxes, 1947-1979

Year[a]	Property Taxes as a Percent of	
	Federal, State, and Local Revenue Combined	State and Local Revenue Combined
1946	9.0%	40.4%
1950	12.6	35.1
1956	11.2	33.9
1961	10.8	33.3
1965-1966	13.1	29.7
1970-1971	13.7	26.1
1975-1976	13.0	22.3
1976-1977	12.3	21.9
1977-1978	11.7	21.0
1978-1979	10.1	18.9

Source: U.S. Bureau of the Census, *Historical Statistics on Government and Employment* (Washington, D.C.: Government Printing Office, 1978), pp. 27-29, 44-46; and U.S. Bureau of the Census, *Government Finances in 1977-78* (Washington, D.C.: Government Printing Office, 1979), pp. 17-18; and *Government Finances in 1978-79* (1980), p. 17.
[a]Data are for fiscal years ended in calendar year indicated or ended between July 1 and June 30 of the years indicated.

Of course, in 1946, federal revenues included high wartime taxes. In later years the figures also reflect the fact that a substantial portion of federally collected revenues were disbursed as grants to state and local government. By contrast, the property tax as a percent of state and local general revenue (including grants) has declined substantially and continually in the period covered by Table 3.3. The local finance picture shows similar trends. Table 3.4 reveals that the property tax provided 57.6 percent of local government revenue in 1946. By 1978-1979 the percentage had declined to 29.5 percent.

Tables 3.5 and 3.6 permit an examination of the changing role of the property tax in financing various types of local government. In 1952, county governments obtained less than half of their total general revenue from property taxation, but almost all (95.7 percent) of their tax revenue was from the property tax. By 1978-1979, the property tax provided about one-fourth of total general revenue and about one-half of own-source revenue. Significantly, county governments now get only 77.1 percent of their tax revenue from the property tax. This indicates that counties have moved significantly into nonproperty taxation. The situation with respect to the municipal government differs somewhat. In 1952 municipal

Table 3.4. Property Taxes as a Percent of Local General Revenues, 1946–1979

Year[a]	Local Property Taxes as Percent of Local General Revenue
1946	57.6%
1950	50.2
1956	48.8
1961	48.4
1965–1966	44.8
1970–1971	39.9
1975–1976	33.7
1976–1977	33.7
1977–1978	32.9
1978–1979	29.5

Source: U.S. Bureau of the Census, Historical Statistics on Government Finance and Employment (Washington, D.C.: Government Printing Office, 1978), pp. 52–54; and U.S. Bureau of the Census, Government Finances in 1977–78 (Washington, D.C.: Government Printing Office, 1979), pp. 17–18; and Government Finances in 1978–79 (1980), p. 17.

[a]Data are for fiscal years ended in calendar year indicated or ended between July 1 and June 30 of the years indicated.

governments were already substantial users of nonproperty taxes but still received almost half of their general revenue from property taxes. By 1978–1979, however, this figure had declined to 22.8 percent.

The striking feature of school district finance (Table 3.6) is that in most states the property tax is almost the only form of tax revenue, although districts receive much state aid. Nationwide, in 1979 school districts received 37 percent of their revenue from property taxes but received 96.7 percent of the tax revenue from that source.

The portion of township general revenue received from the property tax actually rose from 1952 to 1971–1972 and then showed a sharp decline in the next five years. At the end of the period analyzed, townships were the only unit of government still obtaining more than half of their general revenue from property taxation.

At the beginning of the period, special districts received all tax revenue from the property tax but also received large amounts of own-source, nontax revenues. This reflects the fact that many special districts are financed primarily from fees and charges for services and by special assessments against benefited property.

Table 3.5. Changes in the Importance of Property Taxation in County and Municipal Finance, 1952–1979

| Year[a] | County Governments | | | Municipal Governments | | |
| | Property Taxes as Percent of | | | Property Taxes as Percent of | | |
	General Revenue	Own-Source Revenue	Tax Revenue	General Revenue	Own-Source Revenue	Tax Revenue
1952	46.7%	76.5%	95.7%	49.5%	61.2%	75.2%
1957	46.5	75.0	93.7	46.3	57.1	72.7
1962	45.7	74.5	93.5	44.2	55.6	73.2
1966–1967	42.1	70.5	92.1	38.1	51.8	70.0
1971–1972	36.5	63.0	85.6	31.3	46.6	64.3
1976–1977	31.0	56.7	81.5	25.8	42.7	60.0
1977–1978	30.4	55.7	80.4	24.9	41.1	58.5
1978–1979	26.0	49.7	77.1	22.8	37.6	55.8

Source: U.S. Bureau of the Census, *Historical Statistics on Government Finance and Employment* (Washington, D.C.: Government Printing Office, 1979), p. 46; U.S. Bureau of the Census, *Government Finances in 1977–78* (Washington, D.C.: U.S. Government Printing Office, 1979), pp. 64–65; and *Government Finances in 1978–79* (1980), p. 64.

[a] Data are for fiscal years ended in calendar year indicated or ended between July 1 and June 30 of the years indicated.

There are, obviously, still very important sources of revenue, but it is significant that special districts now receive 10.5 percent of their tax revenue from taxes other than property taxes.

THE FUTURE

I have argued that the property tax can usefully be viewed from a political systems perspective. In this view, it appears that the general property tax was adopted as a way of responding to stress and demand overload created by legislative enactment of specific property taxes. This innovation created a formal structure of universal, uniform, ad valorem property taxation that not only had the ring of fairness and equity, but transferred difficult decisions from state legislators to local officials. These changes did not permanently eliminate stress but fragmented responsibility and promoted de facto modification of the general property tax. As stress rose in periods of crises, legislators, courts, and local officials often became involved in seeking solutions. Sometimes laws were modified to bring them into closer conformity with practice, and

Table 3.6. The Changing Role of Property Taxation in School, Township, and Special District Finance, 1952–1979

Year[a]	School Districts			Townships			Special Districts		
	Property Taxes as a Percent of			Property Taxes as a Percent of			Property Taxes as a Percent of		
	General Revenue	Own-Source Revenue	Tax Revenue	General Revenue	Own-Source Revenue	Tax Revenue	General Revenue	Own-Source Revenue	Tax Revenue
1952	51.6%	89.7%	98.6%	58.5%	86.7%	95.4%	23.9%	26.9%	100.0%
1957	50.1	86.5	98.6	63.6	84.6	93.6	29.1	33.9	100.0
1962	51.0	86.2	98.6	65.3	84.3	93.3	25.0	31.7	100.0
1966–1967	46.9	84.2	98.4	61.8	81.8	92.8	21.5	28.0	100.0
1971–1972	47.3	86.0	98.1	64.9	83.2	93.5	17.3	24.5	94.9
1976–1977	42.1	84.6	97.5	54.3	80.8	91.7	14.0	22.7	91.2
1977–1978	41.2	83.8	97.1	55.5	79.8	91.0	13.0	20.9	92.3
1978–1979	37.0	81.2	96.7	53.9	77.5	90.7	11.9	19.6	89.5

Source: U.S. Bureau of the Census, 1977 Census of Governments, *Historical Statistics on Government Finance and Employment* (Washington, D.C.: Government Printing Office, 1978), p. 46; U.S. Bureau of the Census, *Government Finances in 1977–78* (Washington, D.C.: Government Printing Office, 1979), pp. 64–65; and *Government Finances in 1978–79* (1980), p. 64.

[a]Data are for fiscal years ended in calendar year indicated or ended between July 1 and June 30 of the years indicated.

sometimes practices were modified to bring them into closer conformity with laws. Rarely, if ever, however, did practice come into complete comformity with the general property tax idea.

The property tax and its administrative procedures were closely related to the structure of local government that evolved. No other revenue source could have provided the financial resources to support the particular structure that developed. The fragmented nature of the administrative responsibility and the subjective nature of property values made it possible for the tax to be adapted to local political pressures in a way that made the tax tolerable, but not popular.

The depression years produced a property tax crisis of unusual severity, and state governments turned to other sources of revenue —particularly sales and income taxes. Both forms of taxation soon proved to be feasible sources of state revenue, and the property tax became almost entirely a local tax. In the post–World War II years, local governments received increasing portions of their revenue from state and federal grants and from local nonproperty tax sources.

I have argued elsewhere that local governments cannot continue to exist in their present form without continuing to depend on the property tax for a substantial portion of their revenue.[13] This argument is based on the belief that small, overlapping governments would not be able to levy and administer nonproperty taxes successfully. Administrative and compliance problems would be great. Additional problems would be posed by the unequal geographic distribution of alternative tax bases and the mobility of certain kinds of tax bases.

It was also argued that intergovernmental aid cannot be used to replace own-source revenue completely without fundamentally altering local government. This argument rests on the notion that governments that levy taxes must, in general, control the expenditures of the funds so that opposition to taxation can be countered by support "purchased" by the expenditure. There is also a technical problem of revenue distribution formulas if one attempts to support fragmented local government on a grant basis. Grant formulas can be developed rather easily for school districts, which provide a single kind of service to an easily countable clientele, but it becomes much more difficult when one deals with multipurpose governments overlapped in various ways by other units of government providing various kinds of services. I strongly suspect that attempts to do so would soon lead either to detailed direction from the government providing the grant or to a state-imposed "rationalization" of local government structure that would make it easier to distribute funds. Either would amount to a fundamental change in the structure of local government.

If this analysis is correct, it means we face the following alternatives:

1. Reorganize local government into larger single- or dual-units that will have greater capacity to raise nonproperty tax revenues and to which it will be easier to allocate state and federal aid.
2. Allow local governments to be gradually transformed into administrative arms of the state with little control over either the kind or the level of services provided.
3. Continue to rely on the property tax as the "balancing" revenue source—that is, as the source over which local governments have enough control that it can be raised or lowered in deference to local preference regarding the level of taxation and the level of local services.

I must admit that I have not completely proved my case. It appears from earlier tables that all units of government are increasing their use of nonproperty revenues. It is difficult to prove that this has resulted in a loss of independence or control. It certainly has not resulted in consolidation or "rationalization" of local governments, and Table 3.7 shows that smaller cities and counties have been just about as successful in utilizing nonproperty tax sources as have larger ones.

Like any academician, I am sure of the need for more research. We need to do much more serious research and thinking about the relationship between government structure and finance. If we do not, we may find we have relieved stress on the political system by chipping away at the property tax and inadvertently reducing local government to an inefficient, badly structured arm of state (or federal) government.

Table 3.7. The Role of the Property Tax in Municipalities and Counties of Various Sizes, 1976–1977

	Property Tax as Percent of		
	General Revenue	Own-Source Revenue	Tax Revenue
Municipal Population			
Less than 2500	23.4%	40.3%	66.9%
2500– 4999	25.5	39.3	61.4
5000– 9999	26.4	39.2	62.7
10,000– 24,999	27.5	40.6	63.5
25,000– 49,999	30.7	46.0	69.0
50,000– 99,999	33.4	50.3	71.8
100,000–299,999	29.1	48.1	67.8
300,000 or more	22.6	39.9	53.0
County Population			
Less than 10,000	35.9%	59.7%	89.3%
10,000– 24,999	27.7	52.8	85.9
25,000– 49,999	25.6	47.7	80.6
50,000– 99,999	25.1	48.0	76.4
100,000–149,999	27.9	52.5	79.6
150,000–249,999	30.2	56.6	83.8
250,000–499,999	31.9	57.1	80.6
500,000 or more	35.1	62.3	81.5

Source: U.S. Bureau of the Census, *Finances of Municipalities and Township Governments* (Washington, D.C.: Government Printing Office, 1979), Table 17, p. 37; and U.S. Bureau of the Census, *Finances of County Governments* (Washington, D.C.: Government Printing Office, 1979), Table 11, p. 25.

NOTES

1. David Easton, *A Framework for Political Analysis* (New York: Prentice-Hall, 1965); *Political Systems* (New York: Knopf, 1953); *A Systems Analysis of Political Life* (New York: John Wiley, 1965); and "An Approach to the Analysis of Political Systems," *World Politics* 9 (1957): 383–400.
2. Easton, *A Framework for Political Analysis,* chap. 2.
3. Murray, Edelman, *The Symbolic Uses of Politics* (Urbana: University of Illinois Press, 1964). See also *Politics as Symbolic Action* (Chicago: Markham, 1971).
4. Kansas Legislative Council, *Summary History of Kansas Finance*, Publication no. 60 (October 1937), p. 14.
5. J. H. T. McPherson, "The General Property Tax as a Source of State Revenue," in National Tax Association, *State and Local Taxation* (New York: Macmillan, 1908), p. 475.
6. Jens Peter Jensen, *Property Taxation in the United States* (Chicago: University of Chicago Press, 1931), p. 27.
7. The politics involved in legalizing this system in the 1979 Illinois Constitutional Convention is described in Joyce D. Fishbone and Glenn W. Fisher, *Politics*

of the Purse: Revenue and Finance in the Sixth Illinois Constitutional Convention (Urbana: University of Illinois Press, 1974), p. 199.

8. Kenneth P. Fisher and Gail S. Humphreys, "Costly Misconceptions of Law and Legal Services: The Small Business Owner vs. The Chicago Personal Property Tax," *American Bar Foundation Journal* (Summer 1978): 545–563.
9. Glenn W. Fisher and Robert P. Fairbanks, "The Politics of Taxation," *Administrative Science Quarterly* 12, no. 1 (June 1967): 48–71.
10. Robert Kuttner, *The Revolt of the Haves* (New York: Simon and Schuster, 1980).
11. Neal Peirce, "Industrial Blackmail in the Cities?" *Public Administration Times* (December 1, 1980).
12. For an excellent summary of the changes that have occurred, see Steven David Gold, *Property Tax Relief* (Lexington, Mass.: Lexington Books, 1979) p. 331.
13. Glenn W. Fisher, "The Impact of Inflation on the Tax Base, paper presented at the 1980 Property Tax Forum (International Association of Assessing Officers), Washington, D.C., March 10–11, 1980.

Chapter 4

Property Tax Relief Trends in the Midwest: Where It All (or Much of it) Began

*Steven D. Gold**

For a long time the property tax has been one of the most unpopular taxes. Despite its reputation, until recently the property tax was able to hang on and in fact to rise as a percentage of the market value of the property. This changed in the 1970s, however, when there was an outpouring of property tax relief such as never occurred before. While property tax revenue rose in absolute terms in recent years, it fell relative to other taxes, income, the market value of property, and even prices. Perhaps partially as a result of these trends, surveys in 1979 and 1980 suggest that the federal income tax has dethroned the property tax as the most despised levy in the United States.[1]

The states in the Midwest have been prominent purveyors of property tax relief. Formerly noted for unusually high property taxes, this region did more to de-emphasize the property tax than any other during the past decade. In this chapter, I will describe and analyze the property tax relief provided in twelve Midwestern

This paper represents an update and expansion of material included in Steven D. Gold, *Property Tax Relief* (Lexington, Mass.: Lexington Books, 1979), which should be consulted for a fuller discussion of the issues addressed here.

*Project Director, Intergovernmental Finance Project, National Conference of State Legislatures.

states and attempt to explain why is has proliferated.

First, property tax relief has to be defined. It refers to any action that reduces property tax burdens below the level they would otherwise reach. Relief for some may come at the expense of higher taxes for others. Relief may be provided although taxes are increasing, if the relief avoids even larger increases.

This definition of relief is broader than the definition often encountered. It includes not only circuit breakers and homestead exemptions or credits but also classification, state aid to local governments, state-imposed limitations on local spending or taxes, local nonproperty taxes, and other measures.

It goes without saying that these alternative means of dispensing property tax relief differ greatly in terms of their effects. Some mechanisms benefit only a single kind of property while others benefit all. Some reduce the regressivity of the property tax substantially, others do so more moderately, and, in some cases, any effect on progressivity or regressivity is difficult to determine. Some types of relief are easy to administer while others are difficult or expensive. Some purport to change economic incentives while others have no such pretensions. Finally, most types of relief complicate the tax system, but some do so much more than others.

Table 4.1 traces changes over time in five measures of reliance on the property tax for the nation:

Property tax revenue as a proportion of state–local general revenue, excluding federal aid;
Property tax revenue per capita (eliminating the effects of inflation);
Property tax revenue per $1000 of personal income;
Property tax per $100 of market value of homes;
Property tax per $100 of market value of farm real estate.

Clearly, a turning point occurred around 1972. Although four of these measures had risen substantially in the preceding quarter-century, after 1972 there were declines in per-capita property taxes adjusted for inflation, the proportion of personal income claimed by the property tax, and effective tax rates, on homes and farms.

Within this overall pattern of general decline in property tax reliance, the record in the Midwest is especially impressive because the shift away from the property tax has been especially large. Table 4.2 shows how the property tax as a percentage of total state–local taxes compares in each region to the national average. In 1967, the seven Plains states were, on the average, 10.2 percentage points higher than the national average and the five Great Lakes states were 4.2 percentage points above average. By 1978, they were still above average, but only by 3.3 percentage points and 0.8 percentage point, respectively. Property taxes in no other region declined as sharply.

Statistics comparing the proportion of personal income taken by the property tax reveal the same pattern. In 1972, nine of the twelve states being considered were above the national average (Michigan, Indiana, Illinois, Wisconsin, Minnesota, Iowa, South Dakota, Nebraska, and Kansas), while the only three below average were North Dakota, Missouri, and Ohio. But by 1978, only five states—Michigan, Wisconsin, South Dakota, Nebraska, and Kansas—were still above the national average.

Table 4.3 compares property tax levels in the twelve states in 1979. There is clearly a wide variation in levels of property tax, with the highest state being nearly twice as high as the lowest in terms of per-capita taxes and tax as a proportion of income. Variations of effective rates are even greater.

Before continuing, I should mention a defect shared by most of the property tax statistics used thus far. As reported by the Census Bureau, these statistics reflect property taxes paid directly and do not take into account rebates or credits on the income tax that may depend on property tax bills. This omission is relatively insignificant in most states but it particularly overstates property tax levels in Michigan, Minnesota, and Wisconsin because each state grants large circuit breakers (see the following section). In Minnesota, the benefits of the circuit breaker in 1979 equaled 15 percent of property tax collections as reported by the Census Bureau; in Michigan, 9.5 percent; and in Wisconsin, 5.7 percent. In other states, the comparable percentage was 2 percent or less. As a proportion of residential property taxes alone, circuit breaker benefits are, of course, higher and reach more than 30 percent in Minnesota.[3]

The existence of circuit breakers and other credits and exemptions complicates comparisons of tax levels. Because of these programs, property tax rates vary from household to household due to age, income, or home value. Even if there were no such exemptions or credits, comparisons would be complicated because of variations in the amounts of property taxes paid by nonresidential property owners and by intrastate geographic variations in tax levels.

RELIEF PROGRAMS

Table 4.4 summarizes some of the most important features of the property tax relief mechanisms used in the Midwest. Each will be discussed individually.

Table 4.1. Historical Statistics on Property Tax Usage

| Year[a] | Property Tax Revenue | | | | Property Tax per $100 of Market Value | |
	Total ($ billions)	As a Proportion of State–Local General Revenue (Excluding Federal Aid) (percent)	Per Capita ($ 1967)	Per $1000 of Personal Income	Homes[b]	Farm[c] Real Estate
1979	$64.944	24.2%	$142.96	$35.69	$1.34	$0.64
1978	66.422	27.0	161.63	41.17	1.51	0.70
1977	62.535	28.0	158.91	42.85	1.67	0.76
1976	57.001	28.4	155.39	43.24	1.84	0.80
1975	51.491	28.4	149.57	42.76	1.89	0.93
1974	47.705	28.8	152.42	43.22	1.90	0.96
1973	45.283	30.0	161.69	45.40	2.07	1.06
1972	42.133	31.2	161.01	46.77	2.12	1.10
1971	37.852	31.9	150.07	45.59	1.98	1.08
1970	34.054	31.3	142.92	44.02	1.93	1.05
1969	30.673	32.2	137.83	42.87	1.85	1.01
1968	27.747	33.0	132.67	42.30	1.87	0.98
1967	26.047	34.4	131.08	42.99	1.80	0.98
1962	19.054	37.8	112.74	44.53	1.51	1.00
1957	12.864	37.5	88.73	37.82	1.32	0.95
1948	6.126	39.8	57.95	30.76	1.14	0.87
1936	4.093	55.0	76.94	63.46	n.a.	1.11

| 1927 | 4.730 | 66.1 | 76.42 | 59.46 | n.a. | 1.16 |
| 1902 | 0.706 | 72.1 | 34.30 | 34.95 | n.a. | n.a. |

Source: Columns 1–4: U.S. Bureau of the Census, *Governmental Finances* (Washington, D.C.: Government Printing Office, various years); U.S. Bureau of the Census, *1972 Census of Governments*, vol. 6, no. 4, 1974; *Historical Statistics on Governmental Finances and Employment* (Washington, D.C.: Government Printing Office); Column 5: Department of Housing and Urban Development, *Series Data Handbook Covering Section 203b Home Mortgage Characteristics* (1978); Column 6: Department of Agriculture, *Farm Real Estate Taxes* (various years), and Jerome M. Stam and Ann G. Sibold, *Agriculture and the Property Tax* (Washington, D.C.: Department of Agriculture, 1977), p. 51; income and price data: U.S. Bureau of the Census, *Historical Statistics of the United States; Colonial Times to 1970 and Statistical Abstract of the United States* (Washington, D.C.: Government Printing Office).

[a] Fiscal year, for columns 1–3; calendar year, for columns 4–5.

[b] For existing homes with newly issued FHA insured mortgages under the Section 203B program.

[c] For year in which tax is collected.

Table 4.2. Property Tax Revenue as a Percent of Total State–Local Tax Revenue

(Percentage points above or below the national average)

Region	1978	1972	1967	1962	1957	1942
Northeast	+11.6%	+ 9.0%	+ 7.5%	+ 8.0%	+ 8.1%	+ 7.0%
Mideast	– 4.8	– 5.5	– 5.2	– 5.4	– 3.2	+ 1.4
Great Lakes[a]	+ 0.8	+ 5.1	+ 4.2	+ 7.3	+ 5.9	+ 0.2
Plains[a]	+ 3.3	+ 6.1	+10.2	+10.1	+10.2	+ 6.8
Southeast	–12.3	–14.8	–15.7	–16.5	–16.9	–15.2
Southwest	– 6.9	– 7.5	– 6.1	– 8.5	– 8.0	– 9.8
Rocky Mountain	+ 2.3	+ 2.4	+ 4.2	+ 4.2	+ 6.3	+20.5
Far West	+ 1.7	+ 2.9	– 0.3	– 5.6	– 5.8	– 4.0
National average	34.3	39.1	42.7	45.9	44.6	53.2

Source: Derived from data in *Significant Features of Fiscal Federalism, 1979–80* ed. (Washington, D.C.: Advisory Commission on Intergovernmental Relations, 1980), p. 87.
[a] Plains states include North Dakota, South Dakota, Nebraska, Iowa, Kansas, Minnesota, and Missouri. Great Lakes states include Illinois, Indiana, Ohio, Michigan, and Wisconsin.

Circuit Breakers

Circuit breakers are relief programs in which benefits depend both on one's property tax payment and household income. They are invariably state funded. Every state in the Midwest has a circuit breaker of some sort, making this region the only one in the country where coverage is comprehensive.[3] In 1964, Wisconsin was the first state in the nation to offer a circuit breaker. Three of the four largest circuit breakers in the country are offered in this area, with the only other major one being Oregon. Thus, the Midwest could be termed "circuit breaker country."

Yet, even in the Midwest, for most states the circuit breaker is only a small portion of the property tax relief story. According to Table 4.5 only senior citizens are eligible for the circuit breaker in eight of the twelve states. Excluding Indiana's modest program, average per-capita benefits vary from $122 in South Dakota to $229 in Illinois. Except in Illinois, fewer than half of all senior households receive benefits, and per capita costs are under $5. The three big programs in Michigan, Minnesota, and Wisconsin, where all age groups are eligible for the circuit breaker, had per capita costs of $35.79, $47.22, and $19.77, respectively.[4]

The versatility of the circuit breaker is illustrated by the contrasts among these three programs. Wisconsin targets its relief

Table 4.3. Five Measures of Property Tax Levels, Midwestern States, 1979

| State | Property Tax Revenue | | | Property Tax per $100 of Market Value | |
	As a Proportion of State-Local Revenue^a	Per Capita	Per $1000 of Personal Income	Homes	Farm Real Estate
Illinois	28.8% (4)[b]	$350 (4)	$39 (8)	1.48% (5)	0.74% (5)
Indiana	24.7 (9)	247 (11)	32 (11)	1.14 (7)	0.43 (12)
Iowa	28.5 (5)	339 (7)	42 (6)	1.39 (6)	0.66 (7)
Kansas	30.2 (3)	357 (3)	46 (4)	0.98 (12)	0.70 (6)
Michigan	27.2 (6)	376 (2)	44 (5)	2.45 (1)	1.50 (1)
Minnesota	21.4 (11)	311 (8)	40 (7)	1.04 (9)	0.57 (10)
Missouri	22.1 (10)	205 (12)	28 (12)	1.03 (10)	0.47 (11)
Nebraska	31.1 (2)	389 (1)	52 (1)	2.48 (2)	1.01 (3)
North Dakota	21.0 (12)	257 (10)	36 (9)	1.01 (11)	0.63 (8)
Ohio	25.5 (8)	360 (9)	33 (10)	1.09 (8)	0.62 (9)
South Dakota	33.1 (1)	343 (6)	50 (2)	1.63 (4)	0.84 (4)
Wisconsin	25.8 (7)	346 (5)	46 (3)	1.66 (3)	1.38 (2)

Source: U.S. Bureau of the Census, *Governmental Finances in 1978–79* (Washington, D.C.: Government Printing Office, 1980), first three columns; ACIR, *Significant Features of Fiscal Federalism, 1979–1980 ed.* (Washington, D.C.: Advisory Commission on Intergovernmental Relations, 1980), p. 140, fourth column; U.S. Department of Agriculture, *Farm Real Estate Taxes, 1979* (Washington, D.C., 1981), fifth column.

^aExcluding federal aid.
^bNumbers in parentheses indicate ranking among the twelve states.

Table 4.4. Property Tax Relief Mechanisms in Midwestern States, 1979

State	Homestead Exemption or Credit — All Ages	Homestead Exemption or Credit — Seniors Only	Circuit Breaker	Local Taxes — Sales	Local Taxes — Income	State-Imposed Limits — Levy	State-Imposed Limits — Spending	State-Imposed Limits — Assessments	Percent of State–Local Taxes Collected by State — National Rank
Illinois	local	local	seniors	1359		CMS			10
Indiana	state	local	seniors		37	CMS			32
Iowa	state		seniors		21	CMS	S	yes	20
Kansas			all ages[a]	20		CMS			13
Michigan			all ages		16	CMS			24
Minnesota	state		all ages	1		CM			39
Missouri			seniors[b]	218	2	CMS	S		12
Nebraska	state	state	seniors	4		CMS			5
North Dakota			seniors						31
Ohio	state		seniors	51	417	CMS		yes	9
South Dakota			seniors	46					4
Wisconsin	state		all ages			CM	S		34

Source: Local taxes: ACIR, *Significant Features of Fiscal Federalism, 1979–80 ed.* (Washington, D.C.: Advisory Commission on Intergovernmental Relations, 1980), p. 108; centralization: U.S. Bureau of the Census, *Governmental Finances in 1978–79* (Washington, D.C.: Government Printing Office, 1980); other data: survey of states by author.

Notes: "Local" and "State" refer to whether program is financed at state or local level; figures under "Local Taxes" are the number of jurisdictions levying each tax as of October 1979; letters under "State-Imposed Limits" refer to counties (C), municipalities (M), and school districts (S); last column shows the national rank of each state in terms of the proportion of state–local taxes collected by the state government, an indicator of fiscal centralization; the lower the number, the greater the decentralization.

Relief for farm and business property is not shown in the table; Wisconsin and Indiana have credits for renters; Minnesota and Iowa have classification.

[a] Nonelderly households qualify only if they have a dependent child.

[b] See note 3, end of chapter.

68

most narrowly, limiting eligibility to households with incomes under $14,000. This enables it to offer the highest average benefit per recipient, $292. Minnesota provides relief to more than three-fifths of its households, with average 1979 benefits of $215. Michigan's circuit breaker is narrower, with only two-fifths of households claiming benefits, so it has a somewhat larger average benefit, $261.[5]

Homestead Credits or Exemptions

Seven states have credits or exemptions for homeowners in which benefits do not vary with income levels, as Table 4.6 indicates. All homeowners are eligible for these programs but, several states provide extra exemptions or credits to senior citizens in addition to their general program.

An important distinction lies between programs that are funded by states and those that are not so funded. In five of the eight

Table 4.5. Circuit Breaker Program Characteristics

State	Income Ceiling	Average Benefit	Per-Capita Cost
All Ages Covered			
Kansas[a]	$12,800[b]	$150	$ 3.98
Michigan	none	261	35.79
Minnesota	none[c]	215	47.22
Wisconsin	14,000	292	19.77
Only Senior Citizens Covered			
Illinois	12,000	229	7.75
Indiana	5,000	29	0.18
Iowa	10,000	156	4.16
Missouri	9,000	146	1.84
Nebraska[d]	5,200 single	n.a.	n.a.
	7,700 married		
North Dakota	9,000	150	2.42
Ohio	15,000	144	4.46
South Dakota	4,625 single	122	2.70
	7,375 married		

Source: Survey by author.
Note: Income ceiling is as of 1980 and program statistics are as of 1979.
[a]In Kansas, non–senior citizens are eligible only if they have dependent children under 18 years old.
[b]The ceiling is nominally $13,000, but effectively $12,800.
[c]There is no nominal ceiling, but due to interaction with homestead credit, the effective ceiling is $36,000.
[d]Nebraska is included because exemption levels vary with income and the program is state funded.

Table 4.6. Characteristics of State Homestead Exemption and Credit Programs

State	Description of Program	State Financed	Average Benefit	Per-Capita Cost
Illinois	$3000 exemption for increased assessment above 1977 level	no	n.a.	n.a.
	$1500 exemption for senior citizens	no	n.a.	n.a.
Indiana	$1000 exemption for all homeowners with mortgages or contracts	no	n.a.	n.a.
	$1000 exemption for senior citizens	no	n.a.	n.a.
	10 percent of all tax bills	yes	n.a.	n.a.
Iowa	$4850 exemption for all homeowners (minimum credit of $62.50)	yes	$120	$28.42
Minnesota	55% of tax bill, with $600 maximum [a]	yes	239	59.39
Nebraska	Exemption of varying proportions of assessed valuation up to $4000 for non-senior citizens; varying proportions of assessed valuation up to $25,000 for senior citizens	yes	87	16.32
Ohio	2.5% of tax bill	yes	11	3.91
Wisconsin	12% of tax bill	yes	104	19.11

Source: Survey by author.
Notes: Benefits and costs are for 1979, except for Wisconsin, which are for 1980; program description is for 1981.
[a] In 1980, the audit was 50 percent of the tax bill, with a maximum of $550. In 1979, the maximum was $325 and the credit was 45 percent.

states, homestead programs are financed entirely by states. In two states they are financed locally, and in one state there are programs of both types. Where there is no state funding, the exemption tends to raise property taxes for nonresidental property and for homeowners who do not receive the exemption. But if the state replaces the property tax revenue lost by the localities, the property tax of nonexempt property is unaffected.

The increase of the homestead programs is an important development of the 1970s. While the growth of circuit breakers has generated considerable publicity, the expansion of these programs has gone relatively unnoticed. All states offering these programs either initiated or expanded them during the 1970s. As Table 4.7 shows, the amount of funds for these programs is about two-thirds of those for circuit breakers. The number of households benefitting from homestead programs is more than twice as great as those in circuit breaker programs.

For programs defined by a certain amount of assessed valuation exempted, it is helpful to know the assessment ratio in order to judge their quantitative significance.[6] Table 4.8 shows the assessment ratios for homes in the largest city of each of four states in 1976. While such information is of only limited value because of its date and limited geographic coverage, it is better than no indication at all. Even with this data, the value of the exemption cannot be determined if the state does not replace the assessed valuation exempted, because the tax rate tends to rise in such situations. The value of the exemption in that case varies in each local jurisdiction depending on the proportion of its property tax base exempted. Only in the special case where jurisdictions cannot raise their tax rates due to state-imposed limitations can the value of the exemption be determined without considerable additional information.

Renter Credits

Only two of the twelve Midwestern states have credits specifically for renters, although nationally about one-fifth of the states offer such credits. Wisconsin's credit is based on the assumption that 25 percent of rent represents property tax and provides a credit of 12 percent of that amount. This program, begun as a companion of the 12-percent credit of homeowner property taxes, covered 464,950 households in 1980 at a cost of $21.8 million. The average Wisconsin benefit of $46.98 is considerably higher than that of the other state with renter credit, Indiana, where the average

Table 4.7. Participation and Total State Costs of Circuit Breakers and Exemptions and Credits for Homeowners in 1979

State	Circuit Breaker		Homestead Exemption or Credit	
	Number of Participants (thousands of households)	State Cost ($ millions)	Number of Participants (thousands of households)	State Cost ($ millions)
Illinois	381.0	$ 87.1	372.0 (seniors program)	n.a.
Indiana	32.0	0.9	n.a.	about $33 (10% credit only)
Iowa	77.5	12.1	687.0	$ 82.6
Kansas	62.2	9.3		
Michigan	1257.6	328.6		
Minnesota	885.1	190.0	1012.0	242.3
Missouri	61.1	8.9		
Nebraska	Included with homestead data		294.2	25.6
North Dakota	13.1	1.9		
Ohio	333.4	47.9	3700.0	42.0
South Dakota	15.2	1.9		
Wisconsin[a]	318.0	92.6	910.3	92.0
Totals	3436.2	$781.2	6975.5	$517.5

Source: Survey by author.

[a] Wisconsin data is for benefits paid in 1980; homestead program statistics include some households that were homeowners for only a portion of the year. Data in Table 4.6 is for households that were homeowners for the entire year. When Wisconsin began the 12-percent credit for homeowners, it eliminated the income tax deduction for property taxes. Therefore, the cost to the state was only about half of the $92.0 million shown in the table.

maximum benefit is $28.50. That program provides a credit equal to 1.9 percent of rent up to $1500.

Without doubt, one reason why more states do not have renter credits is that renters are usually covered by circuit breakers. Only the Nebraska, South Dakota, and Ohio circuit breakers do not include elderly renters. The proportion of rent assumed to represent property taxes varies from 15 to 30 percent in the other nine states, with 20 percent being the median percentage. Thus, nonelderly renters who qualify receive some benefits in the four states with general circuit breakers and in Indiana. In Wisconsin, renters with incomes below $14,000 may qualify for both the circuit breaker and the renter credit.

Farm Programs

Only seven states in the country have not enacted laws providing for preferential assessment of farmland. Three of them—Kansas, Wisconsin, and Michigan—are in the Midwest; however, the latter two states are unique in that they have circuit breakers especially for owners of farmland. Minnesota and Iowa also have credits for owners of farmland that do not depend on the farmer's income, as circuit breaker benefits do. Apparently no other states in the nation have such programs.

Thus at least four of the states in the Midwest are highly original in their farm policies. It is difficult to assess the situation in other states, since little information has been collected about how their preferential assessment laws operate. In most states across the country, these laws were enacted in order to perpetuate a previously existing de facto policy of assessing farmland at below-market price levels.

Table 4.8. Home Assessment Ratio in Major Cities of Selected States with Homestead Exemption or Credit Defined by Assessed Valuation, 1976

State	Assessment Ratio
Illinois	26.7%
Indiana	16.3
Iowa	74.0
Nebraska	19.1

Source: ACIR, *Significant Features of Fiscal Federalism,* 1979–80 ed. (Washington, D.C.: Advisory Commission on Intergovernmental Relations, 1980), p. 141.
Note: Assessment ratio is the assessment divided by the sales price.

Table 4.9 lists the dates when each farm assessment law was enacted and categorizes these laws according to whether they provide for deferral or outright forgiveness of taxes and whether participants must sign a contract before they can receive preferential assessments.

Business Tax Breaks

Most states provide exemptions for certain business property as an incentive for attracting new businesses or encouraging expansion. Unfortunately, data on these programs have apparently not been collected systematically.

Personal Property

The Midwest also is a leader in the nationwide trend toward exempting personal property from taxation. In 1976, four of the Midwestern states—Illinois, Minnesota, North Dakota, and South Dakota—had completely exempted personal property, representing half of the states in the nation that had completely abolished this form of taxation. Other states have taken partial steps in this direction, both eliminating certain types of property such as cattle

Table 4.9. Farm Tax Relief Programs

State	Year Enacted	Type
Illinois	1970	deferred taxation
Indiana	1961	pure preferential assessment
Iowa	1967	pure preferential assessment
Kansas		none
Michigan	1974	circuit breaker, restrictive agreement
Minnesota	1967	deferred taxation
Missouri	1975	pure preferential assessment
Nebraska	1974	deferred taxation
North Dakota	1973	pure preferential assessment
Ohio	1974	deferred taxation
South Dakota	1967	pure preferential assessment
Wisconsin	1977	circuit breaker, restrictive agreement

Source: Robert E. Coughlin et al., "Differential Assessment of Real Property on an Incentive to Open Space Preservation and Farmland Retention," *National Tax Journal* (June 1978): 167.

Note: Deferred taxation programs require payment of a penalty if land is withdrawn from agricultural use. Restrictive agreement programs require participants to commit land to agricultural use for a certain period before receiving lower assessments. Pure preferential assessment programs have neither of these conditions.

or inventories, or by exempting certain proportions of all personal property. In Iowa, for example, personal property has been progressively exempted on a ten-year schedule beginning in 1973. By 1983, all personal property will be exempt in Iowa, according to present law.

At least seven of the Midwestern states—Iowa, Michigan, Nebraska, Minnesota, North Dakota, South Dakota, and Wisconsin—make payments to local governments to replace all or part of the taxes formerly collected on personal property. The sums involved are often quite sizable. For example, in Michigan, the credit for inventories in 1977 was $130.7 million.[7] As in the case of homestead exemptions discussed previously, when the state finances these exemptions, their effect is quite different from when it does not do so. With state replacement of forgone revenue, the cost is borne by state taxpayers rather than by other local property taxpayers.

Classification

One type of relief seldom used in the Midwest is classification, defined as unequal treatment by law of various classes of nonfarm real property. Only four Midwestern states have any form of classification: Minnesota, Iowa, Ohio, and Illinois, where classification is confined to Cook County.

Minnesota has one of the oldest and most complicated classification systems in the country, with more than twenty different classes, each with its own assessment ratio. Frequent changes have been made in the ratios in recent years with the objective of offsetting the tendency for homes to assume an expanded share of total assessed valuation.[8]

Iowa's classification system was the first of its kind, taking the form of limitations on assessment increases. Each of several classes of property is permitted to increase 4 percent per year on a statewide basis, excluding new construction. If valuations rise faster than this rate, the assessed value of all property in a class is multiplied by a factor to bring down the total statewide increase to 4 precent. Thus assessment ratios are unequal among classes of property, although they are equal within each class of property. In other words, homes and factories may be assessed at unequal percentages, but each home should be assessed at the same percentage as other homes. Thus the relationship between assessment ratios for classes varies each year. This system was enacted, originally in 1977, to prevent homes from becoming a larger proportion of valuations.

Ohio enacted a similar program in 1980, except that it provides for unequal tax rates rather than unequal assessment ratios.

General Relief

Each of the forms of relief discussed thus far can be characterized as "targeted"; that is, all are directed at a particular type of property or property owner. It turns out that most of the property tax relief provided over the past decade was not of this type, but was rather "general," in the sense that all types of property received it. Targeted relief is appropriate to assist a specific type of property, but when the objective is to lower property taxes across the board, relief should be general.

The most important kind of general relief is state aid to local governments, with local nonproperty taxes and user charges being next most important. In addition, three Midwestern states employ what can be characterized as "universal percentage credits," which cover a flat percentage of property taxes for all property (or at least all real property).

Statistics on state aid are somewhat ambiguous because functional responsibilities are assigned differently in various states. For example, one state may provide no aid at all because it has completely assumed a particular function, while another state may provide some aid, yet leave considerable financial responsibility at the local level.

In general, the more centralized a state's tax system, the more property tax relief is being provided, since the general property tax is almost totally a local tax. Table 4.10 shows the proportion of state–local taxes collected by Midwestern state governments in 1970 and 1979. All states in the Midwest have become more centralized, but they have changed at different rates. North Dakota, Indiana, and Iowa took the largest strides in the direction of centralization and consequently had above-normal rates of decrease of reliance on property taxes. Illinois, Michigan, South Dakota, and Missouri centralized the least during this period.

It is interesting to note that the states with the least centralization (South Dakota and Nebraska) and the most centralization (Minnesota and Wisconsin) maintained their positions throughout the decade. As noted previously, increased centralization could be produced either by expanded state aid or by assumption of formerly local functions.

Table 4.11 demonstrates the shifts away from the property tax in another way. The property tax decreased as a proportion of total local government general revenue in all these states, with the median proportion falling from 50.7 percent in 1970 to 34.0 percent in 1979. The largest decreases were in Indiana and North Dakota,

Table 4.10. Proportion of State–Local Taxes Collected by State Governments, 1970 and 1979

State	1970		1979		Change
Illinois	53.0%	(5)[a]	56.1%	(9)	3.1%
Indiana	55.1	(4)	66.0	(3)	10.9
Iowa	51.0	(8)	61.0	(6)	10.0
Kansas	48.6	(9)	57.1	(7)	8.5
Michigan	58.0	(3)	62.3	(5)	4.3
Minnesota	60.7	(1)	70.4	(1)	9.7
Missouri	51.2	(7)	57.0	(8)	5.8
Nebraska	44.4	(11)	53.0	(11)	8.6
North Dakota	52.4	(6)	65.2	(4)	12.8
Ohio	46.6	(10)	56.0	(11)	9.4
South Dakota	42.5	(12)	48.1	(12)	5.6
Wisconsin	59.3	(2)	68.0	(2)	8.7

Source: U.S. Bureau of the Census, *Governmental Finances, 1969–70, 1978–79*, Series GF70, GF79 (Washington, D.C.: Government Printing Office).
[a] Numbers in parentheses indicate ranking among the twelve states.

Table 4.11. Local Property Tax Revenue as a Proportion of Total Local General Revenue and Total Local Tax Revenue, 1970 and 1979

State	General Revenue		Tax Revenue	
	1970	1979	1970	1979
Illinois	50.7%	37.7%	87.6%	80.2%
Indiana	51.3	32.4	99.6	95.3
Iowa	53.4	36.7	99.0	96.0
Kansas	50.6	42.0	97.2	92.9
Michigan	41.8	34.9	91.1	91.5
Minnesota	35.6	27.8	97.5	95.6
Missouri	44.1	28.7	81.8	65.4
Nebraska	51.4	41.6	94.1	91.2
North Dakota	51.9	33.1	96.6	96.4
Ohio	47.0	29.1	85.4	73.4
South Dakota	65.4	49.6	95.6	89.3
Wisconsin	44.6	30.6	98.7	98.4
Median state	50.7	34.0	96.6	92.2

Source: U.S. Bureau of the Census, *Governmental Finances, 1969–70, 1978–79*, Series GF70, GF 79 (Washington, D.C.: Government Printing Office).

the smallest in Michigan and Minnesota.

Table 4.12 illustrates the different ways states distribute aid among various types of local governments. Of course, in all states, school districts are more dependent on aid than other types of local government. In states like Kansas, Missouri, and South Dakota, cities and counties receive particularly small amounts of state aid relative to their other revenue. One problem with this table is that, in some states, much of what is counted as aid is simply state reimbursement for property tax exemptions and credits. This is particularly true in Indiana, Ohio, and Iowa.

Another source of property tax relief is local nonproperty tax revenue. Table 4.4 showed the number of jurisdictions in each state levying a local sales or income tax. Ohio and Missouri have some local governments using both of these taxes, five other states have some local sales taxes, three others have some local income taxes, and North Dakota and Wisconsin have neither.

In many states local nonproperty taxes yield relatively little revenue on a statewide basis. Only in Ohio, Missouri, and Illinois do they provide as much as 20 percent of local tax revenue, as Table 4.11 indicates. In every state except Michigan, local nonproperty tax revenue rose faster than local property tax revenue between 1970 and 1979.

Local user charges have also risen faster than property tax revenue. Between 1970 and 1979, charges and miscellaneous revenue of local governments more than doubled in all these states.

Table 4.12. State Aid per Dollar of Own-Source General Revenue for Local Governments, 1979

State	All	Municipalities	Counties	School Districts
Illinois	$0.46	$0.18	$0.35	$0.80
Indiana	0.73	0.40	0.56	1.09
Iowa	0.67	0.32	0.41	1.08
Kansas	0.35	0.12	0.14	0.67
Michigan	0.61	0.40	0.95	0.68
Minnesota	0.90	0.39	0.92	1.43
Missouri	0.40	0.11	0.12	0.84
Nebraska	0.27	0.26	0.32	0.30
North Dakota	0.65	0.24	0.45	1.16
Ohio	0.58	0.15	0.74	0.89
South Dakota	0.25	0.08	0.10	0.42
Wisconsin	0.98	0.78	1.25	0.97

Source: ACIR, *Significant Features of Fiscal Federalism,* 1979–80 ed. (Washington, D.C.: Advisory Commission on Intergovernmental Relations, 1980), p. 166.

Their increase was fastest in Wisconsin, where they jumped 310 percent, and slowest in South Dakota and Ohio, where they rose 138 percent.

For the entire nine-year period, local general revenue excluding federal aid in these twelve states rose $27,224.4 billion. This increase breaks down as follows: state aid, $11,238.1 billion; charges and miscellaneous revenue, $6084.2 billion; property taxes, $7762.3 billion; other local taxes, $2139.4 billion. In this context, the relative insignificance of the circuit breakers, costing less than $800 million in 1979, and the homestead credits, costing less than $500 million, is clear.[9]

Two other types of general relief should be mentioned. During the 1970s, Wisconsin, Indiana, and Ohio initiated credits that pay a certain proportion of property taxes for all kinds of property, with no maximum. In Wisconsin, this credit is only for property subject to above-average tax rates. These credits are expensive. In 1977, they cost $163 million in Ohio, $270 million in Indiana, and $210 million in Wisconsin.

Such credits are similar to aid to local governments except in terms of their geographic distribution. Aid is seldom distributed to local governments in direct proportion to their tax levies as these credits distribute their benefits. Thus property owners in jurisdictions with high tax rates benefit much more from this type of credit than they would from a typical aid program.

The final kind of relief is limitations on local spending and taxes. This is another area in which the Midwestern states are pioneers. Wisconsin, Minnesota, Kansas, Indiana, and Iowa were among the first states in the nation to limit increases in property tax or spending of local governments. Iowa's limits on school spending began in 1971 and, in combination with major increases of state aid, were a crucial factor in lowering property tax burdens in that state. Kansas's limits began even earlier, in 1970, and were the very first in the nation in many years.[10] Minnesota's began in 1971 and Wisconsin's in 1973. Indiana localities were subject to a freeze on property tax revenue for a number of years beginning in 1973, part of a major restructuring of the government finance system in that state, which drastically reduced reliance on property taxes. Three of the last states to impose limitations on property tax revenue growth were Michigan (1978), Nebraska (1979), and Missouri (1980).

Prior to the 1970s, most limitations took the form of tax rate limits, which are not effective constraints when assessments are rising. Many states still have such limits. Where assessments do

Table 4.13. Proportion of Property Tax Having an Impact on Residential Property, Selected Years

State	1964	1965	1968	1970	1973	1974	1977	1978
Michigan								
Not considering circuit breaker or inventory tax replacement		46.3%			49.0%			54.3%
Taking circuit breaker into account		46.3			46.6			51.3
Taking both circuit breaker and inventory tax replacement into account		46.3			n.a.			47.0
Minnesota								
Not considering circuit breaker					41.5			47.8
Taking circuit breaker into account					34.6			37.1
Ohio								
Considering all credits					36.7			39.9
Wisconsin								
Not considering circuit breaker			50.7%			52.4%		58.2
Taking circuit breaker into account			50.6			51.7		57.3

80

Iowa
Taking credits into account   25.9%   30.0%   33.4%

Nebraska
Not considering exemption program   31.2   34.0

Source: Michigan, Minnesota, Ohio and Wisconsin: Robert Kuttner and David Kelston, *The Shifting Property Tax Burden* (Washington, D.C.: Conference on Alternative State and Local Policies, 1979).

Iowa: Steven D. Gold, *A Citizen's Guide to Local Government Finance: Iowa at the Property Tax Crossroads* (Des Moines: Drake University, 1977), p. 36.

Nebraska: Steven D. Gold, *Property Tax Relief* (Lexington, Mass.: Lexington Books, D.C. Heath, 1979), p. 27.

not rise, these limits are also very effective in holding down property taxes. For more than forty years, Ohio has combined its tax rate limits with rollbacks of assessment ratios when property is revalued, thus effectively preventing local governments from increasing their property tax revenue much without getting approval from voters in a referendum.

As Table 4.4 indicated, only three states in this region do not have revenue or spending limits—North Dakota, South Dakota, and Illinois. In some of these states, property has not been revalued in many years, so that simple tax rate limits may be effective restraints on property tax levels.

Previous studies have concluded that these limits are of variable effectiveness in restraining property taxes. When they are combined with large increases of state aid, as in Indiana and Iowa, or heavy use of local nonproperty taxes, as in Ohio, they are associated with de-emphasis of property taxation. Where alternative revenue sources are not provided, these limits do not appear to have much effect on property tax revenue.[11]

REASONS FOR INCREASED PROVISION FOR RELIEF

Two phenomena account for much of the increase in property tax relief during the past decade—assessment reform and inflation. In the "bad old days," assessments generally were set at the discretion of local assessors, who often betrayed a wanton disregard for the letter of the law. Market values might rise or fall, but assessments did not usually follow in proportion, even though the law dictated that they should. Moreover, although laws usually provided that all property should be assessed at the same proportion of market value, this was commonly not the way things worked out in the "real world."

This situation began to change in the 1960s, frequently as a result of court rulings calling for adherence to the laws that had been flaunted. A common reaction to legal dictates from the courts was to change the laws rather than to make the practices conform to existing laws. This explains the spread of use-value assessment laws, passed to perpetuate the de facto underassessment of farm realty, and also the classification provision in Cook County.

A second major factor in the tax relief movement has been inflation. Because of the manner in which property is assessed, inflation tends to increase the assessments of homes faster than those of business properties. Consequently, if the assessment system is typical, homes will become a larger proportion of the property tax base, resulting in rising taxation, even if the total tax levy is unchanged.

Here is an example: Suppose that homes are originally valued at $10 million and that business properties are valued at $10 million. If the total tax levy is $1 million, the tax rate will be 5 percent, or $5 per $100 of assessed valuation. In this situation, homes and businesses will each pay $500,000 of property tax.

Now suppose that inflation increases home assessments 75 percent and business assessments 25 percent. Homes will be valued at $17.5 million and businesses at $12.5 million, for a total of $30 million. To raise the same amount of tax revenue as before, the tax rate will now have to be only 3 ⅓ percent. With this tax rate, homes will pay $583,000 and businesses $417,000. A shift has occurred in tax burdens, lowering business taxes and raising those for homes.

In addition, tax exemptions granted to business may lower their assessment or inhibit their growth. This has apparently occurred, for example, in Wisconsin and Ohio.[12] The most spectacular example of a tax shift occurred in California prior to the passage of Proposition 13. In just four years, the proportion of the residental tax base jumped from 32.1 percent to 42.2 percent.[13] The shift was especially dramatic in California because home values rose faster than elsewhere and because California's assessment system was particularly efficient in keeping assessments in line with rising market values with a relatively short time lag.

Many states do not even collect data that allow an analysis of the extent to which a shift has occurred, but Table 4.13 summarizes information from Michigan, Minnesota, Ohio, Wisconsin, Iowa, and Nebraska. In each case, there would have been a significant shift if the states had not acted to offset it. In most cases, state actions did reduce the extent of the shifts but in each state at least a small shift occurred and in many states a sizable one.

Some states have not experienced a tax shift because they seldom revalue property. For example, between 1966 and 1976, the assessed value of realty rose less than 60 percent in Illinois, Indiana, Kansas, Nebraska, Missouri, and North Dakota.[14] With new construction being added to tax rolls a rise of this small magnitude over an entire inflationary decade leaves room for little or no revaluation of existing property.

The property tax relief that has been provided can be divided into three categories—autonomous, induced, and incidental. *Autonomous* relief is given to correct a perceived long-standing defect of the property tax. *Induced* relief, on the other hand, reacts to a specific, recent change in the tax system, such as a change of assessments. *Incidental* relief is provided inadvertently or as a side effect when another goal is being pursued. A portion of the relief resulting from increased state aid to local governments is probably of this nature; certainly, much of the lower property taxes resulting from expanded federal aid is of this type.

ANALYSIS OF RELIEF ALTERNATIVES

In many situations, the question to be confronted is not *whether* to provide relief, but rather *how* and *for whom.* Much of the property tax relief of the past ten years has been *induced,* in that it reacted to a change of assessment practice, or inflation, or both. A new or increased homestead program or circuit breaker often simply offsets a tendency for home taxes to rise due to forces described earlier. Such a program targeted at residential property is necessary if a tax shift is to be avoided. A form of general relief, such as increasing state aid to local governments, does not avoid a tax shift.

Space does not allow an exhaustive discussion of the five major ways of preventing a tax shift to homeowners—a homestead exemption, a homestead credit, a circuit breaker, classification, and limitations on the growth of assessments. Three major distinctions will be emphasized: first, whether relief tends to expand, remain constant, or contract over time; second, how progressive the relief is, if at all; and third, how complicated the relief is.

1. If a continuing shift is taking place, a one-shot form of relief will not prevent it. Benefits from a homestead exemption, a credit for a specific amount of tax, classification, or a circuit breaker with a fairly low income ceiling will not expand over time, so they must be periodically changed to offset a continuing shift. On the other hand, the benefits of credit that pays a certain percentage of tax, a threshold circuit breaker with no income ceiling, or assessment limits can provide continuing relief that will offset a continuing shift. The issue faced by a state is similar to that confronted by the federal government in dealing with inflationary income tax increases. Is it better to rely on an automatic formula or to make regular discretionary adjustments in the tax system? The distinction should not be overdrawn; even with a relief mechanism that provides continuing relief, periodic adjustments may be needed because of the difficulty of foreseeing how rapidly a tax shift will occur.

2. Relief programs differ greatly in terms of their progressivity. At one extreme is a circuit breaker with benefits skewed toward low-income citizens. But the progressivity of circuit breakers differs greatly according to how they are designed. In many programs average benefits fall as income goes up. The proportion of households at each income level that qualifies for circuit breaker relief invariably decreases with rising income, so all existing circuit breakers are decidedly progressive.

Next along the progressivity continuum is a homestead credit, which provides equal benefits for all homeowners. It is considerably more progressive than a locally financed homestead program because locally financed programs result in increased tax rates, which are likely to raise the amount of taxes shifted to renters, who have lower income than homeowners on the average.

Least progressive is a general form of relief, which simply lowers the tax rate, since its benefits per household rise as income goes up. However, if the property tax is regressive over the income range covering most households, [15] a proportional cut of property taxes will produce tax benefits that constitute a larger proportion of income for low-income citizens.

3. A final issue in comparing tax relief programs is how complicated they are. Ideally, citizens should be able to understand the tax system so that they can make informed voting decisions. Some of these tax relief measures are much more complicated than others. In Iowa, for example, it is widely believed that only a handful of citizens fully understand the system of assessment limitations. Tax credits seem desirable on these grounds because they are simple, and their immediate benefits can easily be measured and their distribution shown. On the other hand, the level of public understanding about property taxation may already be so low that a complicated tax relief system would make little difference in the level of incomprehension.

SPECULATIONS ABOUT THE FUTURE

If there is anything we can confidently predict about the next decade, it is that inflation will continue at an uncomfortable rate. This implies that pressure on the property tax will continue. Unless action is taken to prevent it, tax burdens will shift toward homeowners. It would be political suicide to allow this to occur, however, so property tax relief will continue to be provided. This leads to the question; *What kind of relief?* The answer depends to a considerable extent on the financial condition of state governments. Unfortunately, the outlook in that department is not particularly rosy either. State budgets will be tight for many reasons. First, taxpayers will not usually tolerate general tax increases in the present environment, with real living standards stagnant or falling. Second, tax limitations and income tax indexing are likely to continue to spread. And finally, federal aid will decrease moderately in nominal terms and sharply in real terms, due to higher military and Social Security spending and pressure to reduce budget deficits.

Thus most states not blessed with large mineral wealth, booming defense industries, or large influxes of industry—which is to say, nearly all the states in the Midwest—will not have a great deal of money available to fund property tax relief programs like circuit breakers or other credits and exemptions.

To prevent tax shifts toward homeowners, states will have to employ measures that do not drain state coffers, like locally financed exemptions, assessment limits, and classification. I view this as unfortunate because such measures complicate the tax system excessively and have effects that are often difficult to measure.

Tight state budgets also imply limited resources to fund state aid to local governments. In cases where the demand for property tax relief is strong, increased employment of local nonproperty taxes and user charges can be anticipated.

One important force will operate to alleviate pressure on the property tax: local spending will increase more slowly than it did until the last few years. One reason is that the lower school-age population will moderate the increase of school spending, which accounts for nearly half of property taxation. Public antipathy toward taxes will also play a role here, as will state-imposed limitations on local spending or taxes.

Thus property tax relief will continue to grow, local governments will be ever more restrained by state controls (except perhaps by having increased latitude to levy local nonproperty taxes), and the tax system will become more and more complicated. But relief will not take the form of more Proposition 13s. That blunderbuss approach will have little appeal as long as legislatures act to prevent runaway tax shifts such as occurred in California. To conclude on a note of optimism, I think they usually will act in time.

Relief granted in the past decade has helped remove the property tax from the top of the public's tax hate list. With wise policies, it need never attain its old unpopularity again.

NOTES

1. The U.S. Advisory Commission on Intergovernmental Relations (ACIR), *Changing Public Attitudes about Government and Taxes* (Washington, D.C., 1979 and 1980).
2. These percentages are only approximations, because the circuit breaker data in some cases is for the calender year whereas the property tax revenue data is for the fiscal year.
3. The ACIR has not counted Nebraska as a circuit breaker, I have classified it as such here because part of its program bases exemptions on household income, with the proportion of assessed valuation exempted varying by income level, and the program is state funded.
4. Oregon's per-capita circuit breaker cost was $36.32 in 1979, making it the second largest in the nation.
5. The proportion of households in each state receiving the circuit breaker in 1977 is reported in Gold, *Property Tax Relief*, p. 57.
6. For example, a $5000 exemption exempts $10,000 of market value when the assessment ratio is $\frac{1}{2}$ and $20,000 when the ratio is $\frac{1}{4}$.
7. Gold, *Property Tax Relief*, pp. 245, 255.
8. The great majority of property in Minnesota, however, falls into one of three classes. Changes of assessment ratios during the 1970s also made the tax less regressive by setting lower ratios for homes of lower value.
9. U.S. Bureau of the Census, *Governmental Finances in 1969-70* and *1978-79*, (Washington, DC: Government Printing Office, 1971, 1980).
10. Colorado, Arizona, and Oregon are usually identified as the only states with other than tax rate limits prior to 1970. ACIR, *State Limitations on Local Taxes and Expenditures* (Washington, D.C., 1977).
11. Steven D. Gold, "The Results of Local Spending Limitations: A Survey," in John M. Quigley, ed., Perspectives on Local Public Finance and Public Policy (Greenwich, CT: JAI Press, 1981).
12. Robert Kuttner and David Kelston, *The Shifting Property Tax Burden* (Washington, D.C.: Conference on Alternative State and Local Policies, 1979).
13. William H. Oakland, "Proposition XIII—Genesis and Consequences," *National Tax Journal* 32 (June 1979): 391.
14. John Behrens, "Property Taxes and Property Values: What's New about Base, Burden, and Other Mysteries," in Esther O. Tron, *Public School Finance Programs, 1978-1979*, (Washington, D.C.: Government Printing Office, 1980), pp. 38-39.
15. Even under the "new view" of property taxation, studies generally find a U-shaped pattern on incidence, with the low point of the U occuring at an income above that for most households.

PART III

Alternate Revenue Sources

Chapter 5

Trends in Intergovernmental Relations: Getting Less, but Enjoying It More (Maybe)

*Paul R. Dommel**

The outlook for intergovernmental aid in the 1980s is likely to be one of mixed satisfaction for state and local offcals: less money but with more spending discretion. The less-money part began during the Carter administration, which ushered in the age of the constant pie for intergovernmental aid. Greater spending discretion is the likely contribution of President Reagan, who favors a reduced federal role in intergovernmental decision making. Thus what seems to lie ahead is a partial return to the New Federalism of the Nixon administration, in the sense that the decentralization policies of the New Federalism were accompanied by more federal dollars. Revenue sharing was new money, accompanied by the political sweetener of consolidating some categorical programs into block grants, which added more money to the pot. In Reagan's version of New Federalism, the word "management" is substituted for "money."

This paper represents the views of the author; it does not necessarily represent the views of the officers, trustees, or other staff members of the Brookings Institution.

*Senior Fellow, The Brookings Institution

HOW WE GOT TO WHERE WE ARE

Before taking a closer look at some of the possible directions of federal aid in the 1980s, it would be useful to examine briefly past trends in intergovernmental aid.

Increases in Federal Aid

Overall, federal aid grew from $2.3 billion in 1950 to an estimated $99.8 billion in 1982 (Table 5.1). In 1950, federal assistance represented 10.4 percent of state and local expenditures; it now represents approximately 25 percent. This growth in the absolute amount and relative importance of federal grants is the most prominent feature of federal aid since World War II.

The greatest increases have come since 1965. Between 1965 and 1970, as the Great Society programs of Lyndon B. Johnson went into operation, aid increased by more than $13 billion, largely in the form of categorical grants with an urban emphasis. Between 1970 and 1976, during the Nixon and Ford administrations, General Revenue Sharing greatly expanded environmental protection aid, and some antirecession programs went into effect. In the 1977–1979 period, President Carter significantly expanded antirecession pro-

Table 5.1. Growth in Federal Aid, 1950–1982

Year	Total Dollars (millions)	Percent of State–Local Expenditures
1950	$ 2,253	10.4%
1955	3,207	10.1
1960	7,020	14.7
1965	10,904	15.3
1970	24,014	19.4
1975	49,834	23.1
1976	59,093	24.4
1977	68,414	25.8
1978	77,889	26.4
1979	82,858	25.6
1980	91,472	25.3
1981 (est.)	95,343	n.a.
1982 (est.)	99,829	n.a.

Source: Special Analysis: Budget of the United States Government, Fiscal Year 1982 (Washington, D.C.: Government Printing Office, 1981), Table H-7, p. 252.

grams, which raised the amount of federal aid going directly to local governments, particularly distressed cities.

Changes in Federal Grants

The politics of federal grants have changed since the early 1970s: there has been growing interest in shifting spending authority from national to state and local governments. From 1950 through the mid-1960s, grants were primarily "categorical" directed at specific kinds of problems and carrying with them a significant amount of federal control. These grants could be viewed as *supplier grants:* the supplier of the money, the federal government, primarily controlling the kinds of goods and services that the money could buy. Nixon's New Federalism sought to convert some federal grants to *consumer grants*. With consumer grants, the needs existing and demands registered at the local level are the principal determinants of the kinds of goods and services the federal money will buy. General Revenue Sharing, enacted in 1972, signified the most notable shift to consumer grants. Under this program, until fiscal 1981, about $7 billion per year was distributed to state and local governments, who were given virtually no conditions on spending these funds. A related development was the consolidation of some narrow-purpose grants into block grants, which prescribed that federal money by spent in a broad functional area, leaving the picking and choosing among specific activities to local participants in the decision-making process. The decentralization momentum of the New Federalism went into dormancy during the Carter administration.

Shift in Federal Aid Allocations

The decentralization period was accompanied by an important shift in the system for allocating federal aid, from an emphasis on project or discretionary grants to a greater emphasis on formula grants. In addition, the number of communities receiving grant funds through formula entitlements increased.

As the number of narrow-purpose grants increased, especially in the mid-1960s, the national bureaucracy was frequently given considerable discretionary authority to determine which communities and which projects would receive funding. Though it was presumably a system of relatively open competition, it was often perceived as a system that tended to bias funding toward communities that had sophisticated bureaucracies able to navigate the grant maze or that could afford to hire people with such expertise. This perception was probably true in part, but some large cities with large and sophisticated bureaucracies simply chose not to particpate in the federal programs because of conditions attached to the money. The New Federalism programs spread federal funds more widely by significantly enlarging the number of communities entitled to the formula grants; the extreme case was General Revenue Sharing, with nearly 40,000 entitlement jurisdictions. As these grants allowed considerable local discretion on spending decisions, few places with entitlements declined the money.

Under the Carter administration—as set forth in Carter's 1978 urban policy—there emerged an interest in targeting a greater share of assistance to the neediest jurisdictions. Targeting achieved only some small successes, however, since it was politically difficult to reallocate funds from one jurisdiction to another. The best prospects (although still not great) for targeting are produced when there is new money to be distributed and there can be a fresh determination of who is eligible to receive funds.

Federal Aid to Local Governments

There has been a continuing tendency to bypass the states and provide an increasing share of aid directly to local governments. Excluding welfare programs, about half of all federal aid to state and local governments now goes directly to localities. The New Federalism programs tended to direct aid to general-purpose units of local government, as opposed to special districts and public authorities. Aid to special districts and semiautonomous authorities remains, however, a significant feature of the intergovernmental aid system.

The preceding are the apparent general trends in the broad intergovernmental aid patterns over a three-decade period. Some crucial changes have occurred, however, in very recent years in the most visible past trend—the amount of assistance. Since 1979, the growth in nominal aid dollars has been much slower than before that date; and in real dollars the trend is downward. For an analysis of more recent trends, the data are divided into two periods: the 1976 and 1977 budgets of President Ford and the budgets from 1978 to 1982 of President Carter. Although the basic budget for fiscal year 1978 was Ford's, it is included here in the Carter years since Carter made major increases in countercyclical aid to state and local governments in the budget revisions he proposed to Congress in February 1977, shortly after he took office.

As noted in Table 5.2, the final Carter budget projected that aid would increase from $59.1 billion in fiscal 1976 to $118.6 billion in fiscal 1984. It must be stressed, however, that the 1983 and 1984 figures were estimates made in the 1982 budget based on general multiyear planning figures and were not firm budget proposals. Over the 1976–1984 period, federal aid was projected to double. The average annual increase in the two Ford budgets was 17.2 percent; for the firm Carter budgets (1978–1982), the annual average increase dropped to 7.9 percent. In addition to the slower nominal dollar growth rate of the Carter budgets, there has been a marked trend toward an actual decline in real federal aid dollars as a result of high inflation rates. The Advisory Commission on Intergovernmental Relations reported that the real purchasing power of federal aid to states and local governments declined for the latest years and the real dollar loss was accelerating.[1] The decline was 8.3 percent from 1980 to 1981, 2.9 percent in 1980, and 2.7 percent in 1979. In the 1960s, constant dollar aid (in 1972 dollars) rose at an average annual rate of 8.6 percent, and 8 percent from 1969 to 1978. Thus what state and local governments face is a shrinking pot in both nominal and real dollars.

Federal aid has also been declining as a percentage of both total and domestic budget outlays. From a high of 17.3 percent of the total federal budget in 1978, federal aid declined to an estimated 14 percent in fiscal 1982 and was projected in the final Carter budget to decline to 13.3 percent in 1984. The same trend occurred as a percentage of domestic spending, decreasing from a high of 22.9 percent in 1978 to a projected 18.6 percent in 1984. These dropoffs in shares partially reflect the fact that 1978 was the year for peak outlays for the three countercyclical programs— antirecession fiscal assistance, local public works, and public service employment.

Another important aspect of analyzing past trends and future prospects for intergovernmental aid is the distinction between assistance given to states and localities for payments to individuals and grants given to carry out the functions of state and local governments. The major programs in the "payments to individuals" category are Medicaid, welfare, housing assistance, and nutrition programs for the elderly and children. When the two categories are separated (Table 5.2), it can be seen that, except for 1978 when the largest countercyclical outlays occurred, growth in programs to

Table 5.2. Intergovernmental Assistance, Fiscal Years 1976–1983

	Total (millions)	Percent Change from Previous Year	Payments to Individuals (millions)	Percent Change from Previous Year	Other (millions)	Percent Change from Previous Year
Ford						
1976	$ 59,093	18.57%	$21,023	20.53%	$38,070	17.50%
1977	68,415	15.77	23,860	13.49	44,555	17.00
Carter						
1978	77,889	13.84	25,981	8.88	51,908	16.50
1979	82,858	6.37	28,765	10.71	54,093	4.20
1980	91,472	10.40	34,174	18.80	57,298	5.92
1981 (est.)	95,343	4.23	39,855	16.62	55,488	-3.16
1982 (est.)	99,828	4.70	42,751	7.27	57,077	2.86
1983 (est.)	109,961	10.15	47,841	11.91	62,120	8.83
1984 (est.)	118,599	7.85	52,840	10.44	65,759	5.85

Source: Based on Special Analysis: Budget of the United States Government, Fiscal Year 1982 (Washington, D.C.: Government Printing Office, 1981) Table H-7, p. 252.

aid individuals was significantly greater during the Carter years than the growth in aid to state and local governments for their use. And, if Carter had not added about $8 billion to countercyclical spending in 1978, there would have been a decline in "other" aid that year instead of a 16.5-percent increase. Overall, payments to individuals were projected to increase from 35.6 percent of total intergovernmental aid in 1976 to an estimated 44.6 percent in 1984.

Budget Discretion

A key term is assessing past, present, and future trends is "budget discretion." Under *the current rules of the game,* the major area for short-term, discretionary growth or shrinkage in federal aid was the "other" category of assistance, as was evidenced by the sudden jump in this category when Carter and Congress decided to inject more countercyclical spending into the economy. The best discretionary example is public service employment under the Comprehensive Employment and Training Act (CETA). The final Ford budget proposed to let the employment program expire in September 1977; projected 1978 outlays were $1.4 billion. Immediately upon taking office, Carter proposed expanding the program and, with congressional approval, outlays increased to $5.9 billion. Similarly, when attention turns to cutting budgets, the "other" category is the prime target. For example, in March 1980, when Cater proposed revisions in his original budget that had been submitted to Congress two months earlier, 94 percent of the proposed $5.2 billion in identifiable net reductions in state and local aid was in the "other" category, with the biggest targets being public service employment, the state share of General Revenue Sharing, and a proposed new version of countercyclical revenue sharing.

Payments to Individuals. What is suggested is that the "payments to individuals" category is difficult to adjust, at least for near-term fiscal impact, unless the rules of the game are changed. At the same time, this is the category showing the greatest growth. As shown in Table 5.3, three programs—Aid to Families with Dependent Children (AFDC), Medicaid, and housing assistance— represented 70 percent of the money in the category ($30.1 of $42.7 billion) in 1982. As currently established, the level of welfare assistance and range of Medicaid services are primarily determined by the states that make the crucial decisions on program

Table 5.3. Outlays for Medicaid, AFDC, and Housing Assistance, 1979–1982 ($ millions)

Outlay	1979	1980	1981 (est.)	1982 (est.)	Percent change, 1979–1982
AFDC	$ 6,584	$ 7,273	$ 7,747	$ 7,638	16.0%
Medicaid	12,407	13,957	16,452	18,120	46.0
Housing assistance	2,119	2,610	3,626	4,327	104.2
Other "payments to individuals"	7,655	10,334	12,030	12,666	65.6

Source: Calculated from *Special Analysis: Budget of the United States Government, Fiscal Year 1981* (Washington, D.C.: Government Printing Office, 1980), Table H-11. pp. 264–271; Ibid., *Fiscal Year 1982*, pp. 263–270.

cost. Because these programs are funded through open-ended appropriations, the federal government must pay the appropriate matching share to the states, regardless of cost. A large part of the housing assistance outlays are to pay for obligations already contracted and are thus not subject to near-term cuts. It is worth noting that housing assistance outlays have been growing at a rate exceeding the other major items in this category (Table 5.4). The housing assistance category, in this case, includes only that portion involving transfer payments to state and local governments. For AFDC, the federal cost has been growing at a moderate nominal rate, but below the inflation rate; in the final Carter budget it was expected to decline in fiscal 1982. Medicaid has been going up at a relatively high rate, primarily because of escalating costs of hospitals and doctors providing services.

"Other" Category. The "other" category remains the larger part of federal aid to states and localities. Given the limits to near-term budget cuts in programs to assist individuals, the "other" category is more vulnerable when one is looking for immediate cuts. Within this category, seven "big-ticket" grant programs constituted nearly two-thirds of the category in 1982 (as shown in Table 5.5). Except for highways and general revenue sharing, the final Carter budget estimated small increases for each of these programs in 1982. The estimated increases were very small except for employment and training, which Carter proposed to increase by 11 percent with a new youth unemployment program; if the proposed youth program is excluded, the employment and training aid declined.

In the near term, outlays for mass transit capital aid, highways,

Table 5.4. Percent Changes from Previous Year in AFDC, Medicaid, and Housing Assistance, 1980–1982

Program	1980	1981 (est.)	1982 (est.)
AFDC	10.46%	6.51%	–1.41%
Medicaid	12.49	17.88	10.14
Housing assistance	23.17	38.92	19.33
Other "payments to individuals"	35.0	16.41	5.28

Source: Calculated from *Special Analysis: Budget of the United States Government, Fiscal Year 1981* (Washington, D.C.: Government Printing Office, 1980), Table H-11, pp. 264–271; Ibid., *Fiscal Year 1982*, pp. 263–270.

and waste treatment facilities will be difficult to cut significantly because they largely represent payments for projects already begun. In the longer term, however, they will be susceptible to a "no new projects" or "stretch-out" approach to cut spending. In spite of the reductions, the stretch-out approach ultimately means a cost for each individual project if inflation continues. The highway spending program is currently operated as a trust fund, and any savings from reduced outlays cannot be diverted to other purposes. The Community Development Block Grant is susceptible to immediate cuts without seriously upsetting projects underway.

The most vulnerable areas of spending are tied to current operating budgets of state and local governments, rather than capital projects, particularly if they do not represent progress payments, reimbursement for previous expenditures, or commitments. An example is assistance to education, including the large Title I general assistance of the Elementary and Secondary Education Act. Another area particularly vulnerable to near-term and sharp reductions is the employment and training category, particularly the public service employment (PSE) program, which accounts for about half the money in this category in fiscal 1982. PSE cutbacks would be especially painful to older, declining cities that have tended to work a large share of this program into their basic city services, such as refuse collection and parks maintenance.

General Revenue Sharing was extended in 1980 for an additional three years. The extension continued payments to local governments, but state governments were cut out for at least fiscal 1981. This left open the possibility of their again receiving funds for fiscal 1982 and 1983. However, Carter had originally proposed totally eliminating the states from the program, and his final

Table 5.5. Outlays for Selected Programs, 1979–1982 ($ millions)

Program	1979	1980	1981 (est.)	1982 (est.)	Percent change, 1979–1982
Mass transit	$2408	$3129	$3556	$3672	52.49%
Highways	6825	8675	8222	7955	16.55
Waste treatment	3756	4343	4200	4230	12.61
Community Development Block Grants	3161	3902	3938	3998	26.47
Elementary and secondary education	3115	3536	3345	3592	15.3
Employment and training	8682	7987	7339	8143	–6.21
General Revenue Sharing	6848	6829	5156	4559	–33.43

Source: *Special Analysis: Budget of the United States Government, Fiscal Year 1981* (Washington, D.C.: Government Printing Office 1980), Table H-11, pp. 264–271; Ibid., *Fiscal Year 1982*, pp. 263–270.

budget did not request reinstating the state share in 1982.

In summary, in his final budget Carter chose a "hold the line, and make no enemies" approach. Very few programs were significantly cut, many were given small increases, and at least two notable increases were proposed (youth unemployment and expanded medicaid coverage.) In real dollars, most programs were losers.

Control. In comparing prior and current estimates of aid costs, it is also evident that the "payments to individual" category has been less susceptible to control than have other types of intergovernmental aid. Table 5-6 compares aid estimates made in the 1980 budget with estimates made in the 1982 budget. The data show that, over a three-year period, federal aid to assist individuals has grown much faster than estimated, currently about 30 percent per year over the earlier estimate, while aid in the "other" category has actually dropped below the prior estimate. This strongly indicates that the "other" category is more controllable; it also means that the larger long-term task for those seeking to obtain aid under budgetary control is to adjust the payments in the individual category.

FISCAL OUTLOOK FOR THE 1980S

The extent of fiscal cutbacks may be a function of who is in the White House and who controls Congress, but some factors inhibiting expenditures are, in essence, apolitical. Budget con-

Table 5.6. Comparison of Outlay Estimates of the 1980 and 1982 Budget ($ billions)

Year of Outlay	Total			Payments to Individuals			Other Grants		
	1980 Budget	1982 Budget	Percent Change	1980 Budget	1982 Budget	Percent Change	1980 Budget	1982 Budget	Percent Change
1980 (est.)	$82.9	$91.5[a]	10.4%	$28.1	$34.2[a]	21.7%	$54.9	$57.3[a]	4.4%
1981 (est.)	88.0	95.3	8.3	30.4	39.8	30.9	57.6	55.5	-3.3
1982 (est.)	91.9	99.8	8.6	32.7	42.7	30.6	59.2	57.1	-3.5

Source: Special Analysis: Budget of the United States Government, Fiscal Year 1980 (Washington, D.C.: Government Printing Office, 1979), Table H-7, p. 225; Ibid., Fiscal Year 1982, Table H-7, p. 252.

[a] In the 1982 budget, the 1980 outlays were actual outlays rather than estimates.

straints began to appear in fiscal 1980 in the Carter administration, and there is little prospect for any near-term real change upward. The election of Ronald Reagan and a more conservative Congress virtually assured reductions, or at best much slower growth, in federal aid for the first half of the decade, at least in selected programs. Although the total amount of nominal dollars may increase, it is likely to be at a notably slower rate, which means significant reductions in real dollars. The following basic factors acccount for the changes: (1) There is something of a national mandate to get the federal budget under control. Because there is an accompanying pressure for more defense spending, the domestic part of the budget is more vulnerable; intergovernmental aid is one of the likely targets. (2) The countercyclical spending that sharply increased federal aid in the latter 1970s is ending and, given existing fiscal pressures, it would be very difficult to initiate another program of the same proportions. (3) The federal government may be better off than some hard-pressed cities and states, but within the federal system as a whole the federal government is no longer the strongest level fiscally.

Five fiscal scenarios could be adopted in budgeting federal aid, although each does not have an equal probability of being chosen, and a single scenario may not be dominant throughout the 1980s.

Great Leap Forward.   This fiscal model would involve large amounts of new federal aid money and major new programs, as occurred in the decade from the mid-1960s to the mid-1970s. We are not likely to see it again soon.

Incrementalism.   Continue business as usual, maintain programs, and give all claimants a bit more money. This approach has demonstrated considerable staying power over the past forty years of our political and budgetary history and cannot be easily dismissed. Unless the rate of inflation drops appreciably, this program would involve a loss in real dollars.

Constant Pie Budgeting.   Simply cap everything and let inflation take care of the real cuts.

Decrementalism.   This approach would involve small cuts in a wide number of programs for which discretion on outlays is possible; these programs could include the trust funds, although these savings could not be used elsewhere. Small nominal cuts combined with continuing losses in purchasing power would mean a significant cut in federally aided goods and services at the state and local levels.

Great Leap Backward. Large cuts would be made in a large number of programs, and some programs would be liquidated. This approach challenges the rules of business-as-usual pluralistic politics.

President Reagan, in his changes to Carter's 1982 budget, proposed to reduce intergovernmental aid by approximately $12.3 billion.[2] When this chapter was prepared, the changes had just been announced, and it could not be known how successful Reagan would be in obtaining Congress's approval. If all his proposed changes are adopted, 1982 intergovernmental aid would decline to about $87.5 billion, putting it below the nominal level of the 1980 budget. However, achieving all reductions would require some major changes in the rules of the game for some programs, not just agreement by Congress to cut or slow spending.

In assembling his fiscal plan, Reagan adopted a mix of the five fiscal scenarios. He proposed that some programs, such as those of the Economic Development Administration and Public Service Employment, be terminated immediately. Other programs, such as mass transit operating subsidies, will be phased out over time. A stretching-out strategy will be applied to some others, including highway construction and modernization of public housing.

It was evident that the most severe and immediate of the proposed actions would involve grants used by state and local governments rather than grants used directly by individuals. However, some changes were proposed in the latter category, including reducing child nutrition grants, holding welfare costs relatively constant, and slowing the growth of Medicaid and housing assistance expenditures. Reagan's proposal to slow the increase in Medicaid expenditures illustrates the problem of controllability. As noted earlier, Medicaid is funded as an open-ended appropriation. Reagan proposed, as an interim solution, putting a cap on the amount of the federal commitment, but even such a short-term solution requires legislative approval. Longer-term controllability would require important legislative changes in the rules of the game, such as establishing copayments for recipients of services and/or eliminating the recipients' freedom to choose hospitals and doctors. However, the first puts an added cost burden on the poor while the second is seen by some as establishing a second-class system of health care for the poor.

The proposed budget changes suggest an important dimension of the future prospects for intergovernmental aid. In the past, the choices of budgetary "winners" and "losers" tended to be relative outcomes; that is, a losing program was generally one that got less of an increase than a winner, but nearly all would get some increase—relative incrementalism. Further, a loser in one budget year had some prospects of recouping the losses in the next budget and becoming a winner. But times may have changed. The current prospects are that program cuts approved by Congress have greatly reduced possibilities for recovering losses the next time around; in fact, a cut may signal that a program is particularly vulnerable and that what lies ahead is not recovery but long-term decline or termination. We have little experience with program termination except in cases such as the Community Development Block Grant, which came from the consolidation of a number of urban grants, most notably Model Cities and urban renewal. In that case, however, the consolidation was accompanied by an increase in the amount of money going into the block grant, nearly doubling in five years. Some observers would argue that terminations and reductions on a large scale are not possible in our complex setting of pluralistic, interest-group politics. Testing of that argument is what the clash and clang of the politics of federal aid will be about over the next few years.

General Revenue Sharing may be an exception to this winner-loser calculus and the future trajectory of funding. President Reagan did not ask for a reinstatement of the state share of General Revenue Sharing, although he has spoken strongly and often about his support for that kind of decentralized financial support program. Not including the state share for 1982 did not necessarily mean permanent exclusion or opposition to congressional efforts to put the states back in. In deciding on his initial fiscal strategy, Reagan may have preferred to maximize the total proposed budget cut and chose not to reduce the net effect of the package of cuts by requesting the state portion of revenue sharing as provided in the authorizing legislation.

Does the magnitude of the proposed cuts mean that the fiscal pressure is so great that there are no prospects for new initiatives to deal with old problems? Not necessarily. There is considerable interest in the so-called urban enterprise zones, which are advanced as a means of attracting private-sector business investment into inner-city poverty areas. Such a program may gain a foothold while other programs are the targets of budget cuts because the urban enterprise zones would be financed primarily through "tax expenditures" rather than through budget outlays. Tax expenditures "reduce tax liabilities for particular groups of taxpayers to encourage certain economic activities or in recognition of special circumstances."[3] The federal government has been in the tax expenditure business for a long time in a very big way. Among the largest and most familiar tax expenditures are the deductions allowed homeowners on their mortgage interest and local property taxes; in fiscal 1982 these two tax expenditures, which are revenue losses to the federal government, totaled an estimated $36.2 billion. The urban enterprise zone proposals contemplate a variety of tax expenditures such as reductions in Social Security payroll taxes, capital gain taxes, and business taxes, and a more generous system for depreciating capital investment. Thus, the tax structure can be used to substitute for budget outlays as a source of new indirect federal assistance.

PROGRAM REFORM OUTLOOK FOR THE 1980S

Overarching any fiscal scenario that may be chosen are likely to be administrative reform through the regulatory process and a legislative strategy aimed at more fundamental change. There is every reason to expect considerable deregulation of federal programs in a way that will give state and local officials more flexibility in implementing programs and that will reduce the amount of federal red tape attached to some of the programs. The word "expect" must be emphasized. Presumably, deregulation can be executed merely by scrapping some of the bureaucratic regulations attached to a program, but in practice this is likely to be more complex than realized, and state and local officials would be wise to hedge their expectations.

Block Grants

Changes in regulations could have an important effect on program operation, red tape, and the scope of federal control. But the changes likely to have the greatest influence on the intergovernmental aid system in the second half of the 1980s involve major legislative alterations. In his program for economic recovery, President Reagan proposed the establishment of two block grants.[4] One, if approved by Congress, would consolidate forty-five education programs into two block grants, one to local education agencies and one to the states. A second proposal would consolidate about forty health and social service grants into a single block grant to the states.

State and local officials usually welcome the added discretion that goes with such consolidations, but some costs are involved. The president's block grant proposals called for cutting the funding levels, a 20-percent cut for education and 25 percent for the health care block grant; thus grant reform and fiscal policy become intertwined. This tradeoff between greater state and local discretion in the use of the money and the level of funding represents a marked departure from earlier block grants. In those cases, greater local decision-making authority was accompanied by additions to the total amount of the grants.

State and local officials should also consider that they would be directly exposed to considerable political conflict among established groups over how the money is spent. Much of that political pressure is currently felt at the federal level. Further, the two block grants initially proposed are likely to be the forerunners of others to come, such as block grants for welfare and housing assistance. It can be argued that the added decision-making authority that goes with block grants make the programs work better because solutions can be better related to diverse local conditions. There is some evidence to support this in the Community Development Block Grant (CDBG). However, there is the question of how much of a load state and local decision makers can handle when the decisions involve highly contentious and politically charged issues. The programs that would be consolidated and decentralized are programs that have primarily directed their benefits to lower-income groups. The CDBG gives evidence that the initial tendency of the recipient communities was to spread the money to meet a broader and more diverse set of demands. Established constituencies for programs to be blocked are thus likely to be very vigorous in pressing their demands on governors, state legislators, mayors, and city councils.

Interestingly, while the Reagan administration contemplates greater decentralization of program authority through block grants as a means of cutting federal costs, the Advisory Commission on Intergovernmental Relations (ACIR), which reflects a state and local viewpoint, has pressed for full federal assumption of certain functions, specifically citing welfare, employment, housing, medical benefits, and basic nutrition.[5]

Targeting

Another aspect of the relationship between fiscal policy and intergovernmental aid concerns targeting of funds. Targeting was a central feature of the Carter urban policy presented in 1978. President Reagan also adopted a targeting policy in saying that people with the greatest needs would not suffer from his fiscal policy. He was referring particularly to programs such as the Social Security Retirement and Supplemental Security Income program, which he proposed to reduce.

However, this people-targeting, or safety net, approach was not applied to places as well. No mention was made of the possible elimination of well-off communities from such federal programs as CDBG. At least one-third of the more than six hundred entitlement recipients in the CDBG program probably fall into the category of those who can support themselves. They could meet their development needs and responsibilities from their growing tax bases or by borrowing on their good credit ratings. Such place-targeting, or providing a safety net for needy places, is good fiscal conservatism. It is cheaper than spreading money to places that do not really need it. Such a targeting policy could begin with CDBG and be extended to other block grant programs that Reagan is likely to propose.

Other Grant Reforms

One likely part of the legislative strategy is the renewal of a proposal allowing some administrative consolidation of smaller grants, similar to the president's authority to reorganize the bureaucracy. The ACIR would go a step further. It has proposed terminating or phasing out approximately 420 small federal categorical grants that together account for only 10 percent of all grant funds.[6] There has also been some discussion about getting the federal government out of some functions altogether, such as highways, and letting the states take over; such a strategy assumes that the states would raise their own auto- and truck-related taxes as a substitute for the current federal levies. There would likely be a heavy political cost to state governors and legislators who make such an effort, and they are more likely to prefer that the federal government continue to collect the money but let state officials choose between maintenance and construction uses. There also is some discussion about returning a part of each individual's income tax payment to the taxpayer's state. This approach was proposed back in the early 1960s as an alternative to General Revenue Sharing.

Regardless of what ideas reach the stage of being legislative proposals, the point stressed here is that there is no shortage of schemes for substantively overhauling the intergovernmental aid system as a whole and specific programs in particular. The pro-liferation-of-ideas phenomenon is not new. What is new is that the discussion has never taken place within a context of very real resource scarcity and strong presidential support for major changes. That may make the crucial difference in what the inter-governmental aid system looks like at the end of the 1980s.

NOTES

1. U.S. Advisory Commission on Intergovernmental Relations, *Intergovernmental Perspective* (Washington, D.C.: ACIR, Summer 1980), p. 19.
2. The proposed budget changes are included in *America's New Beginning: A Program for Economic Recovery*, issued by the Press Office of the White House, February 18, 1981.
3. *Special Analysis: Budget of the United States Government, Fiscal Year 1982* (Washington, D.C.: Government Printing Office, 198) p. 204.
4. *A Program for Economic Recovery*, pp. 24–26.
5. U.S. Advisory Commission on Intergovernmental Relations, *The Federal Role in the Federal System: The Dynamics of Growth* (the *In Brief* publication) (Washington, D.C.: ACIR, December 1980), p. 28.
6. Ibid., p. 29.

Chapter 6

Financing Local Government in the 1980s: Expansion Through Diversification

Catherine L. Spain* and Blue Wooldridge**

The decade of the 1970s was a turbulent one for public officials and other citizens interested in local government finances. Local revenue-raising capacity was buffeted by good news and bad news; unfortunately, most of the good news came at the beginning of the decade while the "bad" commenced at the mid-point and lasted throughout the remaining years. This sequence provides little room for optimism for the 1980s. In the early 1970s, the advent of federal revenue sharing and the existence of surpluses in the current-year state budgets led some students of public finance to write that, with the exception of the central cities, fiscal crisis for most local governments seemed to be a thing of the past.[1] Yet, within six years, a study of the fiscal condition of cities with a population greater than 10,000 conducted by the Joint Economic Committee of Congress concluded:

> Despite the fact the period under study was one of economic recovery, cities, generally, have not flourished. An increasing proportion of cities experienced operating deficits in 1978 and 1979, a trend which is projected to continue in 1980. In the coming decade, one can expect a growing number of cities to experience severe fiscal stress.[2]

* Government Finance Research Center, Municipal Finance Officers Association
** Virginia Polytechnic Institute and State University

The causes of this dramatic reverse are numerous. In many large communities, especially in the Northeast and North Central states, the tax base has shrunk as households and firms leave for the suburbs and the Sunbelt. Levels of intergovernmental assistance from the federal and state governments have leveled off, and inflation has eroded the buying power of that remaining.[3] Inflation has also increased the cost of everything government buys,[4] while at the same time citizens appear to expect not only the same level of services but even more. In addition, the proliferation of federal and state mandates imposed great burdens on the local revenue base. The revolt of the taxpayer was manifested in voters' disapproval of spending proposals appearing on local ballots and in the passage during the decade of tax and expenditure limitations (TELs) in at least twenty-three states. Sixteen states passed TELs in the second half of the decade.[5]

Faced with the prospects of an ever-increasing demand for services, an increase in the cost of providing these services and an existing revenue base that does not increase in line with demand, local public officials are faced with four possible strategies:

1. Actual cut-backs in service obviously require the ability to identify priorities, rank them, and make reductions in a rational manner.
2. A challenge that is perhaps new to many in the public sector is to increase organizational productivity.
3. Local governments can attempt to shift service responsibilities to other levels of government, i.e., the state or the federal level.
4. Public officials may attempt to expand the use of existing financial resources or to identify new resources to supplement existing ones.

While governments will probably consider all four alternatives to meet their needs, the last—raising new revenue from existing or new sources—will certainly be given greatest consideration.

This chapter provides a brief overview of how the local government revenue base has changed during the past decade with an emphasis on those receipts raised from local governments' own sources. This analysis is followed by some brief speculation concerning expectations for the first half of the 1980s.

CHANGING THE LOCAL REVENUE BASE

As many governments have already learned, it is not easy to find new revenue sources. Arguments can be found against almost any new source as being politically infeasible, too hard to collect, not a large enough revenue producer, too difficult to administer, or not equitable. Despite these difficulties, however, many local governments have decreased their long-time dependency on the property tax in recent years and diversified their revenue system in order to acquire additional revenue to support governmental services.

From the early to mid 1970s, local governments, with approval from their state legislatures, expanded their tax bases to include such things as general sales and income and increased tax rates almost at will. As the 1970s neared an end, local revenue-raising capability changed markedly. Strong antitax sentiment emerged, hampering local governments in financing burgeoning local expenditures. To complicate matters the growth in intergovernmental revenues slowed, leaving a small but growing gap to be filled in some other way. The outcome of these changed circumstances brought increased interest in charging for public services and somewhat greater interest in what have been termed alternative taxes. These consist of the less visible and less familiar nonproperty taxes that local governments are permitted to levy.

The general revenue of local governments consists of own-source revenue including taxes, charges, and miscellaneous revenues, and intergovernmental revenue received mainly from state and federal governments. Over the years, the financial mainstay of local governments has been property tax receipts and intergovernmental aid. However, recent political events and already evident trends suggest that the local revenue base is undergoing fundamental changes that will most likely continue into the mid 1980s.

Published and unpublished data from the U.S. Bureau of the Census in Table 6.1 show how the percentage of local government general revenue from various sources has changed within the past decade. Property taxes have declined in relative importance while other sources have increased, with the greatest increment coming from intergovernmental sources.[6]

Table 6.1. Percent of Local Government General Revenue from Various Sources

Year	Property Taxes	Nonproperty Taxes	Charges	Miscellaneous Revenue	Intergovernmental Revenue
1972	39.6%	7.7%	10.5%	4.5%	37.7%
1977	33.7	8.1	10.6	4.7	42.9
1979	29.5	8.6	11.6	5.7	44.7

The outlook for the future level of intergovernmental assistance is uncertain as the current administration works toward implementing policies aimed at reducing the size of the federal budget. Unless state governments are able to shore up local revenue with more assistance, local governments will be required to increase revenue coming from their own sources. The exact nature of the changes will depend on two factors: the structure of current local revenue systems and the priority given to various criteria for selecting potential revenue sources.

Property Taxes

An analysis of recent trends shows that significant changes occurred during the 1970s in the relative importance of various local sources of general revenue. The property tax as a local revenue source diminished, with the greatest change taking place within the most recent two-year period for which data are available — 1977 to 1979. Data on government finances collected and compiled by the U.S. Bureau of the Census for the periods 1972-1977 and 1977-1979 show that property taxes have experienced a continual decline in relative importance, while nonproperty taxes, charges, miscellaneous revenue, and intergovernmental aid, in comparison, have increased (see Table 6.1).

In general, what is seen is a complementary shift in reliance on nonproperty taxes and nontax sources as the role of the property tax has diminished. The change in use of charges and nonproperty taxes from the years 1972 to 1977 is rather gradual, suggesting that intergovernmental revenue and miscellaneous revenue sources such as interest earnings, special assessments, and the sale of property were able to provide the needed additional funds. However, from 1977 to 1979 the rapidity with which the property tax was declining picked up, as did the level of interest in employing charges and nonproperty taxes to finance local government expenditures. This implies that intergovernmental revenue and miscellaneous revenue could no longer bridge the ever widening revenue gap.

Nonproperty Tax Revenue

Another way of assessing trends in local government revenue is to examine the change in composition of local revenue from own sources, that is, the funds raised locally such as taxes, charges, and miscellaneous receipts. Table 6.2 demonstrates how the level of dependency on the property tax has changed from state to state and what adjustments in local revenue systems are occuring to compensate for the lessened presence of property taxes.

Recent Census data show total taxes (property and nonproperty) as a percentage of local own-source revenue dropping significantly. In 1972, on average, taxes accounted for 75.9 percent of local own-source revenue while charges provided 16.8 percent; miscellaneous receipts accounted for 7.3 percent of local own-source funds. In the five-year period from 1972 to 1977, tax receipts dwindled by 1.6 percentage points, charges grew by 1.8 percentage points, and the miscellaneous category decreased 0.2 percentage points. This slight change was followed by a dramatic shift in the composition of own-source revenue in the two-year period from 1977 to 1979. Taxes as a percentage of own-source revenue for all local governments declined from 74.3 percent to 68.8 percent, and charges and miscellaneous revenue increased by 2.4 and 3.1 percentage points, respectively. No doubt, the effect of Proposition 13 and other tax limitation measures began to take their toll on local revenue structures.

Surprisingly, local sales and income taxes did not show as much strength as local revenue producers. There are several explanations: state legislators may have been reluctant to expand local-option taxes for fear that these actions would be tagged as tax increases and used against them in future election campaigns; or they wanted to preserve the states' tax bases. Similarly, local policy makers may not have been anxious to impose these taxes for fear of taxpayer reprisal.

As of 1972, local governments in twenty-six states received sales tax revenue. In 1977, the number increased to twenty-seven and remained the same in 1979. As for local income taxes, eleven states had locally imposed levies in 1972, nine in 1977, and eleven in 1979. General sales and income taxes raised 8.5 and 4.5 percent of local revenue in 1972. In 1977 the percent of general sales revenue fell to 7.3 percent and income increased to just 5.0 percent. This poor showing is a direct result of the sluggish economy and a shrinking tax base caused by the growing number of exemptions. The latest figures from Census show local sales revenue proceeds providing 8.7 percent of local own-source revenue—an overall increase of 0.2 percentage points in the seven years from 1972 to 1979—and local income taxes growing to 5.3 percent of local own-source revenue.

Nonproperty taxes, excluding sales and income taxes (not shown in Table 6.2), have been the big gainers during the period under study, moving from 3.3 percent of total own sources in 1972 to

Table 6.2. Local Government Own-Source Revenue

	Property Taxes as a Percent of Own-Source Revenue			Nonproperty Taxes as a Percent of Own-Source Revenue			Charges as a Percent of Own-Source Revenue		
	1972	1977	1979	1972	1977	1979	1972	1977	1979
U.S. Average	63.5%	60.0%	53.5%	12.4%	14.3%	15.5%	16.8%	18.6%	21.0%
New England									
Connecticut	89.3	86.3	84.7	0.8	0.7	0.9	6.0	7.7	8.1
Maine	87.0	80.9	82.4	1.9	0.7	0.5	6.7	12.5	12.1
Massachusetts	87.1	86.0	84.3	0.7	0.5	0.6	9.3	10.9	11.3
New Hampshire	87.0	82.7	83.3	1.2	1.8	1.4	8.0	11.9	10.4
Rhode Island	89.2	90.7	89.9	0.9	1.0	1.0	5.4	5.8	5.4
Vermont	88.9	86.2	85.9	1.5	1.1	0.5	5.2	8.2	6.8
Mid Atlantic									
Delaware	51.8	50.0	51.6	10.2	9.0	8.1	30.5	34.6	32.8
New Jersey	79.0	77.6	73.5	6.8	8.5	9.6	10.2	9.7	11.5
New York	57.3	54.5	52.9	23.6	25.1	25.2	13.7	14.1	15.6
Pennsylvania	54.6	50.2	47.3	23.1	25.6	24.6	15.5	15.3	15.8
North Central									
Illinois	71.0	64.5	61.2	10.8	14.3	15.1	12.6	14.6	15.7
Indiana	75.5	69.1	62.6	1.5	2.5	3.0	18.9	22.7	26.1
Iowa	72.8	65.7	64.8	1.5	2.0	2.7	17.7	22.0	21.7
Kansas	72.2	63.9	62.2	2.7	3.9	4.8	16.2	18.9	19.0
Michigan	66.0	64.9	66.1	5.9	5.9	5.7	19.3	21.5	23.6
Minnesota	68.2	59.9	57.5	2.1	2.5	2.6	16.9	22.3	22.0
Missouri	57.0	50.1	46.6	16.7	21.7	24.0	18.3	20.7	21.1
Nebraska	67.5	63.4	58.0	4.7	4.6	5.6	15.8	19.9	21.0
North Dakota	69.7	62.9	59.9	2.7	2.1	2.2	13.2	17.0	16.6
Ohio	60.2	53.2	50.9	13.9	16.5	18.5	16.7	18.9	18.5
South Dakota	77.2	72.6	70.7	5.3	7.2	9.7	10.4	11.3	12.0
Wisconsin	80.0	69.1	62.5	1.0	0.9	1.0	12.4	21.2	25.8

Southeast									
Alabama	24.0%	18.8%	18.2%	27.5%	27.5%	29.5%	34.7%	42.7%	40.1%
Arkansas	49.0	42.5	43.8	4.3	4.8	5.0	29.6	32.7	35.7
Florida	49.2	47.7	46.5	10.9	8.8	9.6	30.1	32.2	33.1
Georgia	48.8	45.7	40.2	6.6	10.5	12.5	36.4	36.5	36.7
Kentucky	44.4	42.2	33.2	18.4	20.8	25.1	25.1	22.4	25.6
Louisiana	39.8	30.7	25.4	27.9	32.7	37.1	18.5	23.3	23.3
Maryland	55.0	49.6	45.8	23.7	26.5	27.9	13.3	16.0	16.5
Mississippi	46.7	44.5	42.5	5.9	2.7	2.6	36.1	40.1	40.8
North Carolina	59.6	52.7	50.2	6.6	11.2	11.8	24.0	27.3	28.7
South Carolina	56.8	54.4	50.3	3.4	4.0	3.7	29.6	32.0	34.5
Tennessee	46.4	42.4	38.7	19.4	20.0	21.8	27.3	30.3	29.4
Texas	60.1	58.8	54.7	9.0	9.7	10.3	22.5	22.4	25.0
Virginia	53.0	54.5	50.6	24.8	24.6	23.9	16.2	15.2	17.3
West Virginia	57.0	53.7	46.0	9.9	11.7	11.0	24.7	24.2	26.6
Mountain									
Arizona	61.0	45.8	53.5	15.4	13.4	13.8	15.2	16.9	18.6
Colorado	62.4	55.0	49.5	13.7	17.5	19.5	16.8	18.1	17.5
Idaho	66.5	53.6	60.5	1.8	1.8	2.0	25.0	28.5	29.0
Montana	76.8	71.3	68.1	3.8	3.1	2.8	11.8	14.9	14.8
Nevada	43.8	40.9	40.6	18.9	19.2	20.8	27.6	29.4	27.2
New Mexico	47.2	47.6	38.1	5.6	10.8	11.6	34.2	26.2	29.5
Oklahoma	51.8	46.3	40.6	13.2	19.8	21.6	26.8	25.6	26.4
Utah	65.6	59.0	55.1	9.4	13.1	22.0	17.0	18.0	17.0
Wyoming	61.3	60.1	56.5	1.8	5.4	7.5	27.0	22.2	23.7
Pacific									
Alaska	35.8	48.7	39.6	15.1	13.2	10.1	34.9	28.2	22.7
California	69.2	65.8	43.6	9.6	11.5	17.9	14.4	15.5	25.0
Hawaii	63.6	62.8	66.2	18.2	15.7	16.3	7.8	10.1	9.1
Oregon	71.7	66.8	60.8	2.6	5.7	7.1	16.0	18.6	19.2
Washington	51.5	40.1	37.0	11.5	17.3	18.4	26.2	27.5	26.8

Source: U.S. Bureau of the Census, *Governmental Finances* (Washington, D.C.: Government Printing Office, 1974), Table 46; *Governmental Finances* (1979), Table 47; and U.S. Bureau of the Census, "Worksheets of Revenues of State and Local Governments by Source and Level of Government, by State," (Washington, D.C.: Government Printing Office, 1978–79), Table 5.

7.2 percent in 1977 and 8.5 percent in 1979. Nonproperty taxes used most frequently by local governments are taxes on amusements or admissions, alcoholic beverages, business privileges, gross receipts, lodgings, motor fuels, net profits, real estate transfers, and tobacco products.

User Charges for Public Services

For all local governments in the United States, charges increased by 19.0 percent from 1972 to 1979. This nontax revenue source is not a new phenomenon in public finance, but local governments have not yet relied on these devices extensively to pay for public services. As has been shown, their use is becoming more widespread in the current era of tax limitations.

Charges can and have been used to finance a wide range of services in different areas. However, many officials are often unaware of the great diversity of applications. The list of potential charges available to local governments is quite extensive, covering such areas as recreation, education, health, transportation, and sewer system services. The three main types of charges currently collected by local governments fall within the broad categories of education, hospital, and sewerage charges.

There is tremendous diversity among the states in their dependency on charges for financing the functional areas already identified. While there are numerous "other" charges collected in each of the states, individually they are typically small amounts. A closer examination of the detailed data gathered by the Census suggests that the generation of charge revenue is state specific once the three major categories are netted out. For example, states having a situs on a major waterway, such as California, Oregon, Washington, and Florida, typically receive significant revenue from water and transportation terminal charges, while states blessed with spectacular natural sights receive higher charges related to parks and recreation.

Miscellaneous Revenue

An examination of own-source revenue for the three years under consideration shows that not only were charges and nonproperty taxes becoming more important, so was miscellaneous revenue. From 1972 to 1979, this category of local receipts increased 41.6 percent. In 1972, this source accounted, on average, for 7.3 percent of local own-source revenue. At 7.1 percent in 1977, this item did not have a strong presence in local revenue systems. Between 1977 and 1979 miscellaneous revenue jumped 2 percentage points to 10.2 percent of local own-source revenue.

It is difficult to surmise exactly what is the cause for this formidable increase. One suggestion is that improved financial management in the form of better cash management practices is helping by putting idle cash balances to work to earn more interest. Other possibilities are that governments, large jurisdictions in particular, are collecting payments in lieu of taxes from tax-exempt properties; or that more special assessments are being levied against tax-exempt and other properties. These tactics take the financing burden off the tax base by requiring payments from those persons directly benefiting from a public service.

Diversification of Local Revenue Systems

While there have been some rather strong advances toward revenue diversification nationally, state-level data reveal that local governments in some states are not nearly as inclined to tap a variety of sources. A cursory review of the data for the 50 states gives some feel for how different local revenue systems are.

As of 1979, the New England states were still highly dependent on the property tax, which makes up more than 45 percent of local general revenue in each of the six states in the region. As a result, revenue from nonproperty tax sources including other taxes, charges, and miscellaneous revenue are below the national average. In the North Central states, property taxes are still at above-average levels but there is more diversification in the revenue structures. Seven of the twelve states exceed the national average in percentage of revenue from charges, and three outpaced the average for nonproperty taxes.

The Mid Atlantic states as a group have already diversified their revenue sources, undoubtedly as a consequence of their propensity to spend at higher than average levels. They, too, have shifted away from the property tax and placed greater reliance on the other revenue sources. Two states, New York and Pennsylvannia, stand out among all states in their use of nonproperty taxes. In each, close to 14.0 percent of local general revenue and more than 24.0 percent of own-source revenue is generated from taxes other than the property levy. Delaware collects an unusually high level of charges—32.8 percent of own-source revenue in 1979.

The states in the Southeast have historically had the lowest property taxes and appear to be unwavering in this practice.

Instead of using the property tax to meet their current revenue needs, they are following the national trend and further reducing their dependence on this tax. For the two-year period from 1977 to 1979, twelve of the fourteen states in this region saw reductions in the percentage of their local governments' general revenue coming from the property tax. The most striking declines occurred in Arkansas and Kentucky, where property taxes as a percentage of local general revenue fell from 23.1 to 15.0 percent and 21.8 to 14.3 percent, respectively.

Like the North Central states, local governments in the Mountain states show a high level of variability in their fiscal structure, with local governments in several states (four of nine) collecting higher than average nonproperty taxes and higher than average charges.

The Pacific states follow the national tendency toward diminishing reliance on the property tax. These states are noteworthy for their high level of revenue diversification, with California making the greatest changes over the years, due in large part to the passage of Proposition 13. In 1972, local governments in California received 42.8 percent of their general revenue from the property tax, 6.0 percent from nonproperty taxes, 8.9 percent from charges, and 38.2 percent from intergovernmental sources.

In the fiscal year prior to the passage of Proposition 13, these percentages stood at 38.3 for property taxes, 6.6 for nonproperty taxes, 9.0 for charges, and 41.8 for intergovernmental revenue. In the two-year period surrounding the passage and implementation of Proposition 13, these numbers dropped precipitously. The preliminary Census data for FY 1978–79 show property taxes as a percentage of local general revenue falling to 19.4 percent, a decline of more than 18.9 percentage points in two years. Nonproperty taxes increased 17.6 percent during the same period to 8.0 percent of local general revenue. Charges rose 24.4 percent and accounted for 11.2 percent of local revenue in the states. Additional revenue from the state pushed the intergovernmental category up 32.8 percent in the same period to 55.5 percent of local general revenue.

What the experiences of California local governments and local governments in other states seem to suggest is that there is room for expansion through diversification in many local revenue systems. However, those local governments that already have diverse structures will without doubt encounter the greatest difficulty in finding room for expansion in their mature fiscal systems.

THE LOCAL REVENUE BASE IN THE 1980S

The federal government is a major influence in determining the need for local own-source general revenue. This is true for many reasons. It is the federal government that plays the major role in determining economic conditions, such as inflation and unemployment, that place demands on local budgets. In a similar manner, the federal government's decisions as to the magnitude of intergovernmental fiscal assistance to state and local governments play an important role in determining the amount of local own-source revenue required. Unfortunately, all signs point to an increased burden being placed on local own-source revenue. Many economists project relatively high inflation and unemployment for the first three or four years of the 1980s. It is anticipated that most state and local government assistance programs such as Community Development Grants, Comprehensive Employment and Training programs, Mass Transit and Wastewater Treatment Grants will experience substantial cuts in light of the administration's proposal to cut the fiscal year 1982 budget by nearly fifty billion dollars. Eliminating the states from General Revenue Sharing for one year and subjecting them to the annual congressional appropriation process in the future will probably mean they have fewer funds with which to aid local governments. The states, themselves, are in no position to make up for the cuts in federal assistance. This is in spite of the conventional wisdom holding that states are well off with large budget surpluses. Energy-exporting states do appear to be doing quite well. However, the *Wall Street Journal* reported in 1980 that twenty-nine states may end the year with balances below the danger point.[7]

If the federal government can be said to hold the key as to demands on the local own-source revenue base, the states are the key to determining if local governments will be able to expand this base. The states can determine what taxes, charges, fees, and investment opportunities a local government can tap, as well as place limitations on the use of the source and the use of the funds derived.[8]

A recent inventory of TELs indicates that thirty-nine states place a limit on the property tax rate; eighteen impose a levy limit, that is, establish the maximum revenue that can be raised by a jurisdiction in the form of property taxes; nine states require "full disclosure" on the setting of the property tax rate; and eight states have some other form of local revenue and expenditure limitation. Only four states (Connecticut, Maine, New Hampshire, and Vermont) have none of these forms of limitations.[9]

There is little evidence to suggest that the relative importance of the local property tax will be reversed. Assuming that trends occurring most recently are more important in forecasting the future, one would expect the proportion of local own-source general revenue derived from the property tax to decrease during the early 1980s. In thirty-three states the average annual percentage increase in property tax revenue declined between 1972 and 1978. As an additional indicator, 17 states adopted property tax levy limits and five additional states adopted legislation placing a constraint on assessment during the 1970s.[10]

The relative importance to local government of the general sales tax changed little from 1972 to 1979. However, there was a net increase of more than five hundred (568) jurisdictions imposing this tax between July 1976 and October 1979, suggesting that increased revenue was offset by a shrinking tax base. This expansion might suggest that the general sales tax will increase in relative importance in the near future.[11]

Again, as the earlier discussion indicated, there was little change in the relative importance of the local income tax. In 1972 income taxes raised 4.5 percent of local revenues; this increased slightly to 5.3 percent of local own-source revenues by 1979. However, there was a net increase of 406 localities raising revenue from this source when comparing the 1979 data with that of 1976.[12]

As was stated earlier, other nonproperty taxes made a dramatic increase in relative importance, raising from 3.3 percent of total own-source tax revenue in 1972 to 8.5 percent of the same base in 1979. The partial results of an informal survey of state municipal league directors showed a continued interest by local governments to broaden their accessibility to these taxes. The outlook for these taxes is strong, and they will most likely grow in importance (1) if state governments are willing to grant local governments the authority to tap new sources, and (2) if local governments, in turn, are willing to impose either new or higher levies.

Working under these assumptions, local governments will be choosing new sources of revenue based on several criteria. Almost every writer in the field of public finance has something to say about the appropriate criteria, and from their writings, it is possible to compile a list of points to consider in evaluating a revenue source. Of course, no revenue source will be perfect, thus requiring trade-offs to be made among the various criteria.

Legality is one of the most important criteria. Regardless of the strength of its economic, social, or administrative attributes, a revenue cannot be collected if it contravenes legal limitations. As creations of the states, local governments can raise revenue only from sources for which they are specifically authorized. The stipulations are usually spelled out in state laws, but state constitutions may also impose limitations on local revenue-raising power.

An effective revenue system must have sound *administrative qualities*. A "good" or administratively feasible revenue source is economical to administer. That is, its collection costs are a relatively small percentage of the revenues produced, and its compliance costs are low. It is easily enforceable and understood.

The public must consider the revenue system acceptable and consistent with their notion of fair play. It cannot be considered too onerous as compared to the public's perception of what they get for their tax dollars. What is meant by a fair or equitable revenue system is not a question of technical economics but of personal philosophy. Two major philosophical schools of thought have emerged; one rests on the benefit principle, the other on the ability-to-pay principle. The benefit principle calls for payments for government goods and services to be made in accordance with the benefits received. The other standard of fairness calls on the richer members of a community to pay more taxes than the poor.

Revenue elasticity is a term used to describe the responsiveness of a tax or other revenue source to changing economic conditions. A revenue source is considered elastic if its yield increases at least as fast as the economic activity of the jurisdiction. While growth responsiveness can be a positive factor, it has one drawback: it fails to provide revenue stability.

Ideally, revenue sources should achieve a balance in terms of *stability*. This means that provisions for revenue fluctuations over the business cycle should be made by having revenue that does not rise and fall with the economy. For example, there is more fluctuation in the yield of a tax based upon net income than there is in revenue from taxes based on property values or sales.

Neutrality has long been considered one of the virtues of a good revenue system. If private economic decisions are unintentionally affected by the methods used to collect revenues, the revenue source is not neutral. It should be noted, however, that governments may deliberately choose to influence private behavior through the revenue system.

No single revenue source would score high on each of these criteria. In fact a local government might choose a revenue source in order to achieve balance in its tax base, especially in view of the elasticity-stability dichotomy. A local government that wishes to diversify its revenue base by "tapping" nonproperty tax resources would be well advised to consider each source in light of these criteria.

The following section summarizes the findings cited in the literature that relate the characteristics of the more popular nonproperty tax revenues to the selection criteria.

Income Tax

Legality. It should not be surprising that the first major use of local income taxes was made by larger cities. In 1939 the city of Philadelphia adopted an earnings tax, the state of Michigan in 1964 enacted a "uniform city income tax" enabling legislation, and a year later New York added a city income tax that had a comprehensive income base and that allowed exemptions and deductions. In 1967 counties in Maryland were authorized to levy income taxes on residents at rates up to 50 percent of the state tax liability.[13]

To date, thirteen states have granted local governments the authority to tax income. As of October 1, 1979 no local jurisdiction in two of these states (Arkansas and Georgia) had taken advantage of this opportunity. However, in the eleven states where local income taxes were levied, approximately 4456 localities tapped this revenue source in 1979, an increase of approximately 400 over the number in 1976.[14] Most local income taxes use personal income as the base although there are at least sixteen cities with populations greater than 125,000 that also levy a corporation income tax.[15]

Administrative Qualities. A revenue source should be judged by its sound administrative qualities, including the degree to which the tax can be understood by the taxpayer, and complied with at a low cost.

Most taxpayers complete their federal income tax returns before beginning their state or local tax returns. The "cost" of filing a local return is therefore a function of the degree of conformity of the local income tax to the federal.[16] Since most local governments utilizing this revenue source tax at a flat percent of taxable income, the degree to which the definition of this term conforms to that used in the federal or state income tax return would reduce compliance costs also.[17]

Since income tax administration benefits from economies of scale, administrative costs would usually be lower by having the local tax collected by the state.

Social Acceptability. As far as we can determine, no comprehensive information has been gathered on the acceptability of the local income tax. Perhaps some insight can be gained by an analysis of the state income tax. The state income tax was ranked the most favorable when compared with the federal income tax, the state sales tax, and the local property tax in a 1980 survey.[18]

In response to the question, "Which do you think is the worst tax—that is, the least fair?" only 10 percent of the respondents indicated the state income tax. This rating did not vary by more than 3 percent when the total response was disaggregated and analyzed by age categories, sex, educational achievement, profession, household income, region or rural/suburb place of residence. It was ranked most favorable (receiving a response of 7 percent to the question) by respondents from households with annual incomes from $7000 to $9900, and least favorable (13 percent) from respondents with children from ages 12-17 years.

Elasticity and Stability. As indicated earlier, elasticity and stability can be considered the flip sides of the same coin. A highly elastic tax does not provide for revenue stability. We were unable to find research providing estimates of the elasticity of many local income taxes. Estimates would have to be judged based on the conformity of the local income tax to the federal or specific state income tax. For example, using 1970-1974 data the elasticity of the income tax in the District of Columbia, which is being brought into increased conformity with the federal income tax, was 1.4, about the same as the federal tax.[19] Estimates of state personal income tax elasticities range from 1.3 for New Mexico in 1966, to 2.4 in Arkansas in the same year. Nationwide the estimate for state personal income hovers around the 1.7 mark, that is, for every 10 percent increase in income the revenue from the state personal income tax would increase by 17 percent.[20]

Equity. A major argument in favor of the income tax rests upon equity grounds. It can be assumed that a tax on income is much more likely to be distributed in relationship to ability to pay than taxes imposed on other bases. The income tax also can be adjusted to take into account other factors influencing tax capacity, such as the number of dependents and medical expenses.[21] The degree of progressivity that could be achieved by the use of an income tax is often thwarted by special exclusions from income, different treatment of income from various sources, and deductions that are relatively more advantageous to persons in the higher income levels. Pechman and Okner came to the conclusion in 1974 that the incidence of the tax burden of the combined federal, state, and local income tax is progressive on almost the entire income scale but becomes regressive at the very top.[22]

Productivity. The local income tax constituted 5.3 percent of local own-source revenues in 1979 as a national average. This figure is slightly misleading, however, since in six of the eleven states reporting income tax revenue in 1979, such revenue represented at least 10 percent of own-source general revenue. In Kentucky and Maryland this revenue source represents more than 25 percent of own-source revenue.[23]

Neutrality. We indicated earlier that neutrality has long been considered a characteristic of a good revenue system. According to Due and Friedlander, "a perfectly designed income tax does not create excess burden by distorting consumer choices and thus resource allocation."[24] However, in practice the introduction of an income tax produces some alterations in resource allocation because (1) investments in select economic activities receive favorable treatment, and (2) relative prices of some factors of production will be changed by the tax. And of particular importance in the consideration of the imposition of an income tax by a local government is the fact that the burden of the tax might influence residential location decisions.

Sales Tax

Legality. New York City was one of the first local governments to adopt a retail sales tax when it levied such a tax in 1934; four years later Philadelphia and New Orleans followed suit, although the Philadelphia sales tax was repealed the following year; in 1967 Texas authorized local government to levy local sales taxes.[25] In fact by 1973 twenty-five of the states allowed at least some of their jurisdictions to levy a general sales tax. By October 1, 1979, 5,464 localities in twenty-six states made use of the general sales tax, an increase of approximately 500 since July 1976.[26]

Administrative Qualities. The cost of compliance to the taxpayer is low if total retail sales is the tax basis, since the sales tax is collected from a vendor rather than from individual consumers.[27] There are significant compliance costs to vendors, however, especially when adjustments have been made to the broad base tax in order to lessen regressivity.

Local sales taxes can be administered either by the state or locality. For example in 1979, of the twenty-five states that authorized local sales taxes, nineteen provided state administration, four had local administration, and two had both.[28] In those states with locally administrated local sales taxes, approximately half compensate the vendors for collection.[29] Approximately the same percentage of states administering local sales taxes compensate vendors for their costs to the extent of 1 to 5 percent of their tax obligation.[30]

Severe administrative problems can occur by the local administration of a local sales tax in states with state sales taxes. Tax administration is duplicated without gain; two sets of officials conduct the collection audit and enforcement programs for the same transactions.[31] However, the state administration of local sales taxes has proved a practical and efficient technique for giving financial assistance to localities with collection fees not exceeding 2 percent.[32]

Social Acceptability.   Again, as far as we are aware, no data have been gathered on the acceptability of the local sales tax. However, to the extent that the local sales tax is "piggybacked" onto the state sales tax, an analysis of the acceptability of the state tax might be useful.

Of the survey respondents, 19 percent rated the state sales least tax fair in 1980. Of those aged 17–29 years, 22 percent use this response as compared to only 16 percentage of those over 60 years. For respondents from households with an annual income of less $17,000, 23 percent ranked this tax least fair as compared to only 13 percent of those with annual incomes between $10,000 and $15,000. One quarter of those in the Northeast region had strong negative opinions against this revenue source as compared to only 15 percent of those living in the South.[33]

Elasticity and Stability.   Again this chapter will have to rely on the degree of conformity of the local sales tax to that of the state in order to estimate income elasticity. Estimates of income elasticity ranged from 0.80 in Tennessee in 1962 to 1.27 in Arkansas in the same year. Nationwide the income elasticity of the general sales tax ranges around 1.00, although one investigator determined it to be 1.27 in 1965.[34]

Equity. A major criticism of the sales tax is the regressivity of its burden. As Maxwell and Aronson point out: "Beyond question the most weighty criticism of the sales tax has been its equity. The tax is on consumption, and since consumption must absorb a higher percentage of income for poor rather than for rich persons, a tax that rests on consumption is regressive."[35]

Much research has been conducted to examine the effects on equity of exempting some commodities from the base. Schaefer found that exempting food consumed at home would change the New Jersey regressive levy into a proportional tax, and that including clothing in the base would make the tax more progressive.[36]

Productivity. For those states that do allow local government use of this tax, the revenues constitute from less than 1 percent of local taxes (Arkansas) to more than 49 percent (Louisiana). Overall in 1979 the general sales tax contributed 8.7 percent of local tax revenues.[37]

Similar analyses should be carried out for taxes in the "other tax" categories such as taxes on amusements or admissions, alcoholic beverages, business privileges, gross receipts, lodgings, motor fuels, net profits, real estate transfers, and tobacco products. The literature contains less information relating each of these taxes to the criteria identified above. User charges, which are obviously growing in importance in local own-source revenues, are subject to criticism on equity grounds and under the criteria of sound administrative qualities. Space does not permit a discussion here, but Due and Friedlaender[38] provide an excellent basis for study.

The 1980s will be challenging for all local officials. But for none more than those charged with obtaining the financial resources needed to meet the needs of their commodities. Such officials will need all of the insights provided by a systematic approach to revenue planning in order to diversify their local revenue base in a rational manner.

NOTES

1. George E. Peterson, "Finance," in *The Urban Predicament*, ed. by William Gorham and Nathan Glazer (Washington, D.C.: The Urban Institute, 1976), p. 38.
2. Joint Economic Committee, Trends in the Fiscal Condition of Cities: 1978–80" (Washington, D.C.: Government Printing Office, 1980), p. 5.

3. Anthony H. Pascal et al., *Fiscal Containment of Local and State Government* (Santa Monica: Rand Corporation, September 1979), p. v.
4. Roy Bahl et al., *The Fiscal Outlook for Cities* (Syracuse N. Y.: Syracuse University Press, 1978), p. 16.
5. Pascal et al., *Fiscal Containment of Local and State Government*, p. vii.
6. See U.S. Bureau of the Census, *1972 Census of Governments*, Vol. 4, *Governmental Finances*, Table 46 and *1977 Census of Governments*, Vol. 4, *Governmental Finances*, Table 47; and U.S. Bureau of the Census, "Worksheets of Revenues of State and Local Governments by Source and Level of Government, by State: 1978-1979," Table 5 (both Washington, D.C.: Government Printing Office).
7. *Wall Street Journal*, March 21, 1980, p. 1.
8. National League of Cities et al., Appendix A, *The Fiscal Plight of American Cities* (Washington, D.C., 1971), p. 141.
9. Friedrich J. Grasberger et al., "State and Local Tax and Expenditure Limitations: An Inventory" (Rochester, N.Y.: Center for Governmental Research, 1980), pp. 1-17.
10. ACIR, *Significant Features of Fiscal Federalism*, 1979-80 ed. (Washington, D.C.: Advisory Commission on Intergovernmental Relations, 1980), p. 185.
11. Ibid., p. 108.
12. Ibid.
13. James E. Maxwell and J. Richard Aronson, *Financing State and Local Governments*, 3rd ed. (Washington, D.C.: The Brookings Institution, 1977), pp. 167-168.
14. ACIR, *Significant Features*, p. 126.
15. Ibid., p. 139.
16. Emil M. Sunley and Gail R. Wilensky, "The Personal Income Tax," in Committee on The District of Columbia, *Technical Aspects of the District's Tax System*, 95th Congress, 2nd Session, p. 69.
17. ACIR, *Significant Features*, pp. 127-133.
18. Compiled from ACIR, "Changing Public Attitudes on Governments and Taxes 1980" (Washington, D.C.: Advisory Commission on Intergovernmental Relations, 1980), p. 21.
19. Sunley and Wilensky, "The Personal Income Tax," p. 69.
20. ACIR, *Significant Features*, p. 254.
21. John F. Due and Ann F. Friedlaender, *Government Finance*, 6th ed. (Homewood, Ill.: Irwin, 1977), p. 295.
22. Joseph Pechman and Benjamin Okner, *Who Bears the Burden?* (Washington, D.C.: The Brookings Institution, 1974), p. 57.
23. U.S. Bureau of the Census, "Worksheets of Revenues of State and Local Governments: 1978-79."
24. Due and Friedlaender, *Government Finance*, p. 296.
25. Maxwell and Aronson, *Financing State and Local Governments*, pp. 167-171.
26. ACIR, *Significant Features*, p. 126.
27. Due and Friedlaender, *Government Finance*, p. 378.
28. John L. Mikesell, "Local Government Sales Taxes," in *State and Local Sales Taxation*, ed. by John F. Due (Chicago: Public Administration Service, 1971), p. 267.
29. Ibid., p. 279.
30. Maxwell and Aronson, *Financing State and Local Governments*, p. 106.
31. Mikesell, "Local Government Sales Taxes," p. 281.
32. Ibid., p. 294.

128 / *Alternate Revenue Sources*

33. ACIR, "Changing Public Attitudes on Governments and Taxes 1980," p. 21.
34. ACIR, *Significant Features*, p. 254.
35. Maxwell and Aronson, *Financing State and Local Governments*, p. 106.
36. Jeffrey Schaefer, "Sales Tax Regressivity Under Alternative Tax Bases and Income Concepts," *National Tax Journal* (December 1968), pp. 516–527.
37. U.S. Bureau of the Census, "Worksheets of Revenues of State and Local Governments: 1978–79,"
38. Due and Friedlaender, *Government Finance*.

Chapter 7

The Municipal Bond Market: Recent Changes and Future Prospects

*John E. Petersen**

This chapter reviews major changes in the municipal bond market over the past few years and speculates on its prospects in the near to intermediate future. The first major point is that tax-supported bond financing by general units of governments for traditional public service activities has been eclipsed in importance by the limited-obligation securities (revenue bonds), frequently issued by special purpose entities. These bonds are used to support activities carried on in the private sector. This development has shifted the focus of the tax-exempt market from providing capital for public construction to governments acting as financial intermediaries.

The second area examined relates to the first. The dynamics of and growth in the tax-exempt market will be largely determined by the market's ability to continue acting as a means for the private sector to obtain relatively low-cost capital. Unless political actions reduce the allowable scope of such activities, the strong economic incentives to provide such assistance should continue

This paper represents the views of the author; it does not necessarily represent the views of the Government Finance Research Center or the Municipal Finance Officers Association.

*Director, Government Finance Research Center, Municipal Finance Officers Association

to make nontraditional borrowing the area of growth. This stands in contrast to the bleak prospects in the foreseeable future for traditional public-sector borrowing and capital spending. The latter derive both from a secular slowing of growth in the state and local sectors and from immediate pressures on taxes and spending generated by taxpayer attitudes, declining federal aid, and a sluggish economy.

THE RISE OF THE REVENUE BOND

A fundamental change in tax-exempt bond issues over the past decade has been in the nature of the security pledged to the repayment of the debt. There has been a dramatic decline in the relative importance of the traditional form of governmental borrowing, the general obligation, or tax-supported, bond. In 1970, long-term general obligation bonds accounted for 66 percent of the dollar volume of all new issues (see (Table 7.1). Since 1970, the proportion of new issues sold as general obligations has dwindled, accounting for only 29 percent of dollar volume in 1979 and 30 percent in 1980.

In contrast, the nontax-supported obligations—generically referred to as revenue bonds—have rapidly increased their share of the tax-exempt market. In 1970, revenue bonds accounted for

Table 7.1. Proportion of Revenue and General Obligation Bonds Sold in New-Issue Municipal Bond Market, 1970–1980

Year	Total Volume (billions)	Percent Revenue Bond	Percent General Obligation
1970	$18.083	33.7%	66.3%
1971	24.929	34.9	65.1
1972	23.692	39.7	60.3
1973	23.821	44.6	55.4
1974	23.560	42.4	57.6
1975	30.699	48.0	52.0
1976	35.416	48.8	51.2
1977	46.706	61.3	38.7
1978	48.352	63.4	36.6
1979	43.317	71.2	28.8
1980[a]	47.000	70.0	30.0

Source: Compiled from Public Securities Association, *Municipal Market Developments*, various issues. Data do not include estimates of small-issue revenue bond sales.
[a]Estimate based on data for the first eleven months.

only about one-third of the dollar sales of all new issues. By the end of the decade, however, they accounted for 70 percent. A central theme emerges from these trends: the traditional borrowing purposes and financing vehicles of state and local governments have been supplanted by a rapidly growing array of new uses of proceeds and new borrowing devices designed to accomodate those needs. Together, these developments have radically altered the landscape of the municipal bond market and how the investor perceived it. The most common characteristic among these newcomers is that while the securities are tax-exempt obligations, they are designed to avoid (or circumvent) the traditional linkage between a government's ability to incur debt (which is free of federal taxation on its interest income) and its general power to levy taxes in the repayment of such debt. Thus, most debt of governmental issuers no longer can be considered that of the taxpayer with recourse to the public purse.

The rapidly growing areas of tax-exempt financing, as of late, are those that support essentially private-sector investments. Many of these activities were formerly financed through traditional credit channels, employing taxable credit instruments as corporate debt and bank loans. Industrial aid and pollution control bonds, housing bonds, hospital bonds, and debt of public power projects are leading examples of the new tax-exempt instruments in the municipal bond market. Acceptance of these financing needs as public purposes has led directly to the outpouring of revenue bonds, because the flexibility of that security form accomodates these nontraditional purposes. Because the payment of these debts looks to special or restricted sources of funds—such as enterprise earnings, private payments, or special subsidies—the investor looks through the governmental entity to the credit of the ultimate payor of the debt.

Revenue bonds historically have been the favored means of surmounting a variety of constraints on governmental action and for entering new frontiers for the public purpose; this is true today more than ever. Their use has given rise to governmental entities that have the power to borrow and that inhabit a twilight zone between the public and private sectors—special districts and statutory authorities. But, certainly, not all the presence for change comes from the emboldened public official or the recalcitrant taxpayer. Much of the activity on the fringes of public purpose has been generated by the strong economic incentives tax-exempt financing offers private parties who can gain access to the market. The result of these pressures has been to change the municipal market toward a greater blending of public credit and private activity, with the revenue bond serving as the primary capital-raising catalyst.

THE CHANGING FUNCTION OF PUBLIC BORROWING

Traditionally, governments have sold long-term debt obligations for purposes of financing capital improvements. Thus, financing in the bond market has been viewed as a derived demand to meet the capital needs believed necessary by constituents of a governmental unit, but capital expenditures and the sales of debt reflect the interaction of many fundamental forces that change through time. For example, population growth carries with it the need for additional government services of a basic nature—education, public safety, transportation, and utilities. Rising standards of living have also tended to raise expectations of the government's role in fulfilling certain social welfare goals. Leading examples are the new commitments of state and local government to provide adequate housing, to improve facilities and opportunities for health treatment, and to foster higher education. Thus, trends in public capital spending mirror changes in both the population and the wealth of society and in what society perceived government's mission to be.

An example can be drawn from the environmental concerns and the growth of wastewater treatment and other pollution-control facilities. The prevailing public philosophy has been that the purpose was so important in its accomplishment that governments should help provide access to low-cost capital for industries as well as for themselves. Hence, special exceptions were made for the industrial pollution control bond when the Internal Revenue Code was amended in the late 1960s. Expansions of public purpose to accomodate such private activities have been accompanied by a slowing down of economic growth, a changing demography, and a fiscal tightening of the government sector that have lessened public capital expenditure demands. These forces have jointly served to change the composition and character of the municipal bond market.

Up until a few years ago, a rule of thumb was that about 50 percent of state and local capital expenditures would be financed through the issuance of long-term 'debt; however, several forces at work have broken the traditional tie between borrowing and capital spending by state and local governments.

First, capital spending demands have lessened over the past few years. Capital outlays for traditional state and local purposes evidently have not been keeping up with the increase in prices. In other words, real capital outlays (in price-deflated terms) by state and local governments have generally been in decline since the mid-1960s. While various fiscal stringencies no doubt account for part of it, in other cases the desultory performance is due to a lessening of demand for new facilities—such as schools—because of a changing age profile in the population, changing development patterns, and changing public tastes.

Second, the linkage between traditional government capital outlays and borrowing has been further attenuated because of alternative financing available through federal grants. While such grants vary over time, they have in general become increasingly important in determining the composition, volume, and timing of capital outlays by state and local governments. As may be seen in Table 7.2, during the 1950s federal grants represented an estimated 8 percent of the funds used to finance state and local capital spending; however, by the late 1970s well over 30 percent of state and local capital spending was financed by federal grants.

Third, a growing population of state and local long-term debt represents funds raised for purposes of acquiring financial as opposed to real assets. The governmental entity doing the borrowing acts as a financial intermediary, either for purposes of relending within the governmental sector or—as has become increasingly important—acting as a conduit for supplying funds to private sectors in the economy. In the latter case, the capital spending financed by the bond issue is not reflected in the acquisi-

Table 7.2. State and Local Capital Outlay Financing: Percent Composition of Sources of Funds

Revenue Source	1952–1957	1960	1970	1977
Long-term debt	56.0%	37.1%	51.0%	43.3%
Federal aid	8.5	20.0	22.0	32.1
Other sources	35.5	42.9	27.0	24.6
Total	100.0%	100.0%	100.0%	100.0%

Sources: 1952–1957 Alan Manvel, "State and Local Government Financing of Capital Outlays," in *State and Local Public Facility News and Aiming,* Joint Economic Committee (December 1966). Data for the subsequent years: George Peterson, "Capital Spending and Capital Obsolescence," in Roy Bahl, *The Fiscal Outlook for Cities* (Syracuse, N.Y.: Syracuse University Press, 1978).

tion of a physical capital asset, but rather of a financial asset such as a mortgage or a lease agreement.

CHANGING PURPOSES FOR TAX-EXEMPT BORROWING

In response to the changing economic, demographic, and philosophical forces, the purposes for which state and local debt is issued are changing. Table 7.3 shows the major uses of proceeds for long-term tax-exempt borrowing. The total volume of borrowing shown in that table for recent years is larger than that given in Table 7.1 because of the inclusion of the Congressional Budget Office's recent estimates of small-issue industrial development bonds, an area of the market in which there is a very significant underreporting of transactions. The dollar volume of long-term borrowing for the "traditional" purposes of education, transportation, and water and sewerage facilities has declined markedly, from 65 percent of total borrowing in 1960 to 60 percent in 1970,

Table 7.3. Tax-Exempt Borrowing by Purpose ($ billions)

	1960	1970	1975	1977	1978	1979	1980e
Education	$2.3	$5.0	$4.7	$5.1	$5.0	$5.1	$4.9
Transportation	1.3	3.2	2.2	2.9	3.5	2.4	2.0
Water and sewerage	1.0	2.4	2.3	3.3	3.2	3.1	3.5
Utilities	0.3	1.1	2.7	4.8	5.8	5.4	5.1
Industrial pollution Control	—	—	2.2	2.6	2.7	2.1	2.8
Hospitals	NA	NA	2.0	3.3	2.3	3.4	3.7
Single-family housing	NA	NA	NA	1.0	3.2	7.2	13.6
Other housing[a]	0.4	0.1	0.6	2.7	2.9	2.6	
Industrial aid[b]	—	0.1	1.2	2.3	3.5	7.0	9.5
Other[c]	1.7	5.6	13.6	18.7	19.5	10.3	10.0
Total	$7.1	$17.5	$31.3	$46.7	$51.6	$48.7	$55.1

Source: R. Forbes, P. Fischer, and J. Petersen, "The Remarkable Rise of the Municipal Revenue Bond" (unpublished paper, January 1980); U.S. Congress, Congressional Budget Office, "Small Issue Industrial Development Bonds" (draft report, November 1980), with update based on Public Securities Association, *Municipal Market Developments* and *Daily Bond Buyer,* various issues.

[a]Includes single-family housing before 1977.

[b]Based on Congressional Budget Office estimates of "small-issue" industrial development bonds.

[c]Includes heavy refundings of more than $10 billion in 1977 and 1978.

plummeting to an estimated 19 percent by 1980. New areas for growth have more than taken up any slack in traditional capital demands. Among these new uses, bonds sold to meet social welfare purposes have mushroomed. Housing and hospital bonds accounted for 31 percent of all new issues in 1980, up from 2 percent of the market in 1970 and 8 percent in 1975.

Other uses of public credit, typically financed by revenue bonds, have increased in volume and proportion compared to general-obligation financing. Utility financing has more than doubled in the decade and accounted for approximately 10 percent of the total market in the late 1970s. Many of these utility issues are extremely complex and specialized financing, involving joint undertakings between one public entity or a collection of municipalities and one or more private firms. Several projects involve the construction of entirely new utility systems, including ancillary capital facilities such as railroad cars and other features of the vertically integrated system.

Table 7.3 underscores the fact that industrial aid bonds and industrial pollution control facilities combined, accounted for an estimated $12.3 billion in 1980 (including $8 billion in apparently unreported small-issue transactions). These issues, which primarily benefit private firms, accounted for an estimated 22 percent of municipal borrowing in 1980, double the 11 percent market share recorded in 1975. In 1970 such aid to private firms accounted for less than 1 percent of tax-exempt borrowing.

The major incentive for the growing use of public credit by private purposes is economic: the lower cost of tax-exempt financing compared with conventional taxable financing. As Table 7.4 shows, the spread between taxable and tax-exempt bond issues exceed 2 percentage points over the 1970s, and since 1976, the margin has widened. In 1978 and 1979, high-grade tax-exempt issues carried interest rates more than 3 percent below corporate issues. By 1980, the gap, in extremely turbulent markets, swelled to over 4 percentage points. Thus, interest costs that appeared excessive to conventional state and local borrowers continued to represent a bargain for private firms.

NEW BORROWING ENTITIES

Table 7.5 gives another perspective on the changes in the municipal market, depicting the percentage composition of new bond sales by type of issuer over the past few years. The propor-

Table 7.4. Yields on New-Issue Long-Term Municipal and Corporate Bonds Rated Aaa by Moody's

Year	Aaa Municipal Rate	Aaa Corporate Rate	Spread Between Rates
1970	6.12%	8.04%	1.82%
1971	5.22	7.39	2.17
1972	5.04	7.21	2.17
1973	4.99	7.44	2.45
1974	4.89	8.57	2.68
1975	6.42	8.83	2.41
1976	5.65	8.43	2.78
1977	5.20	8.02	2.82
1978	5.52	8.74	3.22
1979	5.89	9.65	3.76
1980[a]	7.81	12.10	4.29

Source: Moody's Investor Services, Moody's Bond Record (December 1980).
[a]First ten months.

tion of new issues sold by traditional units of government—states, counties, municipalities, and school districts—has declined, while the volume of debt raised by special districts and statutory authorities has increased. Nationally, the proportion of debt sold by traditional governmental units has decreased from 68 percent of all issues in 1966–1970, to 61 percent in 1971–1976, and to 50 percent in 1977–1979.

The use of revenue bonds has accompanied the significant shift to special authority and special district entities, many of which are established primarily for the purpose of making possible such financing. Until the 1930s, most state and local bonds were tax supported and represented full-faith-and-credit obligations. During the Great Depression, the use of "special fund" obligations grew in order to overcome the problems of severely eroded property tax bases and restrictive debt limits, and to circumvent problems of pledging the public credit to certain uses. Use of limited-liability financing expanded rapidly in the post–World War II period as the courts became more lenient about and the public more accepting of a growing number of applications of tax-exempt financing.

Often, it has been easier for a state legislature to permit the creation of a special district or authority with new bonding authority and have it do the financing for a general unit of government rather than to try to amend restrictive constitutional limitations. In other cases, the argument has been that projects could be

Table 7.5. New Bond Sales, Percent Composition as Classified by Type of Issuer, 1966-1979

Type of Issuer	1966-1970	1971-1976	1977-1979
States	23.3%	21.9%	12.4%
Counties	8.5	7.8	9.2
Municipalities	24.0	23.0	22.4
School districts	12.6	8.2	6.1
Special districts	5.3	4.6	4.5
Statutory authorities	26.2	34.4	45.5
Totals	100.0%	100.0%	100.0%

Source: Based on Municipal Finance Study Group (State University of New York at Albany) data files.

established as self-supporting enterprises and that the users rather than the taxpayer would foot the bill; hence, there was no reason to treat the debt as a public responsibility.

Whatever the pros and cons of political expediency versus the principle of public accountability, insulation of special authorities and districts from the general government sphere has both been accommodated by and has encouraged the use of revenue bonds. Furthermore, these special authorities have injected greater flexibility into government in order to meet specialized problems. For example, statutory authorities have made possible the combining of many underlying jurisdictions in a state or a region to accomplish areawide, highly technical, and capital-intensive solutions that would not be possible for any one of the units to do alone. This has been particularly important in the case of programs for pollution control, water resource management, public power, regional transportation, and at the state level, public housing. While such entities often rely heavily on user charges, the underlying security may in some cases rest on the taxing powers of the consortium of local governments that is pledged in contracts to support the bond issue.

Of particular note has been the growing reliance on lease-rental revenue bonds, which are secured on lease agreements between the issuing authority and the operator of the facility. Lease revenue bonds are very flexible and have been used to finance both traditional purposes (such as office buildings or local schools) and newer acitivites (such as housing, pollution control facilities, and stadiums) that are frequently quasi-public or privately operated facilities. The lease rentals may be secured on either user charges or on tax revenues. In the latter case, the usefulness of this type of borrowing vehicle to circumvent debt limits and reference requirements is most evident.

WHAT'S AHEAD FOR THE MARKET

Speculating on the future direction and size of the municipal bond market is particularly difficult for two reasons. First, there is the extreme uncertainty and volatility endemic to all the nation's credit markets as the economy continually falters and inflation roars ahead. Second, there is a rising dependency of the tax-exempt market on factors largely outside the state and local governmental sector and subject to alteration through political action. The latter respect refers to the major growth coming in those uses that represent a conduit for private capital demands. Hence, changes in the legal parameters of what can and cannot be financed through use of tax-exempt bonds have the greatest potential impacts on the supply of bonds in the tax-exempt market.

Were the tax-exempt bond market being used to finance only those activities financed 10 years ago, it would be approximately half its present size. Tax-exempt interest rates would be lower, but by how much no one can say for sure.

The near-term prospects for the market appear far from promising from the prospect of lower costs of borrowing and greater availability of credit. Although the economy will be in a recessionary or slow-growth condition in 1981, the continuation of inflation and high interest rates will probably retard much reduction in long-term rates. It is unlikely that the monetary authorities will permit another rapid expansion in credit and decline in interest rates such as occurred in the spring of 1980. Conventional demands for local government capital—sewers, roads, schools, and public buildings—will continue to be dwarfed by the demands for industrial and commercial development. An easing in supply, however, is likely to occur in the case of mortgage and housing bonds under the amendments approved as part of the Federal Budget Reconciliation Act passed in November 1980. How restrictive this measure will prove to be remains to be tested, but there are enough legal uncertainties and legislated restraints to reduce the supply of housing bonds appreciably. While this should bring some relief in the demand for credit, my own speculation is that the small-issue Industrial Development Bonds and other forms of private sector assistance borrowing will expand and, resultingly, sop up much of the money available for tax-exempt investments.

Taking a somewhat longer view, it is true that state and local governments will be hard pressed to continue the financing of capital improvements from federal grants, a source that has been of major importance over the past decade. This should mean that the sector's infrastructure capital needs will be increasingly met by borrowing. That may be, but the overall penury and slow growth of the sector argue against any new expansionary spending. Monumental efforts will be needed to maintain and operate existing facilities. Governments are clearly less interested in signing up to finance debt service out of tax receipts. The public's mood will remain sour about new public structures and programs during the next few years of general economic retrenchment.

Correctly or not, the economic and social reversals of the past years are identified with "big government spending and high taxes," and that attitude seems pervasive. I believe these tendencies to check the sector's growth will be reinforced by the continuing shift of economic activity (and congressional representation) to the South and West, both of which have "less public and more private" traditions. But even with the regional shifts, the prognosis remains that the general economy, and the domestic public sector specifically, will grow much more slowly (and, perhaps, not at all) in real terms.

Ironically, one consequence of these changes will be to further cloud the separation between the public and the private sectors in an effort to continue supplying needed services. For example, activities will be increasingly shifted to government enterprises where public services are financed using user charges and other market-oriented devices. Fiscal pressures on governments will no doubt foster much experimentation along these lines. Those activities that can prove themselves to be self-supporting will have a great financing advantage over those that must contend for tax or grant dollars. This argues for the continuing dominance of the revenue bond, in all its complicated glory.

A collateral development to the market model of public goods delivery will be less concerned about the equity and distributional effects of public spending and revenues. Promoting the good life and an equitable distribution of wealth and income will not be a concern of local governments, which will not be able to afford the cost of good intentions.

On the technical side, the volatility of the financial markets will put a premium on efficient use of money and timing in transactions. It appears, for example, that short-term tax-exempt borrowing has staged a comeback after languishing in the mid-to-late 1970s. In 1980, short-term note sales were approximately $27 billion, or $6 billion more than in 1979. Another aspect of the emphasis on short-term borrowing has been the development of a tax-exempt commercial paper market, providing large borrowers with great flexibility in their debt management. If done prudently, such borrowing can avoid costly lock-ins of high borrowing costs.

The variable rate security is another innovation spawned by the high and fluctuating rates of interest. Here, the interest coupon is tied to some market index and—within ranges—moves to protect investors from large losses in capital value in down markets. By the same token, of course, issuers are faced with uncertainty about what their debt service requirements will be in the future. The chaotic conditions have led to other financial packages designed to tempt investors into long-term obligations by offering them protection against interest rate risk. For the greatest part such devices require a flexibility in debt administration (and project revenues) that makes them most suitable to revenue bond obligations. The municipal mortgage bond and its assorted housing finance cousins have proved to be especially fecund in this regard.

SUMMARY

The tax-exempt bond market has been transformed dramatically over the past few years, as the types of securities, nature of the issuers, and uses of proceeds have changed. Reacting to a multitude of forces, the market's greatest growth has been at what were formerly its fringes of involvement. Its center of gravity has shifted away from the financing of traditional government functions and units toward the support of activities carried out in the private sector. This shift toward governments acting as financial intermediaries rather than final users of capital has meant increasing reliance on limited-obligation ·debt instruments, and has spawned the creation of special borrowing entities that have access to the tax-exempt market without the constraints faced by traditional, tax-supported governments.

These changes are not merely of historic interest. Much of the new uses and many of the new borrowing entities are controversial and may be faced with extinction as the federal, state, and local governments review their long-term desirability. Therefore, the municipal bond market's shape and behavior will be greatly influenced by how far the rapidly running tide toward financing private-sector activities advances.

The short- to intermediate-term prognosis for the municipal bond market, as for all capital markets, is not favorable. First preference in national policies will be given to stimulating private investment, and this will need to be done in the context of inflationary and uncertain conditions. Furthermore, so long as interest differentials between taxable and tax-exempt interest rates are large, there will be continuing pressure to use the municipal market as a conduit for private sector financing. What may be historically high, unaffordable rates of interest for governments will be relatively economical for private sector activities.

Meanwhile, public sector capital needs—while considered great —will not translate into high levels of effective demand for capital because of severe and unrelenting budgetary constraints. In the absence of the boost that was provided by federal aid over the past, capital spending will continue to lose out to current operating outlays in state and local budgets.

PART IV

Fiscal Capacity and Economic Development

Chapter 8

The Fiscal Status of the State–
Local Sector:
A Look to the 1980s

*Donald Phares**

The financial plight of many states and, even more so, local governments in the United States is a well-publicized issue. One need only turn almost any day to a local or national newspaper to read about the "balancing the budget act." Often the situation is severe, schools are closed or threatened with closure; municipalities are cut back in basic services; and states are forced to absorb a larger share of financing local services. The scenario has become a familiar one and was brought clearly into focus by the fiscal debacle in New York City in the spring of 1975.

There appears, however, to be a crucial distinction between past cries of fiscal woe and what the decade of the 1980s may hold in store. States, and to a greater extent local governments due to their inferior fiscal status, have echoed such misery for decades. Their pleading occurred, however, during a period of generalized growth in government at all levels. As a percentage of gross national product, using one benchmark statistic, total public spending went from 9.9 percent in 1929 to 31 percent in 1969 to an estimated 32.4 percent for 1980. The same percentages for just the state–local sector are 7.3, 10.4, and 10.3, respectively.[1] Thus, we experienced a tripling of the relative size of government over this

* Department of Economics and Center for Metropolitan Studies, University of Missouri–St. Louis

145

fifty-year period, but a recent marked slowdown in the overall growth rate and even a slight drop at the state–local level. While spending for this latter sector in dollar terms has attained new heights, its share has begun to show signs of tapering off or falling.

Herein lies a fundamental shift from the earlier period of almost continual expansion for the state–local sector, once referred to as the "Most Dynamic Sector,"[2] to what will be played out over the next decade. The combined impact of inflation, recession, a low rate of real economic growth, a steady upward drift in the overall burden of taxation, increased regulation, unionization of public employees, rising input costs, and the fiscal limitation movement has generated a new environment. The affluence that had enabled government to increase its share of the economic pie and to fund expensive new programs, without eroding private income, is no longer there. As one writer has put it, *"all growth in income in the United States since 1973 has been either eaten away by inflation or gone into government spending."* While real disposable income per worker, adjusted for the growth in the federal debt, rose by an average annual rate of 2.9 percent per year between 1947 and 1973, it fell by 0.3 percent between 1973 and 1977.[3]

State and local governments, being the most proximate to citizens, have responded in the past to citizen needs for a variety of public goods related to the general growth in population as well as to the particular demands induced by urbanization and suburbanization and a desire to ameliorate a variety of social ills. The question to be addressed here is what public resources will be available to finance these needs in the 1980s.

The text that follows will focus on the resource base of the state–local sector and how it might be influenced by public policy, laws and regulations, and economic factors. The term "resources" will be viewed in a broad context rather than in the more traditional, limited sense say of fiscal capacity or tax capacity.[4] An attempt will be made to sketch an overview of the resource base of the state–local sector and then to speculate concerning what will happen over the next decade.

One caveat must be noted at the outset. Since we are implicitly discussing the fiscal status of about 78,000 separate jurisdictions, there is no way to spell out the financial fortunes of each. Even doing this state by state would be a formidable task. Rather, an overview will be presented with a highlighting of the major trends that seem most probable. The discussion will be couched in terms of the general forces in operation, with due recognition of the wide

variations that exist across governments.
To accomplish this, the text will evolve in three main segments:
(1) a discussion of the options for balancing the budget; (2) a
survey of the financial pressures that will serve as a background
for the 1980s; and (3) an elaboration of some major policy issues
for this decade.[5]

HOW TO BALANCE THE BUDGET

There are a variety of ways by which a state or local government can bring a budget into balance. Given that this is an ubiqui-
tous requirement, insight into the financial dilemma can be gained
by a review of the financial options that can be used to equate
revenues with expenditures.

Increase Tax Yield

The most obvious first step to raise additional funds is to alter
the specific provisions of taxation to increase yield. This can be
done in two general ways: (1) increase the rate(s) that apply to a
base, or (2) broaden the base itself by somehow making it more
inclusive. To a large extent, this is exactly how additional funds
have been derived in the past. Thus, in addition to any automatic
expansion of revenue due to economic growth, yield has been
increased through overt policy manipulation.[6]

At the state level over the period 1959–1976, for example, there
were 586 separate legislative actions affecting just the six major
state taxes. In addition, forty-one new taxes were also put into
effect. A general sales tax is now in place in all but four states,
and only nine do not currently have a broad-based tax on individual income.[7] These taxes have become the two major revenue
generators producing billions of dollars in additional revenue for
states over the last couple of decades.

At the local level the picture has not been quite so rosy, but it
has generally been one of expanded options. State enabling legislation has allowed local jurisdictions in thirteen states to tap into
the income base. In some instances such as New York City, Detroit,
or Philadelphia hundreds of millions of dollars are produced annually. A somewhat more liberal situation prevails with the local
general sales tax, currently in place in twenty-six states. All in all,
about 10,000 local jurisdictions now have the option of taxing
income and/or sales.[8] Without invoking the plethora of statistics

that could be conjured up to document this point, the fiscal environment of the 1960s and 1970s was one of wider use of existing and previously untapped tax sources. The demands of expanding budgets were met, in large part, with a broader, more intensively used tax base.

The prognosis for the 1980s, however, does not at all mirror the 1960s or 1970s. Legislative activity at the state level between 1977 and 1980 manifests a new trend. During this period there were thirty-six instances of a major decrease in the personal income tax and twenty-two for the general sales tax. In addition, nine states have indexed the income tax, cutting its yield, and eighteen have enacted either statutory or constitutional fiscal lids.[9]

At the local level the picture is obfuscated by the sheer number of jurisdictions, but full disclosure laws, property tax levy limits, assessment constraints, and classification have occurred on about forty-eight occasions in thirty-one states since 1970.[10] A separate but related issue is the requirement for a referendum vote to increase local property taxes. The success rate has reflected a growing reluctance on the part of citizens to react positively to increased taxes. Beyond this, local governments are restricted in a variety of other ways by state law in being able to increase property tax yields through overt policy action.[11]

In summary, the prospects for obtaining major new sources of funds through legislated tax increases look dim. While some automatic growth will undoubtedly result as the economy revives, the environment necessary for intentionally expanding tax yield seems unlikely. It seems even less promising at the local level due to the burdensome nature of the property tax and the severe lack of fiscal flexibility afforded this sector.

Cut Expenditures

Virtually everyone seems predisposed to the general notion of cutting back on government. This is no less true at the state and local level than at the federal level, in principle. There is a fundamental difference, however, when one accounts for the proximity of states, and especially local jurisdictions, to their taxpayers. The typical citizen is much more aware of, concerned with, and dependent on services available locally, or at the state level, simply because they affect one's day-to-day life. Education for children, safety on the streets and in the home, transportation to get to and from work, emergency health-care facilities, access to higher education, and so on, are the core of public goods that affect a citizen most directly. National defense, getting an astronaut on Venus, or providing aid to foreign countries are distant in impact and concern. In a very real sense it is the collection of local governments (school district, municipality, special districts, etc.) that one is most aware of and concerned about.[12]

When it comes to the nitty-gritty of cutting state–local budgets the problem arises of what to cut. Everyone wants reduced expenditures but not if it concerns a program that directly affects him. In other words, cut someone else's services but not mine.[13] Obviously, this produces a paradoxical situation for any policy maker attempting to order priorities for a budget reduction. If cuts are attempted in education, health care, or public safety, the services that probably affect the most people the most often, officials are confronted with cries of anguish.

Curiously, the situation is even more of a paradox than this. In a general milieu of reducing budgets, it is not uncommon to have citizens clamoring for even greater services from government. More police protection, quality education, better health care, faster transportation facilities, are all fairly common requests. The high degree of interdependence and the problems relating to congestion and density in urban areas (involving most of the U.S. population) elicit greater demands for government to "do something" at the same time it is being asked to do less.[14] We have come to depend heavily on government to accomplish objectives that private activity shuns or to clear up problems that private behavior has created.

Cutting spending is clearly an option to balance the budget but it is a painful one, difficult for officials to put in place, difficult for taxpayers to accept, and often hard to rationalize given the conditions of our nation's urban areas, the poor and aged, or the environment. That cuts will occur is a certainty; they have already begun. That pressure will come to bear for further public commitment of resources to urban and social problems is also certain. Reconciling these two forces will place added strain on the state–local sector since this sector is likely to be called on to do even more as federal involvement diminishes under the Reagan administration.

Increase Fees and Charges

One expanding contributer to revenue has been a heavier reliance on a panoply of fees and charges levied by state and local governments spanning the spectrum from university tuition to parking meters. Over the period 1962–1976 fees and charges went from

12.5 to 14 percent of state–local own-source revenues. Some local governments have reached the point where this source accounts for as much or even more revenue than taxes.[15]

The use of fees and charges is an attempt to establish a quid pro quo or benefits-related linkage between the costs and benefits of certain public services. This enables the activity to be priced separately and the user assigned a charge for services received. To this end it has lessened pressure on the tax base, provided revenues for expanded operations, and increased the efficiency of public resource utilization.

The question arises, can this trend in the "marketization" of public sector financing be extrapolated into the 1980s? While it is safe to assume that this source will continue to account for significant amounts of revenue, it also seems likely that increasing its relative role will be difficult.[16] Local governments, and to a lesser extent states, may continue to experience an expanded yield from fees and charges, but it is not feasible to use these charges for the financing of many of the most expensive crucial services such as education or public safety. The more collective or public an activity, the less feasible it is to attach a "price" to it. Most public services with easily assignable benefits already have an associated charge.

Intergovernmental Revenue

The past two decades have seen a dramatic shift in the fiscal relationship among federal, state, and local governments. Federal aid has steadily grown with the advent of general revenue sharing, housing and community development, and Comprehensive Employment and Training Act funds and the shift from categorical aid to formula funding. States have also increased aid flows to local units. While this aid has been heavily concentrated on school districts, there has been a marked growth in other types of state aid to local governments during the last twenty years as well. These involve revenue sharing schemes using a variety of distribution formulas as well as aid for support of specific local functions. Even local aid flows have been implemented as in tax base sharing in Minneapolis-St. Paul.[17]

Federal grants-in-aid have risen dramatically from about thirty-eight programs and 4.7 percent of federal budget outlays in 1955 to hundreds of programs peaking at over 17 percent of outlays in 1978. Federal aid has grown to the point where it is a large component of state budgets and a dominant source of funds for major older central cities such as Buffalo, St. Louis, or Newark.[18] States have also poured greater aid into their local jurisdictions to support education and other local services or to lessen pressure on the local fisc. Equalization of resources for local education, as a prime example, became a major focus of state policy and a major claimant for new state revenues.[19]

Looking forward to the 1980s, however, does not suggest a continuation of such a trend. At the federal level, aid has already fallen as of 1980 to roughly its 1975 proportion of federal budget outlays. With the advent of "supply-side" economic policy and Reaganomics, federal aid to states and to local governments seems destined to drop further. At the state level, the environment is exacerbrated by the tension of the taxpayer revolt. Legislators are generally looking for ways to cut taxes, not to increase them for greater support of local programs or fiscal relief. The rapid expansion of aid for education or state revenue-sharing programs, as examples, is likely to suffer as fiscal retrenchment worsens.

In summary, there seems to be little hope to expect the continuation of increases in intergovernmental revenue to the state–local sector that characterized the 1960s and 1970s.

Issue Debt

As an option for providing funds for day-to-day, current operations, issuance of debt by state and local governments is not viable. While debt can be used to finance capital projects or, in some cases, to encourage industrial location, subsidize certain types of urban programs, or ease a short-term cash flow problem, it cannot be relied upon to provide operating funds for the core of state–local activities. While funds are fungible to some extent and plans to finance capital projects out of current revenues could be shifted to debt proceeds—thus de facto freeing up current revenues—there is a limit to how much this can be done. Beyond this, the burden of debt maintenance remains as a claim on future state–local revenues.

The situation in New York City notwithstanding, state and local governments face rigid legal constraints on their use of debt instruments, are less and less able to bear the maintenance cost with double-digit interest rates, have increasing difficulty selling issues or obtaining an underwriter, and face strong citizen opposition whenever taxpayer approval is required.[20] Therefore, the sale of securities to provide current funds for balancing the budget does not hold much promise.

Fiscal Reassignment

A final major alternative to achieving a balanced budget would entail a formal reassignment of fiscal responsibility for certain state or local functions. This could occur on two levels. First, the federal government could assume a greater portion of the cost of state–local programs. Probably one of the most notable, often discussed instances of this is federalization of welfare and poverty programs, which would take pressure off of the state–local sector. Over the years, there have been numerous suggestions for making poverty programs a federal responsibility.[21] Education was also at one point targeted for federalization. During the Nixon administration, as *Serrano* and its progeny began to raise serious constitutional issues about financing local education, a national value-added tax was suggested as a replacement for the local property tax.[22] The proceeds from this new form of taxation (new at least to the United States) would have been earmarked for the support of local education, thus de facto having the result of a "federalization" of eduation (or its financing, at least). For a variety of reasons it was never adopted.

Second, state governments could assume greater responsibility for what are now local programs. The primary function, in dollar terms, is education.Over the past couple of decades, states have taken on a larger role in providing aid for education. While no instance of a fully state-funded system exists (although Hawaii is virtually there), greater formal state commitment to financing education has helped to reduce the strain on the local sector, particularly on the property tax. In this respect it has eased somewhat the fiscal burden on local government. However, it has resulted in often dramatic increases in state taxes. One can legitimately question whether greater support for local education will be legislatively desirable or even feasible within the milieu of cuts and limitations seen ahead for the 1980s.

A well-thought-out, serious reappraisal of the division of fiscal responsibility not only is desirable on pure economic grounds but also makes a great deal of sense in an immediate policy sense.[23] Re-establishing a semblance of fiscal balance in our federal system would necessitate just such an exercise. To count on such a restructuring as a fiscal savior to state or local government during this decade would be an exercise in self-deception. While some incremental adjustments will undoubtedly occur, the major responsibilities of state and local jurisdictions are most likely to remain where they are. If the full extent of President Reagan's budget cuts are implemented, these responsibilities may even increase.

Summary

In reviewing the primary options for achieving a balanced state–local budget in the 1980s, the situation (admittedly conditioned by the crystal ball nature of such an endeavor) appears to be almost a mirror image of the previous two decades. During this latter period tax rates were increased and new taxes were put into effect, spending grew dramatically, the use of fees and charges became much more pronounced, intergovernmental aid became a financial mainstay for states and local governments, and the federal and state governments were willing and able to assume a larger role in expensive public programs. The age of affluence that characterized the 1960s, and to a lesser extent the early 1970s, spilled over into the public arena. The dividend provided by the continuous real growth of our national economy enabled public programs to expand without encroaching on the taxpayers' standard of living.

Such will not be the case for much of the 1980s. Growth in the public sector will come only at the expense of the taxpayers' standard of living as inflation, unemployment, low productivity, slow (or no) economic growth, and a rising tax burden continually erode the advances made over the past two decades. All this is not to say that no increase in government will occur; undoubtedly some will. However, the forces at operation suggest a leveling off or even a decrease in the relative size of the state-local sector.

FINANCIAL PRESSURES ON THE STATE–LOCAL SECTOR

As we move into the 1980s and reflect on what is likely to transpire, one is struck by the impressive nexus of pressures that seem to be building up. Not to wave the banner of Armageddon, but there is quantitatively and qualitatively a variety of factors that will interact to produce an entirely new fiscal environment for—as far as can be discerned now—the bulk of the decade. Exactly what this will entail can only remain speculation at this point, but one fact seems evident—the state–local resource base will be affected for as long as these forces remain operative. A review of these major pressures helps to set the situation in perspective.

A Changing Legal Environment

The state–local sector has been h¹t with a new wave of legal issues that has exerted a claim on resources. The first set deals with the financing of education and the issue of equal protection under either federal or state constitutions.[24] Beginning with the *Serrano* vs. *Priest* case in California, states were confronted with the legality of using the highly fragmented local property tax base as a means of financing education. The initial challenge was couched in terms of a denial of equal protection under the Fourteenth Amendment to the U.S. Constitution. While the U.S. Supreme Court ruled (in *Robinson* vs. *Cahill*) that the issue was not one to be dealt with by the federal government, this did not absolve individual states from dealing with the equal protection issue under their own constitutions. In response to the demands of *Serrano, Robinson,* and a variety of subsequent cases, states have poured large sums of money into aid for education in order to mitigate fiscal disparities across school districts. California, as one notable instance, spent billions in the early 1970s to comply with *Serrano* only to have this ruled inadequate by the state Supreme Court. In 1977, an additional $4.6 billion over four years was appropriated to comply with the court's decision.[25] A number of other states have responded in a similar fashion by increasing their commitment of resources to support local education.

Beyond equal protection-type cases, litigation has also been introduced to deal with educational inequalities affecting groups such as the handicapped, the disadvantaged, or urban students. The end result has been greater spending in almost every state as a consequence of the expanding legal pressure for equalization, equal opportunity, or equity.[26]

Beyond the pressure of the financial claim of education has been a plethora of other laws and regulations that have influenced virtually all facets of state–local operations. It seems as though the decades of the 1960s and the 1970s have been the heyday of federal involvement in regulating major segments of American life. Environmental quality in all of its many manifestations is now subject to a bewildering array of federal regulations. Many of these impact directly on the state–local budget. For example, the cost of inputs is increased due to the higher costs of production to meet the regulation standards. Or, regulations influence the ways in which governments can "do business", i.e., trash disposal becomes more expensive, sewage plants must meet rigid standards, and so on.

Labor is the single biggest input, and therefore cost, to government. The passage of laws dealing with equal opportunity, affirmative action, antidiscrimination, workplace safety, and pensions has therefore had an impact on the cost of meeting legal mandates. Compliance with federal laws and regulations pertaining to all aspects of the labor force and workplace has added untold amounts to budgets.

Aside from these major areas are literally hundreds of laws and regulations with which state and local governments must comply. Some entail only record-keeping and periodic reporting; others require major commitments; all involve additional resources. While it is extremely difficult to assign a cost to this, in the final analysis laws and regulations of the type and magnitude enacted over the past twenty years stake a significant claim on state and local funds.

Evolving Labor Relations

At one point in the not too distant past, unionization and collective bargaining were almost anathema in the public sector. Public employees, such as teachers or police, were working for society or the commonweal. To engage in strikes or collective bargaining or to join a union was the clear exception to the general rule of behavior. Such is no longer the case.

Over the past two decades we have witnessed dramatic alterations in labor relations for public employees that have led to strikes, unionization, and collective bargaining touching on virtually all facets of public operations.

There are few signs that labor pressures for the state–local sector will taper off during the 1980s. To cite two statistics that portray the trend, union membership for state–local employees increased from 27 to 36 percent between 1968 and 1978 while employee associations had enrolled about 60 percent of all employees in this sector by 1978.[27] The financial burden of greater collectivization will be felt across all facets of public employment from vacations, working conditions, and wage levels to medical insurance, pension and retirement systems, and sick pay. While, hopefully, the New York City model of dealing with workers will be avoided, costs have nowhere to go but up.

Growth in Demand for Public Services

State and local governments are in a position to react more responsively and faster than is the federal government to the myriad concerns of their citizens. Over the recent few decades, as urbanization reached its zenith and suburbanization commenced, all the attendant problems emerged as well. The externalities of urban life were converted into demands on the local fisc, as well as the states, to design and implement policies to cope with a growing array of urban and social ills. Pressure also filtered upward to the federal government, which in turn has adopted a variety of aid programs to help ease the strain on the state–local sector. Thus, there has been a marked upward trend in spending on a much broader array of programs, often involving totally new areas of public involvement.

This growth in reliance on government to ameliorate the ills of urban areas and to cope with social problems such as poverty has led state and local government in directions that a few decades ago were clearly beyond their purview. Pollution control, complex land use and urban redevelopment schemes, expanded criminal justice activities, and drug abuse treatment programs, are merely suggestive of the diversity.

Aside from their own immediate involvement, state and local governments have also been lured into new activities due to the availability of federal largesse. Matching funds, on as favorable terms as 90/10 percent sharing, made involvement seem painless, almost suggesting that scarcity was dead, at least as long as federal dollars kept pouring in. And herein lies the kicker! These governments have expanded their program offerings as well as their funding levels and have tied into a variety of clientele groups that "were in need." Mass transit to facilitate the journey to work; medical care for the young, poor, or aged; urban redevelopment to lure the middle class and businesses back to the central city; and expanded welfare benefits—each provides an example of government fulfilling "needs" based heavily on federal funds.

The dilemma arises when federal funds are phased down or eliminated altogether. The clientele remains but the primary source of capital, and often operating funds as well, does not. San Francisco and Washington, D.C. may be left with BART and METRO to finance fully from local resources. New York City (and state) has a poor population that benefits from a high level of welfare support and comprehensive health care and social services. City after city accepted urban renewal funds to tear down vast areas of old residential and commercial structures only to discover their tax base had diminished and the economy of the city was not benefited as had been hoped.

While one could go on endlessly citing specifics, the bottom line is clear—government has increasingly been called on to do more and more. State and local governments are particularly sensitive to citizens' day-to-day concerns and have responded accordingly with new programs and greater funding for existing ones.

The interesting question is what will happen during the coming decade. A most likely, albeit schizophrenic, scenario is that the demand for more and better services will continue, particularly those that affect people most directly.[28] Citizens will continue to look to government to cope with social and economic issues because in many instances collective action offers the only reasonable medium to ameliorate a situation. This will occur at the same time that taxpayers are clamoring for cuts and limitations in the fiscal operations of state and local jurisdictions and federal involvement is shrinking.

One facet to this seeming paradox is that the taxpayers who favor retrenchment and constraint are not necessarily the same ones that push for higher services. As has been amply demonstrated in California, Massachusetts, Missouri, and elsewhere, tyranny of a minority through the ballot box is a force to be reckoned with. Also to be reckoned with is the apparently strong belief that government can do more with less. In other words, taxpayers can and do simultaneously push for lower taxes and increased budgetary commitments for health, education, urban and environmental problems, and drug addiction.[29] Since state and local services impact with much more immediacy on important needs of taxpayers, reluctance to see them dwindle is going to the very strong. A good slogan for the 1980s might be "cut government services—someone else's."

All this does not even account for the fact that state and local governments are major employers. Cutting their budgets means ultimately cutting jobs. It seems quite probable that the state–local public sector is going to confront the difficult dilemma of cutting back services at the same time that there exists a demand for something to be done about the growing array of urban and social ills, and that unemployment remains high.

Inflation

Inflation exerts an erosive impact on the public sector just as it does on private disposable income. As the cost of purchasing goods and services rises, the real purchasing power of a dollar of public funds falls. Governments are forced to absorb higher prices for goods, services, materials, and labor which at double-digit rates are generally rising relatively faster than their own source revenues. To the extent that labor costs increase more rapidly than other inputs due to collectivization of employees or spin-off effects from the private sector, government is hit even harder since labor is the major input. Needless to say, other factors such as the energy situation have also contributed to the spiraling costs of state–local operations.

One difference, however, between the effect of inflation on private income and that on the public resource base concerns certain taxes used by state and local government. Inflation pushes up the cost of goods and services but it also increases incomes as workers attempt to maintain their standard of living. This may occur due to union pressure, indexation of contracts, or a desire on the part of employers to help offset their employees' loss of real income. The net result is that nominal incomes rise and push taxpayers into higher and higher marginal tax brackets. The situation is particularly acute with the highly graduated rate structure of the federal income tax but also exists for any state that has a progressive rate structure.

All but five of the states with a broad-based individual income tax have adopted a system of graduated rates. Some, such as Alaska, Delaware, and New York, have introduced considerable progressivity in the nominal marginal tax rates.[30] As a result, yield automatically goes up even faster than the rate of growth in income, generating, if you like, a fiscal windfall.

In addition, yields from various taxes on consumption (e.g., the general sales tax) and on property also tend to grow as inflation pushes up the price of taxed goods and services or property. Property values in California provide an excellent example of an inflation-fed market. Inflation, therefore, while eroding the purchasing power of state and local governments on the expenditure side of the budget, increases yield on the revenue side.

The combined effect of both factors has been estimated by ACIR for each year from 1973 to 1976.[31] Table 8.1 summarizes the magnitude of inflation's impact on the state and local budget. Several points stand out from a perusual of these data. First, over this period inflation has provided a cumulative $23 billion net gain to the state–local sector. Second, states have gained relatively more than local governments, $17.1 vs. $6.0 billion. Third, net gains rose each year between 1973 and 1975 but then took a precipitous drop in 1976. Finally, inflationary gains have accounted for a significant percentage of own-source revenue.

In summary, two points need to be emphasized. First, on the

surface it appears as though inflation has improved the revenue status of the state–local sector by much more than it has eroded its purchasing power. One problem with aggregate statistics, however, is that they disguise the distributional effects across jurisdictions. While there have been winners sharing in the windfall, there have also been losers whose net gain has been negative. The relative incidence of losers is much more likely to be concentrated among local governments, given their inelastic revenue sources, than states. Second, one can legitimately wonder if past gains will be maintained so long as inflation continues or worsens. There might well be a point beyond which inflation impacts on the economic base (income, sales, etc.), causing it to reduce the increase in tax yield by more than the growth in input costs. At this point, net gains would become negative. This type of phenomenon is suggested by the sharp drop in net gain between 1975 and 1976.

Recession and Unemployment

The national economic environment has important implications for the budgets of state and local governments. A lag in economic activity tends to exert an adverse impact on each side of the budget; the result is to add to the financial strain.

First, a decline in economic activity with attendant expansion of unemployment increases the demand for a variety of governmental services. State unemployment compensation payments go up as well as does the need for social services to carry people through their period of joblessness. This latter factor may entail greater funding for welfare or medical services, heavier usage of state employment agencies, or the need for job retraining and education. At the local level, similar types of social services may be demanded in addition to the general upward pressure that higher unemployment levels tend to exert on such factors as crime, drug dependence, and family problems. All these factors, while difficult to convert into dollars and cents, do add to the demand of state and local government to assist individuals during a period of joblessness and cope with the spin-off effects of unemployment.

On the other side of the budget, the situation is perhaps a bit easier to state in quantitative terms. As the economy contracts and more people become unemployed, the following scenario comes into operation. Decreased economic activity evenutally leads to unemployment and underemployment. Loss of jobs leads to a loss of income. Loss of income feeds the decline in economic activity and generates lower levels of consumption. These in turn lead to

Table 8.1. Impact of Inflation and Recession on State and Local Revenues, 1973-1976

Fiscal Year	Inflationary Increase in Revenues $ Billions	Inflationary Loss in Purchasing Power $ Billions	Net Gain From Inflation		Net Revenue Change Due to Recession		Net Revenue Loss (−) or Gain (+) From Inflation and Recession	
			$ Billions	Percent of Revenues[a]	$ Billions	Percent of Revenues[a]	$ Billions	Percent of Revenues[a]
State and Local								
1973	$10.3	$9.4	$0.9	0.6%	$+0.3	+0.2%	$+1.2	+0.8%
1974	18.9	12.4	6.5	3.9	−2.5	−1.5	+3.9	+2.4
1975	28.4	18.5	9.9	5.5	−16.0	−8.8	−6.1	−3.6
1976	19.5	13.8	5.7	2.9	−16.4	−8.2	−10.6	−5.3
Totals (1973–1976)	77.1	54.1	23.0		−34.7		−11.6	
State								
1973	6.2	5.0	1.1	1.4	+0.2	+0.2	+1.3	+1.7
1974	11.3	6.7	4.6	5.2	−1.8	−2.0	+2.8	+3.2
1975	17.0	9.9	7.1	7.3	−11.2	−11.6	−4.1	−4.2
1976	11.6	7.4	4.3	4.0	−11.4	−10.6	−7.1	−6.7
Totals (1973–1976)	46.1	29.0	17.1		−24.2		−7.1	
Local								
1973	4.2	4.4	−0.2	−0.4	+0.1	+0.1	−0.2	−0.2
1974	7.6	5.8	1.9	2.4	−0.8	−1.0	+1.1	+1.4
1975	11.4	8.6	2.8	3.4	−4.8	−5.7	−2.0	−2.4
1976	7.8	6.4	1.5	1.6	−4.9	−5.3	−3.5	−3.7
Totals (1973–1976)	31.0	25.2	6.0		−10.4		−4.6	

Source: Advisory Commission on Intergovernmental Relations, *State-Local Finances in Recession and Inflation* (Washington, D.C.: ACIR, 1979), A–70.

[a] Own source general revenue.

160

a contraction of the resource base available to state and local governments to finance public services.[32] As the economy contracts, the state–local sector is caught in a vicious cycle due to its dwindling tax base. Unless it can raise tax rates, revenues decline. It is placed in the peculiar situation of being called on to do more in the midst of less. As the economic milieu worsens, so does the financial pressure.

One facet of this process that can exacerbate the scenario described above is that economic contraction tends to concentrate more heavily in certain localities. For example, Sunbelt states are likely to fare much better than the Frostbelt states during such a period. Or, surburban areas are likely to suffer less than an older central city. What this produces is areas in which the consequences of recession are much more extreme in terms of lost revenues and increased demands for public services.

An aggregate view of the consequences of recession can be gleaned from a recent ACIR study that quantifies the revenue loss component of recession yearly between 1973 and 1976. As the data in Table 7.1 indicate, the revenue loss is substantial and has grown each year. For the entire state–local sector it cumulated to about $34.7 billion for these four years and reached 8.8 percent of own-source revenues in 1975. The impact has been more severe for states since their taxes are generally more responsive (elastic) with respect to the economic environment; they lost $11.4 billion or 10.6 percent of own-source revenues in 1976. The local sector, tied more heavily into the less elastic property tax, lost only $4.9 billion or 5.3 percent of own-source revenues.

The financial condition of the state–local fisc is heavily influenced by the health of the national economy. For the most part there is little that this sector can do to offset the impact except defer to national economic policy to correct the situation. It must, however, at the same time cope with the shrinkage of revenues. For many states and local jurisdictions these losses can be terribly disruptive.

Erosion of the Tax Base

The tax base of state and local governments is a primary source of funds for most jurisdictions. The viability and coverage of this base, therefore, in large part determine relative poverty or affluence. As the tax base expands, either naturally or through overt legislative action, a government is fiscally better off; as it contracts, for whatever reason, it becomes more difficult to meet the cost of public operations. A variety of factors influences the magnitude of the tax base, from the state of the national and local economy to inflation and the internal migration of people and economic activity. There is another consideration, however, that tends to be overlooked since its evolution is slow and is often linked with positive-sounding notions such as equity, fairness, economic efficiency, or administrative ease. This is the intentional shrinkage of a tax base due to explicit policy manipulation.

At the state level there are two prime examples that help to exemplify this point. Twenty-six states currently exclude food entirely from the general sales tax base. This is done to lessen the regressive sting of this tax and thus improve the equity of the tax system. The revenue loss to states, as well as to local governments that piggy-back on the state tax, can be substantial. While the actual loss would vary from state to state depending upon income levels and consumption patterns, it is safe to assume that as much as 15 to 20 percent of yield might be foregone by such legislation. If this tax is a fiscal mainstay for a particular jurisdiction, the loss can be significant.

State individual income taxes have an incredible variety of special provisions, nominally incorporated to adjust for inequities, that also serve to lessen yield. Deductions, exemptions, and credits for a variety of purposes diminish the size of the tax base and, therefore, its revenue potential. One facet of this tax that is gaining greater and greater attention is the extra or windfall yield generated as a result of inflation, the so-called indexation problem. To correct for the perverse consequences of inflation on increasing the tax burden, while nominal incomes increase by less or not at all, nine states have adopted some form of indexation in the last three years. For five of these states the total revenue loss has been estimated at about $618 million for the year 1979–1980.[33] The loss would be even more striking if indexing were designed to neutralize the full impact of inflation and if it were to spread to all thirty-six states with graduated marginal income tax rates.

At the local level there has also been a contraction of the tax base, one which often has been mandated by the state for equity, administrative, or efficiency reasons. The property tax is particularly hard hit and, since it is the primary source of tax revenue for local governments, so is local yield. One distinct trend has been the gradual phasing out of the property tax on personal items of on intangibles. At present only six states continue to tax intangibles while forty-five tax some form of personal property, nominally at least. By type of personal property, however, commercial-industrial remains the dominant component while others are generally being eliminated; only three states, for example, still claim to tax household items.[34] For the most part the taxation of all but real property is either being phased out or has already been eliminated. This is true despite the fact that this component represents a substantial proportion of total wealth in the United States. Usually equity, efficiency, or administrative ease is invoked as the rationale for such an intentional shrinkage of the local tax base.[35]

In addition to shrinkage of the personal property tax base, states have also enacted legislation to relieve the real estate tax burden for a variety of specific groups. Homestead and veterans' provisions eliminate part of assessed valuation from taxation. Businesses are exempted from taxation in an attempt to induce additional investment in a locality or to attract new business. Nonprofit charitable, religious, and educational institutions are tax free to promote their socially beneficial purposes.[36]

More recently exemptions have been provided in the form of circuit-breakers that target relief on the basis of ability to pay. The 1970s have witnessed a dramatic rise in this approach to ameliorating the burden of local taxation. Michigan, one notable example, expends nearly $300 million annually to finance its circuit-breaker program. About $1 billion is spent nationwide on such programs in thirty states.[37]

Whatever the specific form of property tax exemption or relief, two factors stand out. First, most of the erosion of the tax base has been done at the instigation of state government; state legislatures grant relief to a specific group often at the expense of local coffers. Second, even if the revenue loss is compensated for by the state (as is quite often the case with the circuit breaker but less so with other types), the total tax base available to finance state-local public services still has been contracted through overt policy action. If states do assume the cost of reducing the local tax burden, then they are forced to use their own tax base more intensively or extensively.

In summary, one can view the shrinkage of the state and local resource base as a facet of a broader issue. Given the resources that are available to governments within a state, what is the gap between what they could use and what they are actually willing to use? Part of this has been discussed above in the context of equity, efficiency, or administrative motives. Part of it, however, can also be placed under a rubric such as "tradition" or "political reluctance." Things have been done a certain way and there may be very strong resistance to any change. Yet another facet pertains to the limits placed on local jurisdictions by state government concerning use of the property tax base and whether or not they have access to a sales or income base. Locals are subject to a bewildering array of state-imposed constraints concerning how they can use their resources base and just what this base contains.[38]

Viewed as a process, there has been a continuous revision in the resources states and local governments are willing to use for the support of public operations. While each component that is removed may serve some purpose or benefit some group, the cumulative revenue loss can become burdensome.

The Taxpayer Revolt

Rebellion against taxation in the United States has a long-standing tradition that goes back to the Revolutionary period in American history. Since then the fiscal countryside has been littered with attempts—at times, successful—at placing limits on the power of government to raise taxes. In a historical context the state-imposed restraints on local use of the property tax base may represent the most prevalent example.[39]

Recently, however, in the 1970s particularly, limits have taken on a new spectre. They now are increasingly couched in terms of restraints on overall *yield* rather than on *tax rates*. Twenty-three states now have such limits, only four of which pre date 1970; six were enacted in 1978 alone. This places a more severe constraint on revenue-raising capacity since rate limits afford local governments much greater flexibility before reaching the maximum, especially given the recent inflationary increases in housing markets.

A second recent trend is the placing of fiscal limits on the states. During the 1970s eighteen states enacted limits on either revenues or expenditures. Three major points stand out in examining this trend. First, the pace of enactment seems to be gaining momentum as indicated by the number of new "lids" per year—1976 (1), 1977 (2), 1978 (5), 1979 (5), 1980 (5). Second, lids in eight states have been couched in constitutional rather than statutory terms, giving them much more permanence since statutory measures are far easier to alter or revoke. Third, there has been a marked growth in citizen participation with the change process. Many of the recent constitutional amendments were placed on the ballot by citizen initiative rather than legislative referendum. Where an initiative was not possible, citizen groups have brought pressure to bear on legislators to place lid-type amendments on the ballot.

Proposition 13 in California hit the state–local fiscal scene like an earthquake registering 8.5 on the Richter scale. While there has been a long-standing tradition of states imposing fiscal constraints on their local governments such as tax and spending lids or mandated local expenditures as well as a history of attempts to impose cuts or limits by legislators or citizens, anything of such dollar consequence had yet to be seen. A simple 389-word initiative placed on the ballot was approved almost 2 to 1 and cut local property taxes by about $7 billion.[40] In some respects it was a watershed.

Since Proposition 13 there has been a greater use of lids and cuts at the state and local level. Massachusetts, as one prime example, confronts the fiscal ramifications of Proposition 2½, as it has come to be called, which will reduce the property tax burden to 2½ percent of market value and limit the annual growth in yield to the same percentage. The situation here, however, is much more severe than in California due to the relatively poor fiscal health of the state of Massachusetts. While California had resources it could tap into at the state level to help bail out the local sector, Massachusetts is not so fortunate.

The trend for the 1980s seems clearly to hold in store more of the same. Citizens are dissatisfied with government and its bewildering nexus of regulations, an increasing tax burden and inflation that erodes their standard of living, and a crazy-quilt federal system that seems to defy comprehension. States and local governments are the easiest target by far to attack since the federal government is so far removed from direct citizen access. It seems highly probable that the "taxpayer revolt" scenario will continue to be played out over the decade and, accordingly, reduce or constrain revenues available to the state–local sector.

POLICY ISSUES FOR THE 1980s

A review, albeit cursory, of options for balancing the budget and of the financial pressures confronting the state–local sector suggests a number of important policy issues that will loom on the horizon as we move into the 1980s. While the previous discussion has reflected on general trends and made use of the imperfect medium of foresight and historical extrapolation, several phenomena are precipitated out of this discussion that might serve as a prologue to policy considerations for this decade.

Proposition 13 and Its Progeny

One major factor that the state–sector will have to confront head-on is a growing demand from taxpayers to limit or actually cut the scope of government operations. Tax cuts and limits have already become an integral part of the financial scene and are likely to continue to be. Nearly every state has somehow been affected by the so-called taxpayer revolt, at least to the extent of having entertained lid-type proposals.

In response to pressure for fiscal contraction (relative or absolute), eighteen states have enacted either statutory or constitutional lids; twenty-three have cut the individual income tax, twelve more than once; seventeen the general sales tax, five more than once; nine have indexed the income tax; and twenty have imposed overall fiscal limits on their local governments since 1970.[41] Proposition 13 cut local taxes by nearly $7 billion in 1978; Massachusetts is currently in the throes of cutting its local property tax back to 2½ percent of market value (in the face of a 3.4 percent statewide level and a much higher level of 10.2 percent in some cities such as Boston); and Missouri faces an initiative amendment to the state constitution that, aside from limiting the growth in state taxes, requires voter approval to increase virtually any local revenue source.

Successful initiative actions in several states and an increased willingness on the part of legislatures to respond to pressure for lower taxes suggest that the phenomenon has far from run its course. While implicitly much of the discontent may be focused at the federal government and its highly visible income tax, the state–local sector is by far the easier target.[42] As long as the process continues, subnational governments are going to be hamstrung in their capacity to raise additional resources to cope with any upward tendency on the expenditure side of the budget.

The Indexation Issue

As inflation has continued and become more and more a part of the U.S. economic environment, there has been growing sentiment that corrective action should be taken to adjust for the "inflation tax." The argument is that as inflation pushes taxpayers into higher and higher marginal tax brackets, their tax liability rises by relatively more than their income. Thus, not only is their income being eroded by inflation but the marginal rate structure of an individual income tax (federal and state) adds to their tax liability as well. While this problem is particularly acute at the federal level, it also exists at the state level, where thirty-six states currently have some form of progressive rate structure.

If indexation of state income taxes were to become widespread, the revenue losses could amount to hundreds of millions or even billions of dollars annually. A recent analysis by the ACIR of five states that have enacted some form of indexation is summarized in Table 8.2.[43] Revenue loss for these five states alone exceeded $600 million, and none of them has what would be considered a fully indexed system. Were the process to spread to other states and full indexing to be put into effect, the potential loss in revenues would be of major consequence.

Given the persistence of inflation and its perverse interaction with the tax structure, it seems certain that indexing will gain the support of citizens and legislators alike. There is little doubt that correcting for inflation would promote tax equity, increase political accountability for elected officials, and strengthen fiscal discipline. It will also, however, contract state revenues.

Restoring Fiscal Balance in the Federal System

One problem that has plagued fiscal operations at the state and local level is the often severe imbalance existing between needs for a jurisdiction and the resources available to meet those needs. To overcome this imbalance, which has become acute for some localities, an elaborate system of intergovernmental aid flows has been devised. The federal government provides billions for the support of state and local programs and the state, in turn, provides billions for local programs. This complex flow of funds has even

Table 8.2. Impact of Indexation on Tax Collection, 1979–1980

State	Collections: 1978–1979 (millions)	Change in Collections: 1979–1980 (millions)	
		Without Indexation	With Indexation
Arizona	$ 270	$ 79	$ 49
California	5452	1520	1047
Colorado	494	100	76
Iowa	669	81	75
Minnesota	1256	240	155
Totals	$8141	$2020	$1402

extended to local jurisdictions sharing in an areawide tax base, as in the seven-county Minneapolis-St Paul metropolitan area.[44] We currently have a web of hundreds of programs providing aid for scores of social and urban programs ranging from sewer systems and airports to medical care, education, and local fiscal relief.

Looking to the 1980s there seem to be some drastic changes in store that may alter the complexion of our federal system. President Reagan has taken office with the stated goal of reducing the scope of federal operations, balancing the budget, and restoring health to the U.S. economy. Contraction at the federal level will force the states into a position of assuming a greater share of the cost of phased-down (or out) federal programs or bearing the wrath of their citizens as cuts filter down. The billions cut in social and urban aid programs, unless replaced with state funds, are going to force severe cutbacks. The challenge of the 1980s in financing the federal system is going to lie in the states' response to diminished federal support for their own programs as well as those of their local governments. Are they going to respond by increasing their commitment, or will spending be allowed to contract and programs wither?

There is even the question as to whether some states respond at all to take up the slack due to lids on taxing and spending. Pressure on the state-local sector will come from two sides— reduced federal dollars to support state and local programs, and pressure for states and local governments not to increase their taxing or spending levels. Whatever the case, creative federalism in this decade will have to place much greater emphasis on "creative" to cope with the emerging situation. Governmental poverty, fiscal disparities, and fiscal imbalance are likely to become even more pressing issues than they were in the past.

Internal Migration

The Frostbelt-Sunbelt tension epitomizes another phenomenon to be coped with, that is, the internal migration of people, businesses, and economic activity from region to region. Recent results from the 1980 Census reflect the shifts in population that have occurred. States like Florida, Arizona, Nevada, Wyoming, New Mexico, and Colorado have seen their population grow substantially over the last decade. At the same time, New York and Rhode Island have lost people while many of the eastern and industrialized midwestern states have virtually stabilized.

When the migration process is examined within a state, in the context of changes in metropolitan areas, the situation can be even more pronounced. Many major older cities have suffered substantial population losses during the 1970s. The fiscal bifurcation between a central city and its suburbs is becoming more clearly defined and the disparities in the resource base more severe.[45]

As this process of migration, population decline, loss in economic activity, and diminished tax base continues, these older urban areas will be increasingly hard-pressed. They are caught squarely in the jaws of a fiscal vise. On the one side is a dwindling resource base from their own sources compounded by the imminent cuts in federal aid and even state funds. On the other side is a population that requires relatively more in the way of public services and an "environment" that suffers from a variety of ills that include concentrated poverty, crime, pollution, housing abandonment, drug abuse, and a deteriorating urban infrastructure.

Dealing with the dynamics of internal migration, within states and across them, is going to demand some truly creative exercises in federalism unless we intend to adopt a laissez-faire stance and let economic forces (exacerbated by public policy) run their course. The costs of the latter option may indeed be great; the problem is how to restore some semblance of fiscal balance in the face of major spatial rearrangements in people and economic activity.

Who Pays for Government?

One concern of citizens that underlies the recent "taxpayer revolt" is who pays the cost of public operations. Thus, in addition to questions about the size of government (absolute and/or relative), the impact of government laws and regulations on private behavior, public productivity, and so on, is a concern over the fairness or equity with which the cost of supporting the public sector is apportioned among the citizenry. While there is little doubt that the increase in the overall tax burden is disquieting, what with the combined claim of the Social Security system and the array of federal, state, and local taxes plus the impact of inflation, there is also a concern over how the burden impacts on persons with different abilities to pay. Many of the inequities that exist for state and local taxes, as well as for fees and charges to the extent they are not levied on a quid pro quo basis, feed the discontent of state and local taxpayers and increase the pressure for broad sweeping cuts and limitations rather than carefully thought-out, specifically targeted policies to relieve inequities.

We have seen over the recent couple of decades some progress toward improving the equity of the state–local revenue system. As of 1980, twenty-five states exempt food completely from the general sales tax and forty-two exempt medicines as well.[46] This has lessened the regressive impact of this tax. In addition, most states currently have some form of property tax relief for homeowners and more than thirty have a circuit breaker to help mitigate the burden of the local property tax, with the cost being absorbed by the state general sales or income tax. This shift away from the local property tax to state revenues is generally more equitable, especially when the shift involves a state income tax with a progressive rate structure.

While there has been progress toward lessening the inequities of state and local taxation, there remains a great deal yet to be accomplished. Most state tax structures remain regressive and, across states, the "equal treatment of equals" and "unequal treatment of unequals" varies widely depending upon where one lives. Not only is the level of burden affected by place of residence but so also is the pattern of who pays.[47]

In the context of improving taxpayer equity and reforming the state–local revenue system, many issues remain. Given fiscal limitations, will states be willing or able to maintain past reforms? Broad cuts such as adopted in California have proved to be popular with voters but very inefficient in terms of channeling relief to where it is most needed, such as to homeowners or to low-income families. One can make a strong case for targeting reform so that, as in California, nominal homeowner property tax relief does not wind up benefiting out-of-state businesses and property owners or increasing federal tax liabilities.

Maintaining past progress in reforming the state–local fiscal system is going to be hampered by what appears almost certain to be a smaller revenue base constrained by fiscal cuts or limitations as the federal government cuts back on aid and the taxpayer revolt gains momentum. To accomplish reform in this milieu is going to necessitate a much heavier state involvement, one that many states may be unable to or simply unwilling to assume.

CONCLUSION

As we move into the 1980s the state–local sector confronts an array of financial pressures that may well test the fabric of our federal system. The dramatic growth in government that characterized the 1960s and 1970s has already shown signs of tapering off. Inflation and recession have impacted on this sector's financial status and have also eaten into the affluence that allowed for the past expansion in public operations. As a result of a declining standard of living in real terms for most Americans, these taxpayers have begun to exert pressure for cuts and limitations on government, the so-called taxpayer revolt. In addition, state and local governments must cope with the financial demands of a bewildering collection of federal laws and regulations, pressure from employees for more and better of everything, a gradual erosion of the tax base, and, paradoxically, citizen pressure to do more to alleviate a variety of urban and social problems.

On top of all this, the federal government under President Reagan is threatening major cuts for programs that have provided support for state and local operations. In essence, the state-local sector is going to be called on to do as much (or perhaps even more) with fewer resources. The key to what finally emerges from this new environment seems to lie with the response of the states to the phasing down of federal funding. Will they help fill the fiscal void? Will they be able to do so given the fiscal cuts and lids being put in place? For answers to these questions we will have to wait but it seems certain that the role of the state is going to be much more pivotal in the 1980s.

NOTES

1. U.S. Advisory Commission on Intergovernmental Relations (hereinafter referred to as ACIR), *Significant Features of Fiscal Federalism: 1979-80* (Washington, D.C.: ACIR, 1980, M-123), p. 4.
2. Alan K. Campbell, "Most Dynamic Sector," *National Civic Review* 53 (February 1964): 74-82.
3. Michael J. Boskin, "Some Neglected Economic Factors Behind Recent Tax and Spending Limitation Movements," *National Tax Journal* 32 (June 1979 supplement): 38, emphasis in original.
4. For more on fiscal or tax capacity measures refer to ACIR, *Measuring the Fiscal Capacity and Effort of State and Local Areas* (Washington, D.C.: ACIR, 1971, M-58).
5. Since the theme of this paper is so broad, the text could easily become hopelessly cluttered with statistical information to document each point. Instead, references are provided that give substantiation, support, or elaboration. The reader is encouraged to turn to them for more detail.
6. ACIR, *Significant Features,* 1979-80, p. 74, shows the breakdown by political action and economic growth yearly between 1966 and 1979.
7. ACIR, *Significant Features of Fiscal Federalism: 1976-77* (Washington, D.C.: ACIR, 1977 M-110), p. 105.

8. ACIR, *Significant Features, 1979-80*, p. 108.
9. John Shannon, "Statistical Appendix to Accompany Remarks before the State and Local Finance in the 1970's and 1980's Conference," Chicago, Ill. 1/17/81, Appendix 8.
10. Ibid., Appendix 9.
11. ACIR, *State Limitations on Local Taxes and Expenditures* (Washington, D.C.: ACIR, 1977, A-64) elaborates on these restrictions.
12. While many of these programs are supported by federal funds, this complex web of intergovernmental revenue flows is a mystery to most taxpayers.
13. Jack Citrin, "Do People Want Something for Nothing: Public Opinion on Taxes and Government Spending," *National Tax Journal* 32 (June 1979 supplement) discusses this issue.
14. Refer to ibid.
15. Selma Mushkin (ed.), *Public Prices for Public Products* (Washington, D.C.: Urban Institute, 1972) documents the diversity and importance of fees and charges; see Chap. 1.
16. James A. Maxwell and J. Richard Aronson, *Financing State and Local Governments* (Washington, D.C.: Brookings Institution, 1977, 3 rd edition), pp. 184-85.
17. See ACIR, *The State of State-Local Revenue Sharing* (Washington, D.C.: ACIR, 1980, M-121) for detail on state revenue sharing; and Andrew Reschovsky, "An Evaluation of Metropolitan Area Tax Base Sharing," *National Tax Journal 33 (March 1980): 55-66* for a description of the Minneapolis-St Paul arrangement.
18. U.S. Department of Housing and Urban Development, Office of Community Planning and Development, "Whither or Whether Urban Distress—a response to the article 'The Urban Crisis Leaves Town'," reprinted in "Is the Urban Crisis Over?" hearing before Subcommittee on Fiscal and Intergovernmental Policy of the Joint Economic Committee, 96th Congress, 1st Session, March 20, 1979, 53.
19. Walter I. Garms, James W. Guthrie, and Lawrence C. Pierce, *School Finance* (Englewood Cliffs, N.J.: Prentice-Hall, 1978), Chap. 9 discusses this phenomenon.
20. ACIR, *Understanding the Market For State and Local Debt* (Washington, D.C.: ACIR, 1976, M-104); see particularly p. 30 on the trend in bond issue elections over recent years.
21. Committee for Economic Development, *Improving the Public Welfare System* (New York: CED, 1980) provides a good review of this issue.
22. ACIR, *The Value-Added Tax and Alternative Sources of Federal Revenue* (Washington, D.C.: ACIR, 1973, M-18).
23. ACIR, *Governmental Functions and Processes: Local and Areawide* (Washington, D.C.: ACIR, 1974, M-45) examines the assignment issue in depth.
24. Garms, Guthrie, and Pierce, *School Finance,* Chap. 9 reviews this.
25. Michael W. Kirst, "A Tale of Two Networks: The School Finance Reform versus the Spending and Tax Limitation Lobby," *Taxing and Spending* 3 (Winter 1980): 46.
26. For a review of the equity issue in school finance see Allan Odden, Robert Berne, and Leanna Stiefel, *Equity in School Finance* (Denver: Education Finance Center, Education Commission of the States, 1979, Report #F79-9).
27. David Lewin and Shirley B. Goldenberg, "Public Sector Unionism in the U.S. and Canada," *Industrial Relations* 19 (Fall 1980): 239-243.
28. Citrin, "Do People Want Something for Nothing," pp. 116-118.
29. Ibid, p. 117.

30. ACIR, *Significant Features, 1979–80,* Table 82 provides detail on the income tax.
31. ACIR, *State–Local Finances in Recession and Inflation* (Washington, D.C.: ACIR, 1979, A–70).
32. The exact impact is, of course, a function of the elasticity of various taxes. This varies by type of tax and by state, see ACIR, *Significant Features 1976–77,* p. 254.
33. John Shannon and Robert Lucke, "State Experimentation with Indexed Income Taxes—Early Results," paper presented at National Tax Association—Tax Institute of America meetings, New Orleans, 11/17/80.
34. ACIR, *Significant Features, 1979–80,* Table 94 provides detail on the taxation of personal property.
35. Refer to Dick Netzer, *Economics of the Property Tax* (Washington, D.C.: Brookings Institution, 1966), Chap. VI.
36. Steven David Gold, *Property Tax Relief* (Lexington, Mass.: Lexington Books, 1979) reviews all forms of property tax relief.
37. John Shannon and Frank Tippett, "An Analysis of State Personal Income Taxes and Property Tax Circuit Breakers," paper presented at the 46th Annual meeting of the National Association of Tax Administrators, Boston, Mass., 6/78.
38. ACIR, *State Limitations.*
39. Anthony H. Pascal, et al., *Fiscal Containment of Local and State Government* (Santa Monica, Calif.: Rand Corporation, 9/79, R–2494–FF/RC), Chap. 4 reviews this phenomenon.
40. Frank Levy, "On Understanding Proposition 13," *Public Interest* no. 56 (Summer 1979): 66–89 gives a good review of Proposition 13.
41. Shannon, "Statistical Appendix," and Pascal, et al., *Fiscal Containment of Local and State Government, Chap. 4.*
42. ACIR, *Changing Public Attitudes on Governments and Taxes* (Washington, D.C.: ACIR, 1979, S–8).
43. Shannon and Lucke, "State Experimentation with Indexed Income Taxes," p. 10. See also ACIR, *The Inflation Tax: The Case for Indexing Federal and State Income Taxes* (Washington, D.C.: ACIR, 1980, M–117).
44. Reschovsky, "An Evaluation of Metropolitan Area Tax Base Sharing."
45. The disparities existing between a central city and its suburbs is spelled out in great statistical detail in ACIR, *Central City-Suburban Fiscal Disparity and City Distress: 1977* (Washington, D.C.: ACIR, 1980, M–119).
46. ACIR, *Significant Features, 1979–80,* p. 100.
47. Donald Phares, *Who Pays State and Local Taxes?* (Cambridge, Mass.: Oelgeschlager, Gunn & Hain, 1980), Chap. 5 and Appendix A.

Chapter 9

Government Policy to Stimulate Economic Development: Enterprise Zones

Susan S. Jacobs* and Michael Wasylenko**

State and local governments have considerable interest in stimulating economic development within their borders. Typically, these governments use a wide variety of fiscal tools to attract new business establishments and to retain existing ones. These tools include industrial revenue bond financing and other state and local subsidized loans to new business; tax exemptions or tax moratoriums on land, capital improvements, equipment, and machinery; and accelerated depreciation on state corporation income taxes. In addition to these explicit fiscal subsidies, state and local governments attempt to compete for firms by keeping their tax burden on business in line with or more favorable than those in neighboring states and jurisdictions.

Despite the proliferation of these fiscal incentives, most analy-

The views expressed in this chapter are our own and do not necessarily represent the position of the U.S. Department of Housing and Urban Development. We have benefited from discussions with Paul Bardack, Robert Ebel, Sy Herman, Nina Klarich, and John Ross, but we are responsible for the views and any errors in this chapter.
*Office of Policy Development and Research, U.S. Department of Housing and Urban Development
**Department of Economics, Pennsylvannia State University, and Visiting Scholar, Office of Policy Development and Research, U.S. Department of Housing and Urban Development

ses conclude that these programs have surprisingly little impact on business locational choices among sites in alternative states. While these programs may be decisive in a location choice for firms considering similar sites in two or more proximate taxing jurisdictions, the consensus is that local tax differentials have, at best, a secondary influence on business location decisions.

The federal government has not offered geographically targeted tax differentials to firms as yet;[1] however, several federal programs, operating through state and local governments, attempt to influence business location choice by providing "up front" financing. Most prominent among these are the Department of Housing and Urban Development's Urban Development Action Grant (UDAG) Program and the Economic Development Administration's Public Works and Business Loan programs.

In addition, some aspects of the Federal Tax Code and several other federal programs (such as the interstate highway program, water projects, and FHA single-family home insurance) have an indirect influence on firm location. At the same time, other federal programs, such as HUD's Community Development Block Grant (CDBG) program, and its predecesor programs, Model Cities and Urban Renewal, have attempted general revival of portions of central cities in the hope of attracting industry.

Recently, Congressmen Kemp (Buffalo, N.Y.) and Garcia (Bronx, N.Y.) proposed legislation to create "Urban Jobs and Enterprise Zones"[2] in cities to encourage revitalization of distressed areas in cities and create jobs for their residents. In one version of the bill, by designating inner-city poverty areas as Enterprise Zones, new or existing firms in a zone drawing at least 50 percent of their labor force from the zone's residents will be eligible for some federal tax reductions, including reductions in Social Security tax payments, in corporation income tax rates, and in local property tax payments, and depreciation and capital gains tax advantages.

In this paper, the goals of the Enterprise Zone program are discussed. The bill and its fiscal mechanisms to attract and create industry are described and previous research on the factors known to affect firm location choice is reviewed. Given the findings of this research, the types of industry that are likely to be attracted to Enterprise Zones are analyzed. The last two sections describe the factors, in addition to tax incentives, necessary for economic development and suggest modifications that would increase the program's prospects for success.

GOALS AND DESCRIPTION OF THE PROGRAM

Enterprise Zones are designed to stimulate the economic development of inner-city areas. In their purest form, as proposed in England by Peter Hall,[3] the Enterprise Zones are geographic areas in which government-imposed taxes and regulations would be removed. By establishing a site in which business activity would be unencumbered by these restrictions, the costs of doing business would be lower, thereby providing a stimulus for increased economic activity. A unique feature of this concept is its irony; it is a government policy to remove restrictions imposed by the government itself. Hall outlined a plan which "would be based on fairly shameless free enterprise." Enterprise Zones would be "free of—taxes, social services, industrial and other regulations. Bureaucracy would be kept to an absolute minimum. So would personal and corporate taxation."[4] Hall conceived of Enterprise Zones as a National Growth Policy, enabling Britain to recapture its prominence among industrialized nations. He envisioned that British Enterprise Zones would provide the best business climate for the high-risk ventures (mostly taken by small and medium-size businesses) leading to innovation and economic growth, thus attracting entrepreneurs from other parts of Britain and the rest of the world. The British economy would benefit from its linkages to the Enterprise Zones, through both the production of inputs used by industries in Enterprise Zones and the opportunity for employment of British residents in these zones.

In this country, the concept of Enterprise Zones has been articulated by Stuart Butler.[5] In contrast with Hall, Butler views Enterprise Zones as an economic development policy for distressed areas within cities. He and other proponents of an Enterprise Zone—Economic Development Policy for the United States do not argue that the problems of inner cities were caused by governmental restrictions; rather, they assert that removing these restrictions is the best way to revitalize inner-city areas.

Goals

Although the Enterprise Zone concept is new, the goals of the Kemp-Garcia bill are common to those of other economic development programs such as (1) providing a business climate to revitalize the local economy, and (2) providing employment to local residents. Just as the goals of economic development programs are common, so are the market forces that these programs face.

Consequently, Enterprise Zones are likely to encounter similar difficulties in simultaneously achieving these two goals as faced by current urban economic development programs.[6]

Targeting the benefits of development projects to certain individual groups and to specific localities in a metropolitan area is difficult. Development projects that are most profitable in central-city locations—be they privately financed or government subsidized—create jobs that are often filled by residents from outside the central city, and do little to alleviate central-city unemployment. Central-city revitalization policies can be most effective, however, if new central-city industrial and commercial establishments are not restricted to hiring only central-city residents.

By contrast, policies to provide jobs for a city's unemployed residents should be focused on bringing appropriate jobs to the target population, or bringing the people to the jobs. Lower-skilled inner-city residents could be encouraged to commute or migrate to the suburbs, if the industries that employ unskilled labor choose the suburbs as more profitable locations. However, research on this issue has not demonstrated that merely moving low-skilled inner-city residents to the suburbs would necessarily provide them with jobs.[7] Bringing these jobs to the cities could be accomplished by providing incentives for the specific industries that employ low-skilled labor to locate in the cities.

Because an Enterprise Zone is smaller in area than a central city, the problems associated with addressing these two sometimes divergent goals are likely to be exacerbated. The target areas are smaller and have a less diverse labor force than a central city, so that locating within the target area is more restrictive than locating in any part of a city. Both goals could be better served if the mechanism through which the program works —reducing regulations and taxes—is more likely to attract industries employing low-skilled labor than either previous programs or the existing private market.

In order to achieve revitalization and local employment, proponents of Enterprise Zones focus on two vehicles. They wish to stimulate both small businesses operated by local entrepreneurs and latent industry that otherwise would not exist under the present tax laws and regulations. Butler argues that there are two basic reasons for relying on small businesses to provide successful revitalization—job creation and neighborhood externalities. First, citing Birch,[8] he argues that the crucial differential between employment growth and decline in cities is that cities experiencing employment decline have lower rates of both firm births and employment growth of existing business. Because small businesses are responsible for more than half of all employment growth nationally, Butler argues that encouraging the creation and growth of small businesses is the cornerstone of a successful economic development policy. Second, he cites Jacobs,[9] who noted that the small entrepreneur has a stake in the community and will be a community leader, actively working toward maintaining safety in the streets. From this, Butler concludes that local entrepreneurs could create jobs and reverse the tide of decline in inner-city areas, satisfying both goals of employment creation and urban revitalization.

The other mechanism—stimulating net new business activity—is founded on the tenets of supply-side economics. Inherent in this school of thought is the belief that the costs and red tape of taxation and regulation make the operation of some firms so unprofitable that they are never established. Reducing costs by abolishing these restrictions will allow firms to get started and then grow and prosper. Enterprise Zones, then, would create new industry for the nation as a whole, not just attract firms from other locations.

Entwining these two vehicles for development is the belief that the dormant industries are small businesses that could be run by local entrepreneurs currently unable to operate because the tax laws and regulations are financially prohibitive. In turn, these new businesses would employ local labor.

This supply-side mechanism receives support from an unlikely alliance of conservatives and liberals. Some proponents of supply-side economics would prefer to abolish business restrictions nationally, not only in targeted areas.[10] They may think of Enterprise Zones as experiments that would prove their hypothesis. Others who do not accept abolishing taxes and regulations as a national policy find it appealing as a tool for inner-city economic development. They contend that society derives the benefits of stabilization, redistribution, and controlling externalities from taxation and regulation, but support the targeted removal of these restrictions if the benefits (in terms of the area's economic development) are worth the costs (in terms of the value of the restrictions removed and taxes forgone).

Program Description and Mechanism

In June 1980, Congressmen Kemp and Garcia introduced the Urban Jobs and Enterprise Zone Act of 1980. In keeping with the goals previously described, the intent of this proposed legislation is to "provide incentives to attract businesses to areas which face severe depression, unemployment, and poverty... [in the hope that] ...the residents of those areas will be able to get off the welfare rolls and onto the payrolls."[11] The mechanism for achieving these results is a targeted tax cut. Enterprise Zones would be established, and businesses in these areas employing at least 50 percent of their workers from within the zone would be eligible for several tax concessions:

1. reduced corporate income tax rates ranging from a 3 percent reduction in the first tax bracket to a 7 percent reduction in the highest tax bracket;
2. a depreciation schedule calculated with a straight-line method using a three-year asset life for total assets valued up to $500,000;
3. a 50 percent reduction in employer Social Security payments made for workers aged 21 years and over, and a 90 percent reduction for workers under 21 years;
4. a reduction in the capital gains tax to 15 percent; and
5. a 20 percent reduction in the effective local property tax rate, phased in over four years.

The tax advantages would be available to new and existing businesses in the Enterprise Zone, including rental housing. Homeowners in the Zone would be eligible for the 20 percent reduction in property taxes.

These tax advantages form the complete package of incentives designed to attract new businesses to the Enterprise Zone.[12] A zone would be designated after a city applied to the Secretary of Commerce for approval. To qualify, a zone must have a population of at least 4,000 or be an Indian Reservation and meet one of the following three criteria:

an average unemployment rate of at least twice the national rate for the most recent twenty-four–month period for which data are available, and 30 percent or more of the families living in such areas below the poverty level,
an unemployment rate of at least three times the national average,
50 percent or more of the families living below the poverty level.

Once designated, an area would remain an Enterprise Zone for ten years. Businesses operating during this period would remain eligible for the tax incentives indefinitely unless sold after cessation of the zone designation. For the successor business, eligibility for the tax concessions would be lost. The ten-year time limit provides a period of tax relief for business so that the revitalization of the area can begin. After ten years, if revitalization has begun, the area should be able to complete the recovery without government subsidy. If revitalization has not begun in ten years, continuation of the tax subsidy is probably not economically efficient.

The Kemp-Garcia Bill and British Enterprise Zones

It is worthwhile at this point to contrast the Urban Jobs and Enterprise Zone bill with the principles of the Enterprise Zone philosophy and the nine British Enterprise Zones.

The Conservative Party in Great Britain has enacted legislation establishing Enterprise Zones. Somewhat different from Hall's philosophy, the policy objectives are to stimulate regional growth and to demonstrate a political commitment to laissez-faire principles. The nine zones have been designated in regions across the nation and are expected to begin operation during the summer of 1981. The zones are in inner cities, at the edges of cities, and in nonurban areas. Each zone has been chosen for its attributes that are attractive to industry—vacant land and highway access, for example.

Hall's concept of an Enterprise Zone calls for a tax-free environment. In the Kemp-Garcia bill, taxes are not abolished, but tax rates are reduced. By contrast, the British law provides complete exemption from three types of taxes: development taxes, local property taxes, and 100 percent capital allowances. With available data, it is not possible to measure whether the monetary value of the U.S. tax reduction is of more or less value to a firm than the British tax exemption. The difference between no tax and some tax, however, means that, over time, the U.S. firm will continue to make decisions that are influenced by the effective tax rate. In addition, because the taxes must be paid, the administrative costs involved in paying them would not be alleviated in the U.S. bill.

The Kemp-Garcia bill does not require removal of any regulations. Although the British law explicitly preserves standards needed to protect health and safety and to control pollution, town planning procedures would be simplified with some of the current regulations encumbering the development process being abolished. Also, establishments in the zone would be exempt from compliance with Industrial Training Boards (which includes regulations, taxes, and reporting requirements). For some firms and in some cities, simplifying compliance procedures may be more valuable financially than the tax reductions themselves. In many older cities in the United States, municipal planning and zoning procedures and inspections during the development process are time consuming and costly.[13]

The legislation in the two countries also differ in their attempts to minimize bureaucracy. The British law states in general that simplified procedures and speedier administration will be applied in Enterprise Zones. In addition, the government will reduce its requests for statistical information from firms to a bare minimum.

The only U.S. provision reducing bureaucratic activity is one that affects the city rather than a firm; applications submitted to the federal government on behalf of Enterprise Zones to become Foreign Trade Zones will be processed quickly.[14] From a firm's point of view, however, locating in the Enterprise Zone will require at least one additional bureaucratic action to retain its favored tax status. To be eligible for the tax concessions, each year after its first year of operation in the Enterprise Zone, a firm must demonstrate to the federal government that 50 percent or more of its employees live in the Enterprise Zone. Although this creates additional red tape, firms are likely to view it as less cumbersome than applying for a discretionary loan or asking a city to apply for a categorical grant. Usually the grants awarded through competitive procedures involve time delays in processing and involve uncertainty about receiving these awards. The uncertainty and the time delays in the approval process for loan applications—for example EDA programs or even HUD's Urban Development Action Grant program (which has received high praise for its sixty-day response period)—may discourage some firms from participating in these programs. The eligibility criteria for firms in the Urban Jobs and Enterprise Zone bill are clear cut and objective. Firms would not be required to compete against one another for approval, this coverage under the program should be straightforward. As a result, if the annual applications are processed in a timely manner, firms should encounter less bureaucracy through the Enterprise Zone program than through many other existing economic development programs.

Capitalization of Tax Subsidy into Land Prices

Economic theory and the empirical evidence on incidence of local taxes conclude that tax differentials among areas (or between an Enterprise Zone and the rest of the area) are capitalized into the price of land and any other immobile factors.[15] Capitalization occurs when factors of production flow into areas enjoying the tax advantage. If the tax advantages offered in Enterprise Zones attract capital, these advantages may be capitalized into the land prices in the zone.

Because of the ten-year sunset provision on the zone, the capitalization process will take expectations into account, raising land prices at the onset; these prices will gradually decrease through the ten-year life of the zone. Initial investors are likely to bid up the price of land by the discounted present value of the ten years of tax advantages. In the subsequent years, investors will only bid up the price of land by the remaining years of these advantages.

Under capitalization, the investor would enjoy no tax advantage in the zone, because the advantages are reflected in the higher price of land. Capitalization occurs, however, only if enough investors are attracted to the zone to bid up the price of land. Current holders of land or early investors in land in successful Enterprise Zones are likely to benefit from the tax advantages.

Capitalization is not an argument against Enterprise Zones. Rather it is an economic consequence of successful fiscal incentives.

The Subsidy Offered by the Kemp-Garcia Bill

Because the locational incentives offered in the bill are all tax changes, the size of the subsidy that is available to a firm in the zone can be estimated. Tables 9.1 and 9.2 demonstrate the tax advantages accruing to two representative small businesses in an Enterprise Zone.[16] The first is a manufacturer of electronic components, and the second is a commercial firm, a retail food store, each with $500,000 of annual sales. Considering the tax advantages for Social Security payments, property tax rebates, three-year asset depreciation, and changes in the corporate income tax rates, the savings accruing to the firms total $6,959 for the electronic components firm and $2,540 for the food store. They represent about 20 percent of the manufacturer's current cash flow and 8.5 percent of the retailer's cash flow. Clearly, the savings are greater for the manufacturer both absolutely and as a percent of cash flow.

In general, firms with high ratios of value-added payments to land, labor, and capital to costs of raw materials and intermediate inputs are more likely to benefit from the Enterprise Zone tax credits, because costs of raw materials and intermediate inputs are subsidized. Firms having higher value-added-to-raw-materials ratios tend to be in the manufacturing and service sectors. Alternatively, firms that incur high costs for materials (including energy), such as wholesale and retail trade, will not find the tax incentives as attractive.

The present bill does not subsidize capital and labor inputs to the same degree. By providing a larger subsidy for capital, firms have an incentive to use more capital-intensive production methods than they would use in non-Enterprise Zones.

To assess correctly whether this subsidy favors capital or labor, one should measure the ratio of the labor subsidy to the labor cost when one worker is added to a firm and compare it to a similar ratio when a unit of capital is added to a firm. This labor subsidy reduces wage costs about 3 percent for workers 21 years and over and about 5.5 percent for workers under 21 years. The capital subsidy for corporations, in the form of reduced corporate income tax rates, reduces capital costs by 2.5 percent for corporations in the two lowest corporate tax brackets and 4.3 percent for those in the other tax brackets.

The accelerated depreciation allowance increases the relative size of the marginal capital subsidy, especially for firms in the lowest corporate tax brackets. These firms are less likely to have assets in excess of the present $500,000 limit.[17]

As a tool for attracting firms, however, these savings must be placed in perspective. Each firm would weigh these savings

Table 9.1. Cash Flow Analysis of Manufacturer of Electric Components (1979)[a]

Category	Current Tax Laws	Kemp-Garcia Proposal	Difference (col. 1 − col. 2)
Sales	$500,000		
Selected operating costs			
Labor	60,400		
Rent	13,850		
Insurance	6,850		
Depreciation	8,750		
Property taxes	3,324		
Expenses affected by the Kemp-Garcia bill			
Employer payments to Social Security (6.7%)[b]	4,046.80	$ 1,699.66	$2,347.14
Property taxes[c]	3,324.00	2,659.20	664.80
Profit before taxes and depreciation[d]	40,200.00	43,211.94	
Depreciation (depreciable assets $95,500)	8,750.00	31,833.00	
Taxable income	31,450.00	11,378.94	
Income tax[e]	5,540.00	1,593.05	3,946.95
After-tax income	25,910.00	9,785.89	
Cash flow (after-tax income and depreciation)	34,660.00	41,618.89	
Total savings (cash flow col. 2 − cash flow col. 1)			6,958.89
Savings as a percent of current cash flow			20.1%

Note: See Table 9.2 for footnotes.

Table 9.2. Cash Flow Analysis of Food Store (1979) [a]

Category	Current Tax Laws	Kemp-Garcia Proposal[b]	Difference (col. 1 – col. 2)
Sales	$500,000		
Selected operating costs			
Labor	36,150		
Rent	5,000		
Insurance	2,850		
Depreciation	6,450		
Property taxes	1,200		
Expenses affected by the Kemp-Garcia bill			
Employer payments to Social Security (6.7%)[c]	2,422.05	$ 1,017.26	$1,404.79
Property taxes[d]	1,200.00	960.00	240
Profit before taxes and depreciation[e]	34,950.00	36,594.79	
Depreciation (depreciable assets $25,000)	6,450.00	8,333.00	
Taxable income	28,500.00	28,261.79	
Income tax[f]	4,950.00	4,054.50	895.50
After-tax income	23,550.00	24,207.29	
Cash flow (after-tax income and depreciation)	30,000.00	32,540.29	
Total savings (cash flow col. 2 – cash flow col. 1)			2,540.29
Savings as a percent of current cash flow			8.5%

Notes to Tables 9.1 and 9.2

[a] Sales and cost data for a representative firm were obtained from *Financial Studies of the Small Business*, 3rd ed. Financial Research Associates, Washington, D.C., 1979 and Internal Revenue Service, *Statistics of Income—1975 Corporation Income Tax Returns*, U.S. Government Printing Office, Washington, D.C. 1979.

[b] Data for capital gains taxes paid by firms were not available, and were thus omitted from the analysis.

[c] 20 percent of the payroll is assumed to be paid to employees under 21 years of age. We regard this as an upper-bound estimate of the proportion of the payroll earned by youth under 21.

[d] Property taxes are estimated to be 24 percent of annual rent. We assume a 3 percent effective tax rate, and rental value equal to 12.5 percent of market value.

[e] In column 2 (Kemp-Garcia) savings on property and Social Security taxes are added to profit before taxes and depreciation.

[f] Under current law, the corporate income tax structure is as follows: tax rate 17%, taxable income first $25,000; 20%, next $25,000; 30%, next $25,000; 40%, next $25,000; 46%, over $100,000.

The Kemp-Garcia bill changes the corporate income tax structure: tax rate 14%, taxable income first $25,000; 17%, next $25,000; 25%, next $25,000; 34%, next $25,000; 39%, over $100,000.

against the additional costs incurred when operating in the zone. These costs include high insurance rates and additional private costs to combat crime, wage premiums to attract nonzone residents to work in the zone, and possibly higher costs of moving inputs and finished products into and out of the zone. These costs will vary for firms in different sectors of the economy, and will depend on the extent to which these goods and services are provided by the local public sector, thereby reducing the private expenditures that entrepreneurs would otherwise make.

FACTORS AFFECTING FIRM LOCATION CHOICES

As previously described, the aim of the tax incentives in Enterprise Zones is to increase the probability that firms choose an inner-city location. In general, businesses choose their locations from a set of geographic alternatives that vary in the degree to which they offer a series of attributes that are important to a firm's profitability. Clearly, firms of different sizes and in different sectors of the economy will not value the same locational attributes equally. It would also be rare for a firm to find one site that ranks highest on all attributes. The entrepreneur must evaluate the trade-offs and choose a site having the attributes most important to his firm's profitability. The Kemp-Garcia tax advantages add to the desirability of an Enterprise Zone location for some firms, but these tax advantages may not compensate completely for the locational disadvantages of these inner-city areas.

In fact, the subsidies offered in this bill are not likely to be large enough to overcome all the negative features that characterize these zones. Nonetheless, these zones offer some desirable attributes (e.g., a large pool of low-skilled labor), in addition to the tax incentives to some businesses. The industries that can take advantage of these existing attributes are most likely to be attracted. The existing literature on firm intrametropolitan location decisions will identify which types of firms will find Enterprise Zone areas more advantageous.

Intrametropolitan Location Decisions

From the existing research on business location decisions, one can gain considerable insight into the types of industries most likely to locate in Enterprise Zones. Because Enterprise Zones are unlikely to influence interregional migration of firms, especially if several zones are established in each region, the conclusions drawn from the intraregional migration literature are the most relevant here.

Employment change in an area results from an interplay of

establishment births (new businesses), deaths, expansions or contractions of existing establishments, and relocations of establishments into and out of the area. Studies by Birch, Struyk and James, and Schmenner confirm the importance of establishment births and changes in employment of existing firms in determining patterns of employment growth both for SMSAs as a whole and areas within SMSAs.[18] The spatial patterns of establishment births, deaths, relocations, and expansions of existing firms tend to reinforce one another. However, births and expansions and contractions of existing establishments determine the direction and magnitude of employment change, since death rates vary only slightly among areas and only a relatively small percentage of establishments relocate. Given these patterns, it appears that public policies aimed at increasing employment in given areas should focus on fostering the growth of existing establishments and creating new ones. Clearly, the Kemp-Garcia bill is intended to benefit these firms.

Research on intrametropolitan industrial location has focused on establishment relocations and net changes in total employment. Only a few studies analyze the expansion of existing establishments and the spatial pattern of establishment births. More research has focused on the variables influencing the locational decisions of relocating firms than new firms. The relatively few studies on firm births and the expansion of existing ones suggest that the same variables influencing relocating establishments also influence the locational decisions of new establishments and expanding ones. Thus one can draw some conclusions about births and on-site expansion decisions from the relocation studies.

The relocation decision of central-city firms can be usefully viewed as two consecutive decisions. First, an establishment decides to leave its central-city site, then it decides where to relocate. Most studies of firm location consider either one of the two aspects of this relocation decision. The first stage of the location decision is generally analyzed using survey data while the latter is analyzed using both survey data and economic models.

Several studies[19] analyze the determinants of destinations patterns for relocating establishments. The evidence points consistently to a supply of labor for firms in each particular industry and to locational external economies from the presence of firms in the same industry as the two most important determinants of destinations. Fiscal variables, while not irrelevant, are generally found to be relatively less important determinants of destination patterns.[20]

Other studies[21] analyze the decision to relocate. Relocating firms cite three principal reasons for their decision to leave an area: a lack of space to expand at their present location, the desire to modernize their entire plant, and to move closer to a labor supply.[22]

One study[23] focuses on whether Milwaukee industrial and commercial establishments (analyzed separately) are more likely to relocate from relatively deteriorated inner-city areas than from other areas. The rate of establishment relocations was only slightly higher in inner-city areas than in other areas of the city in Milwaukee during the 1972–1977 period. The relocation rate was found not to be related to the percentage of the area's residents in poverty, the incidence of crime, or the percentage of the area's population that is nonwhite. In another study,[24] little variation was found among city subareas in the spatial incidence of manufacturing establishments going out of business. This evidence suggests that it is the availability of labor, and not the external effects of inner city areas such as crime, that is a stronger determinant of firm relocation from subareas of cities.

Two studies provide insight into the reasons for firm expansions rather than relocations. Firms that choose on-site expansion generally cite "keeping their labor force intact" as their primary reason for this decision.[25] Struyk and James[26] find, however, that expansion on-site and creation of new firms has occurred more in the suburbs than in the central city.

In summary, there is no evidence for or against the hypothesis that expanding and new firms avoid central-city areas because of crime, low-income population, or other external factors of the area, although nothing suggests this is not the case. The presence of an appropriate supply of labor to the industry emerges in every study as an important determinant of industry expansion and creation. Space for expansion is also an important element in the locational decision of firms.

Evidence of Manufacturing Employment Growth in Central Cities

All studies of manufacturing industries in urban areas confirm that, overall, manufacturing is shifting out of central cities and manufacturing employment is decreasing in central cities.[27] It is not true, however, that every type of manufacturing industry is declining in central cities; studies provide evidence of establishment births and employment growth in certain kinds of manufacturing in central-city areas.

Kemper[28] examines a sample of firm births in five areas (central business district, central industrial district, core, inner-suburban ring, outer ring) of the New York City SMSA between 1967 and 1969. For each area, he relates the percentage of the births in each manufacturing industry that occur in that area to a set of industry characteristics. He argues that both input requirements for the industry and input prices are important for location choice. He finds that industries using more nonstandard inputs (such as large amounts of water, more professional labor, and more unskilled labor) and manufacturing products for consumer use (as opposed to intermediate products) are more likely to choose central-city sites.[29] Thus, not all manufacturing industries migrate to the suburbs, nor do they all respond to the same locational incentives.

Struyk and James examine employment changes from 1965 to 1968 for two-digit manufacturing industries in poverty areas of central cities in four SMSAs: Cleveland, Minneapolis-St. Paul, Boston, and Phoenix. Two measures are used to analyze manufacturing employment change in these areas. The first, concentration, measures whether the industry accounts for a greater fraction of manufacturing employment in poverty areas than it does in the SMSA as a whole. A second, growth, measures whether the industry grew faster between 1965 and 1968 in poverty areas than in the SMSA as a whole. They find that between eight and thirteen manufacturing industries concentrated or grew in poverty areas in each of these four cities. Moreover, these industries tend to be similar across the four cities. For example, food and kindred products is relatively concentrated in the poverty areas of three of the four cities. This is also true for printing, publishing, and allied industries and for electrical and electronic machinery, equipment, and supplies.

From the perspective of future employment, the industries whose employment is growing in poverty areas may be more interesting than industries concentrated in poverty areas. Lumber, primary metals, and electrical machinery grew more rapidly in the poverty areas of three of the four central cities than in the SMSA as a whole. Rubber and rubber products, and stone, clay, and glass grew more rapidly in the poverty areas of two of the four central cities than in the SMSA as a whole.

In general, industries found to be concentrated in these poverty areas are either nuisance industries—in that they create negative externalities—or primarily employ low-skilled workers. The nuisance industries whose growth is concentrated in poverty areas in two or more of these central cities include chemicals and products, petroleum and products, and primary metals. The authors were not able to determine whether exclusionary zoning in other jurisdictions in an SMSA played a role in nuisance industry location in poverty areas, however.

Most of the other industries that are either growing or concentrated in poverty areas of these cities are labor-intensive, low-wage industries. With their data, Struyk and James admittedly are not able to adequately test whether these industries find the poverty area resident labor force an attraction, or if the establishments offer significant employment opportunities for poverty-area residents. Their results are consistent with both of these hypotheses, however, and indicate that urban poverty areas can be attractive to some firms.

Industries Most Likely to be Attracted to the Labor Force in an Enterprise Zone

An available labor supply appears to be an important factor in firm location choices. Because Enterprise Zones will, by definition, be in poverty areas of cities, the resident labor force is likely to be unskilled. Therefore, low-skilled labor-intensive industries will be more attracted to Enterprise Zones than industries using highly skilled labor. Firms that cannot make adequate use of low-skilled labor would not generally meet the bill requirement that 50 percent of its labor force be drawn from residents of the Enterprise Zone to qualify for the subsidy. Examining the use of low-skilled labor by industrial category will offer insight into the industries that Enterprise Zones areas are likely to attract.

Table 9.3 reports the percentage of total U.S. employment that is unskilled, by industry, in 1970. Industries with high concentrations of employment in these occupations are more likely to be attracted to resident areas of low-skilled workers.

For all industries, the 1970 average of the labor force in unskilled occupations is about 53 percent. According to these figures, industries using an above-average percentage of unskilled employees include mining, manufacturing, transportation etc., hotels and lodging places, other personal services such as dry cleaning and laundries, and public administration.

Because the census occupational categories are aggregated, generalizations can be misleading. This is especially true for clerical and kindred workers, because this occupational category includes

Table 9.3. Percent of Unskilled Employed Persons, 1979, by Industry

Industry	Percent Unskilled[a]
Agriculture, forestries, fisheries	10.0%
Mining	60.0
Construction	30.0
Manufacturing	62.4
Lumber and wood products except furniture	74.0
Furniture	63.0
Stone, clay, glass products	66.4
Primary ferrous industries	57.4
Primary Nonferrous industries	61.6
Fabricated metal industries	61.3
Machinery, except electrical	54.3
Electrical machinery and equipment	59.1
Motor vehicles and equipment	63.3
Aircraft and parts	44.7
Other transportation equipment	43.1
Ordnance	50.8
Other durable goods	63.9
Food and kindred products	67.0
Textile mill products	75.4
Apparel and other fabricated textile products	84.9
Paper and allied products	67.3
Printing, publishing and allied industries	37.2
Chemicals and allied products	52.7
Rubber and miscellaneous plastic products	70.3
Other nondurable goods	71.2
Transportation, communication, public utilities	60.3
Wholesale trade	47.5
Retail trade	49.4
Finance, insurance, real estate	53.6
Business services	55.3
Automobile services	31.4
Other repair services	37.1
Hotels and lodging places	68.9
Other personal services	88.9
Entertainment and recreation services	46.3
Professional and related services	45.0
Public administration	66.5
All industries	52.7

Source: U.S. Bureau of the Census, Census of Population: 1970, *Occupation by Industry* Final Report PC (2)=7C (Washington, D.C.: Government Printing Office, 1972), Tables 1 and 4.
[a]Low-skilled occupations include clerical and kindred workers, operatives except transport, transportation equipment operatives, laborers except farm, and personal service workers. Low-skilled occupations are identified here on the basis of their lower-than-average mean earnings.

secretaries and dispatchers—relatively skilled occupations—as well as file clerks and clerical assistants. The effect of this occupational aggregation may be to overestimate the percentage of unskilled workers in industries using the relatively skilled members of this occupational group.

Transportation may be one instance where industry does not have as high a reliance on unskilled personnel as these numbers suggest. In the case of transportation, if clerical and kindred is removed from the unskilled categorization of occupations, the percentage of unskilled workers employed in that industry declines from 60.3 to 35.3, well below the national average. A similar result occurs for public administration.

Excluding transportation and public administration (and also mining, an unlikely industry for an urban area because it is tied to the location of raw materials), only three industries are likely to be attracted by the labor force in Enterprise Zones. These industries are manufacturing, hotels, and other personal services.

Within manufacturing, there are several subindustries that have 62.4 percent (the manufacturing average) or more of their employees in unskilled labor categories. (See Table 9.3). Given these occupation and industry data, the emphasis on attracting manufacturing establishments to Enterprise Zones by some of the bill's proponents seems appropriate.

Establishments in industries that use unskilled labor will have an incentive to locate in Enterprise Zone areas to take advantage of the available labor force. Because the tax incentives offered in the Kemp-Garcia bill are relatively neutral between capital and labor, they should not change the area's attractiveness for these industries, but strengthen it compared to locations outside the zone. Space availability for the expansion of existing firms and the establishment of new ones would be a prerequisite for any industry. Even with available space and appropriate labor supply, whether the tax advantages are large enough to offset the negative external effects generally associated with these inner-city areas remains an empirical question.

CHANCES FOR SUCCESS

Although tax incentives could attract firms to some inner-city areas, establishing an Enterprise Zone in the worst inner-city areas with the incentives offered by the Kemp-Garcia bill will not significantly stimulate economic development. Incentives based on annual operating costs and profits will not alter the start-up costs of establishing or expanding a business, the risks and additional costs of doing business in the area, or the bank's risk of lending money to new entrepreneurs in these areas. Some existing federal programs could be used in tandem with an Enterprise Zone policy to alleviate some of these problems. In addition, designating places other than the worst areas in the city as Enterprise Zones will also alleviate these problems, significantly increasing the chances for success in revitalizations.

Business Climate in the Zone

Areas likely to qualify as Enterprise Zones are at present generally characterized as poor business location choices. The tax incentives of this bill and the presence of a low-skilled labor force attracting some industries may not be enough to compensate for many locational disadvantages of these zones. A combination of high fire and property insurance rates due to higher crime rates, lack of available venture capital, difficulties in land site assembly, age and quality of existing structures, poor condition of the public infrastructure, limited access to highways or traffic congestion, and a possible low level of police and fire services all determine the viability of these sites for business location. In the absence of sufficiently favorable external conditions, tax subsidies alone may not attract many businesses to Enterprise Zones. Moreover, it is clear that zones will vary in the level of each of these external factors. Thus, some zones are more likely to be successful than others. Federal, state, and local policy for the zones may want to address these external factors as well as grant the tax incentives.

To partially alleviate the external problems, cities may find it productive to link the Enterprise Zone with other federal programs designed to address these problems. The Community Development Block Grant (CDBG) program and the Urban Development Action Grant (UDAG) program could be used for this purpose.

If a city assigns its CDBG funds to the zone for a period of years to improve infrastructure, increase police and fire protection, and upgrade other local public services, it would demonstrate a local public-sector commitment to the Enterprise Zone. To the business community at large, this would minimize the uncertainty faced by locating in the zone and would reduce some costs of operating in an area that traditionally is not well served by the local public sector.

In certain areas of the zone, buildings may be in such disrepair that they cannot be refurbished. Firms may be reluctant to incur the costs of demolition and may avoid these sites. To increase the viability of some areas, cities may find it desirable to clear or demolish, on a selected basis, areas within a zone. This, however, may come at the expense of other city neighborhoods. Additional funds for infrastructure improvement made available to Enterprise Zones through the Block Grant program could be used to alleviate this difficulty.

Currently, the UDAG program funds projects in "pockets of poverty" in otherwise healthy cities. To date, six awards have been made to pockets-of-poverty locations, half of them for infrastructure. Clearly, infrastructure is one of the components of development that is necessary at the onset. As well as fund infrastructure, Action Grants can serve as a vehicle to provide front-end funding for firms locating in Enterprise Zones. To accomplish this, the UDAG selection criteria could be expanded to favor projects in Enterprise Zones.

Operating Insurance

Businesses in Enterprise Zones are likely to face difficulty in obtaining property insurance. If it is available at all, the rates may be much higher in Enterprise Zones than in other areas, and insurance costs in zones would add significantly to the cost of doing business. A successful Enterprise Zone may require the provision of business insurance from a risk pool of private insurance companies. Even so, the cost of business insurance in these worst zones may be a serious stumbling block to revitalization.

Venture Capital

To the extent that Enterprise Zone establishments are branches of corporations, these firms would use internal capital funds for expansion or borrow at prime interest rates. Thus these firms may face fewer problems investing in Enterprise Zones.

New small firms investing in these zones will still face the same, if not more difficult, problems associated with raising the initial capital for a small business enterprise. At the beginning, many small enterprises raise capital from the proprietor's personal and family savings, and from bank loans at interest rates higher than the prime rates. Banks will view loans to a small business located in Enterprise Zones as more risky than a small business located outside an Enterprise Zone, and may choose to make loans only up to the value of the land, which they hold as collateral. Given the additional problems of raising capital for small firms in Enterprise Zones, encouraging the use of Small Business Administration Loans by firms in these zones would tend to reduce the start-up costs for some firms.

Worst-First Selection Method

Using the proposed poverty and unemployment selection criteria, Enterprise Zones can be in the most deteriorated areas of a city. Cities may choose among a set of deteriorated areas with their borders when applying for Enterprise Zone designation. Because of the extreme costs imposed by these external factors in the worst areas, less deteriorated areas may provide an environment more conducive to development. Which type of area to choose as a zone may ultimately depend on the revitalization goal of the program. Placing the zones in the inner-city areas with more potential for development may increase the chances of the program's success and lead ultimately to more employment opportunities. In any case, it seems clear that other existing federal programs will have to be targeted to Enterprise Zones to partially alleviate the adverse factors characterizing these inner-city areas.

Also prominent in the bill is the Enterprise Zone philosophy that overtaxation of returns to capital, and restrictions such as minimum wage laws, both reduce opportunities for employment of low-skilled workers and lead to underinvestment and unemployment. Although nationwide reductions in the taxation of returns of capital and in the costs of labor may stimulate investment and reduce unemployment, it does not necessarily follow that these same tax incentives will significantly stimulate investment in the worst areas of the inner cities. If these incentives do not work there as a tool for economic development, they should not be construed as a fair test of the effectiveness of supply-side economic policies to stimulate national growth.

Designing Investment and Employment Incentives

In its present form, the legislation would allow subsidies to capital through accelerated depreciation of the first $500,000 of assets and reduction in capital gains, property, and corporate income taxes. Its labor subsidies operate through reduced employer contributions to the Social Security system for workers. Although both types of subsides are not likely to be strong enough to provide incentives for firms to locate in these zones and employ low-skilled labor, they could be redesigned and strengthened to accomplish one or both of these objectives. In order to minimize the revenue loss to the U.S. Treasury, these capital and labor subsidies could apply to only new investment and employment, and not existing investment and employment.

Improving the Capital Subsidy

Asset Depreciation Limit. Studies show that accelerated depreciation and investment tax credits, available nationally, stimulate investment.[30] Accelerated depreciation in an Enterprise Zone proposed by the Kemp-Garcia bill applies only to the first $500,000 of physical assets. This may be a generous incentive for small firms that operate in rented space, and therefore have relatively few assets to depreciate, but it provides little incentive for large firms that own their buildings as well as greater amounts of other physical assets. The worst inner-city areas, however, are not likely to have much rentable space for these small firms, and given the high cost of construction, the $500,000 allowance does not provide much incentive for construction or rehabilitation of industrial and commercial space.

The purpose of the $500,000 asset depreciation may be to specifically subsidize smaller businesses and to limit the federal revenue losses that would result from larger subsidies to capital. Revitalization, however, may benefit more from a higher depreciation asset limit that is restricted to new (and not existing) investment in zones.

Corporate Tax Rates. Although any type of business can take advantage of the favorable depreciation schedule, only incorporated enterprises benefit from reduced corporate income tax rates. Ironically, the small firms that the bill's proponents hope to attract are often sole proprietorships or partnerships. Either these tax reductions should be extended to unincorporated enterprises through reduced personal tax rates, or the corporate tax reduction should be eliminated.

Capital Gains Provision. The capital tax reduction may encourage sellers of small businesses in Enterprise Zones to sell to other small businesses rather than larger, stock-issuing firms. Under current laws, selling to smaller firms that would make payments in cash would subject the seller to capital gains taxation, whereas payments made in shares of stock are an exchange of assets and not subject to capital gains taxation.

The capital gains reduction in the Enterprise Zone may add to the turnover of small business, which can be desirable in terms of economic development. Risk-taking entrepreneurs often establish businesses with the intent of selling them later to more risk-averse persons for a profit. Lower capital gains taxes may attract risk-taking entrepreneurs by raising their returned profit from the sale.

Property Tax Provision. Currently the bill requires local government initiation in the designation of an Enterprise Zone. The explicit cost of the local government—the 20 percent reduction in local property taxes in the zone—may deter participation, especially for cities in fiscal difficulty. Moreover, selective local tax reductions may require amending state and local uniform taxation laws for which legislative approval may be difficult to obtain.

An alternative proposal would freeze property tax assessments at current levels for property in the zone. Any new investment in the zone would therefore be exempt (completely or partially) from property taxation for the ten-year period. Local government revenues would not shrink in absolute amounts, but would grow more slowly.[31] Exempting new investments from property taxation is consistent with our proposal to extend accelerated depreciation to new investment.

Maintain Relative Subsidy in Enterprise Zones. Over time, investment incentives may change for the nation as a whole (e.g., the 10–5–3 depreciation proposal). To be effective, Enterprise Zone investment incentives should be designed to maintain their relative advantage over nonzone areas. One method of accomplishing this is to allow Enterprise Zone firms to depreciate their new investment at a fixed percentage rate above the amount allowed nonzone firms, and to similarly peg capital gains and corporate income tax rates in Enterprise Zones to the national rate.

Capital Subsidy and Employment. Although there is evidence that capital subsidies induce the expansion of both investment and employment, high-skilled labor expands more than lower-skilled labor.[32] Thus, although a subsidy for investment may stimulate revitalization, a direct subsidy for employment of low-skilled labor would be a more efficient method of expanding employment opportunities for lower-skilled workers.

Improving the Labor Subsidy

The labor subsidy provision in the Kemp-Garcia bill gives a labor subsidy to firms for all of their employees through reductions in the employer's Social Security tax contribution. The subsidy is larger for employees under 21 years of age than for those 21 and over. While this subsidy favors workers under 21, it makes no distinction among types of workers who are over 21. With the current eligible income ceiling of $29,700 for Social Security tax payments, the employment tax subsidy covers the full wages of all but a few highly skilled employees. Thus, as currently constructed, the subsidy is not directed toward low-skilled workers because the same percentage of wages for almost all types of employees are subsidized.

To provide an incentive to hire low-skilled employees, the subsidy might be in the form of a tax credit for a percentage of wages paid to employees in either certain low-skilled occupations or earning, for example, less than 125 percent of the minimum wage. This would have the additional advantage of avoiding the Social Security tax–general revenue debate. Moreover, to reduce the revenue cost, the subsidy might only apply to net new employment instead of total employment.

To be eligible for the subsidies, the current bill also requires employers to hire at least 50 percent of their work force from among residents of the zone. Although this demonstrates a commitment to providing the benefits of Enterprise Zones to the people in the places as well as to the places themselves, it may be an undesirable restriction on businesses because it creates an incentive for employers to discriminate among potential hires on the basis of their place of residence. Moreover, employers may also be encouraged to fire employed zone residents who choose to migrate from the zone because these employees then reduce the fraction of the firms employees who are zone residents.

EMPLOYMENT ZONES AND ENTERPRISE ZONES: POLICY ALTERNATIVES

The current bill attempts to attack two related but somewhat different problems. Using what are only modest tax incentives, it hopes to revitalize inner-city areas by inducing investment and employment in these areas, and simultaneously, to stimulate employment of the zone's residents. Moreover, it hopes to achieve these goals in the worst areas in cities.

In order to achieve its goals, the types of subsidy offered should attract capital for revitalization of the area, and provide incentives to employ area residents (low-skilled labor). Although the bill does provide both capital and labor incentives, its constraints may prove too restrictive to stimulate development. At best, because the capital and labor subsidies are relatively neutral for small firms (as shown in Tables 9.1 and 9.2) there is no reason to expect to attract industries using low-skilled labor in a greater proportion than under present market conditions. The additional constraint of hiring at least 50 percent of employees from the resident labor force may be a condition that precludes firms that would otherwise be attracted by the tax savings from locating there at all. A result may be that neither, rather than both, of these two goals is furthered. By better separating the tools with which the program operates, both goals—revitalizing an area and employing its residents—could be better accomplished.

The appropriate types of subsidy offered should depend ultimately on the goals and objectives of the program. If the objective is to revitalize certain inner-city areas, then large new investment tax credits or accelerated depreciation targeted to those areas are suggested.

On the other hand, if the objective is to increase employment of lower-skilled workers, employment subsidies for workers earning less than a certain hourly wage are suggested, and those subsidies should not be restricted by place of work. An Urban Jobs and Enterprise Zone Act can encourage the growth of urban jobs, but need not restrict them to Enterprise Zones. This two-pronged approach, using capital subsidies that are place specific and labor subsidies that are people specific, would do much to enhance the probable success of the Urban Jobs and Enterprise Zone Act.

NOTES

1. The only such case is provided under Section 931 of the Internal Revenue Code, which provides U.S. income tax-free status to corporations conducting active trade or business in certain U.S. possessions.
2. H.R. 7563, "Urban Jobs and Enterprise Zone Act of 1980," 96th Congress, 2nd Session.
3. Hall, P., Speech to the Royal Town Planning Institute, June 15, 1977.
4. Department of the Treasury of Great Britain, "Enterprise Zones," *Economic Progress Report* no. 121 (May 1980): 1–2.
5. Butler, S. M., *Enterprise Zones: Pioneering in the Inner City* (Washington, D.C.: The Heritage Foundation, 1980).

6. Chinitz, B., "Toward a National Urban Policy," in *Central City Economic Development,* Benjamin Chinitz, ed. (Cambridge, Mass.: Abt Books, 1979).
7. Dansziger, S., and M. Weinstein, "Employment Location and Wage Rates of Poverty-Area Residents," *Journal of Urban Economics* 3 no. 2 (1976): 127–145.
8. Birch, D. L., *The Process Causing Economic Change in Cities* (unpublished manuscript, M.I.T., 1978); and Birch D. L., *The Job Generation Process,* (unpublished manuscript, M.I.T., 1979).
9. Jacobs, J., *The Economy of Cities* (New York: Random House, 1969).
10. Even if one accepts this aspect of supply-side economics for a national policy and removes taxes and regulations in all areas, it would be naive to believe that the problems of inner cities would be alleviated. The latent industries now kept out of the economy by government rules would not bloom ubiquitously in the absence of regulations, and those that do may surface in more favorable locations than the inner cities.
11. Garcia, R., "Toward a New Federal Role in Urban Redevelopment—A Policy of Opportunity Development," *Congressional Record* (August 19, 1980), pp. E3878–3881.
12. The tax incentives proposed in the Kemp-Garcia bill include a number of tax revisions recommended to the House Subcommittee on Small Business. These revisions simplify taxing procedures for businesses in a way that enables smaller businesses to take full advantage of them. For additional information see McKevit, J. D., "Disproportionate Use of the U.S. Tax Code Advantages," Hearings before the Subcommittee on SBA and SBIC, House of Representatives, 95th Congress, Second Session, Washington, D.C., February 22, 1978; Semo, M. A., "Proposed Small Business Tax Reforms," Hearings before the Subcommittee on SBA and SBIC, House of Representatives, 95th Congress, Second Session, Washington, D.C., February 22, 1978.
13. Harrison, B., and S. Kanter, "The Political Economy of States' Job-Creation Business Incentives," *AIP Journal* (October 1978).
14. Foreign Trade Zones are areas in which industry is exempt from certain customs duties. Cities and counties apply to the federal government for such designation for parts of their jurisdictions; Enterprise Zones would be eligible as Foreign Trade Zones.
15. For a presentation of the theoretical model, see Mieszkowski, P., "The Property Tax: Excise or a Profits Tax," *Journal of Public Economics,* 1 (1972); 73–96; empirical evidence is offered in Bloom, H. S., H. F. Ladd, and J. M. Yinger, "Intrajurisdictional Property Tax Capitalization," Report prepared for the Department of Housing and Urban Development, Grant H–2915G, July 1980.
16. These examples are for illustrative purposes only. Obviously, the subsidy's effects on firms will vary by industry.
17. Other than the accelerated depreciation allowance, noncorporate firms receive no tax reduction. Other versions of this bill may amend this differential treatment of noncorporate and corporate firms.
18. Birch, *The Job Generation Process;* Struyk, R. J., and F. J. James, *Intrametropolitan Industrial Location* (Lexington, Mass.: D.C. Heath, 1978); and Schmenner, R. W., "The Manufacturing Location Decision: Evidence from Cincinnati and New England," Report to U.S. Department of Commerce, Economic Development Administration, 1978.
19. Chinitz, B., and S. S. Jacobs, "Central City Economic Development:: The Post War Experience," presented at the North American Regional Science Meetings,

November 1977; Moses, L., and H. F. Williamson, Jr., "The Location of Economic Activity in Cities," *Papers and Proceedings of the American Economic Association,* 57 (May 1967): 211–222; Schmenner, R., "City Taxes and Industry Location," unpublished Ph.D. dessertation, revised, Yale University, 1975; Schmenner, R. W., "The Manufacturing Location Decision: Evidence From Cincinnati and New England"; and Wasylenko, M., "Evidence on Fiscal Differentials and Intrametropolitan Firm Location," *Land Economics* 56 (1980): 339–349.

20. Wasylenko, "Evidence on Fiscal Differentials and Intrametropolitan Firm Location."

21. Erickson, R., and M. Wasylenko, "Firm Relocation and Site Selection in Suburban Municipalities," *Journal of Urban Economics* 8 (1980): 69–85; Schmenner, R., "City Taxes and Industry Location."

22. Schmenner, R. W., "The Manufacturing Location Decision."

23. Erickson, R. A., "Environment as 'Push Factor' in the Suburbanization of Business Establishments," *Urban Geography* 1 (1980): 167–178.

24. Struyk, R. J., and F. J. James, *Intrametropolitan Industrial Location.*

25. Schmenner, R. W., "The Manufacturing Location Decision."

26. Struyk, R. J., and F. J. James, *Intrametropolitan Industrial Location.*

27. Chinitz, B., and S. S. Jacobs, "Central City Economic Development"; Sacks, S., "Trends in Large City Manufacturing Employment," unpublished manuscript, prepared for U.S. Department of Housing and Urban Development, 1979.

28. Kemper, P., "Manufacturing, Location and Production Requirements" (mimeo), 1975.

29. Most large central cities are located on a large body of water because interregional transportation of commodities was initially via water. The large body of water also facilitated location of industries using water intensively.

30. Abel, A., "Tax Incentives to Investment: An Assessment of Tax Credits and Tax Cuts," *New England Economic Review,* Federal Reserve Bank of Boston (November/December 1978).

31. We owe this suggestion to Professor William Vickery of Columbia University.

32. Ebel shows this to be the case in Puerto Rico as a result of the Section 931 and 936 tax reductions that subsidized capital. See Ebel, R. D., "An Analysis of the Puerto Rican Industrial Tax Incentive Program," Working Paper no. 2, Department of Economics, University of the District of Columbia, Washington, D.C. (October 1978); also see Kesselman, J. R., S. H. Williamson, and E. R. Berndt, "Tax Credits for Employment Rather Than Investment," *American Economic Review* 67 (June 1977): 339–349.

PART V

Issues for the 1980s

Chapter 10

Balancing the Federal Budget: The Intergovernmental Casualty and Opportunity

*Donald Haider**

Coming off a record peacetime deficit of $66 billion, President Ford promised a balanced budget by FY 1980. President Carter set his sights on achieving this goal by 1981. President Reagan hopes to attain this mark during his first term in office, but already acknowledges that, even under favorable economic conditions, budget balance may not occur until FY 1985.

In spite of extensive veto of spending measures, President Ford fell $45 billion short of balancing the budget in his final proposed budget. Mr. Carter's final budget for FY 1982 is likely to miss by an even wider margin. The cumulative Carter deficits for FY 1977–FY 1981 will approach $190 billion, and more than $250 billion in red ink if one includes off-budget financing. In their final budget messages to the Congress, the last three presidents have gone beyond traditional pleas for expenditure moderation and indeed have called for fundamental changes in public expectations concerning the government's role in society. Nixon inveighed against a "momentum of extravagance" propelled by "legislative committees' sympathy to new narrow causes"; Ford railed against the attitude that "income and wealth are produced in Washington"; Carter against those who "make special pleas for exceptions to budget discipline.[1]

*Professor of Public Management, Northwestern Kellogg School of Management

Presidents are not alone in their dedication to the virtues of a balanced budget. Public opinion polls indicate that Americans resoundingly support this goal. A proposed constitutional amendment requiring a balanced budget received considerable support throughout the country. Governors and legislatures have gone on record supporting it, as have most candidates in their quest for public office. The Ninety-sixth Congress in June, 1980, enacted its first budget resolution, which at the time provided a guide to achieve the first balanced budget in eleven years and only the second in twenty-two years. Six months later, the same Congress approved a second budget resolution that moved from a $100 million budget surplus to a forecast $27 billion deficit, with an end of FY 1981 fiscal deficit likely to be double that target.

MEANS AND ENDS

It is reasonable to assume, then, that the United States and its leaders are not divided as much by the goal of achieving a balanced budget as they are by the means. Like so much else in the world of politics, how something is to be accomplished is as important, if not more important, than what is to be accomplished. The means for achieving the ends separates conservatives from liberals; interest groups from political parties; mayors from governors; Keynesians from Monetarists; and rationalists from incrementalists.

The "means gap" spans political parties, levels, and branches of government. The search for means, among other objectives, gave birth to the 1974 Budget Reform Act, which established a new set of ground rules designed to ensure congressional determination of national budget policies and priorities. The new law can be viewed, however, as the outcome of conflict, first between the President and Congress, and then between different interests in Congress. The executive-legislative fight turned on President Nixon's determination to achieve a $250 billion limitation on FY 1973 outlays, and Congress's equal resolve to participate fully in program cuts that fell victim to this expenditure ceiling. In early 1973, President Nixon moved by executive fiat to impound $18 billion in programs substituting executive policies for those established by Congress. A constitutional crisis arose. Support for the Budget Act came from liberals and conservatives alike, each group for its own reasons and each with its own expectations as to what would be accomplished. The net effect of the act was to shift more power over economic and fiscal policy making to the Congress and away from the President.

Critical as the shift in interbranch power became, the shift in power among different interests within Congress seems no less important. The Budget Reform Act resulted as much from an internal power struggle within the Congress as it did from Mr. Nixon's catalytic actions.[2] Growing congressional conflict over the budget stemmed from the fact that increments were no longer available in sufficient amounts to cover both the built-in increase in the budget and claims for new programs. As then Congressman, and now OMB Director, David Stockman wrote in 1975, "For some time now, the built-in momentum of the federal budget and the exigencies of fiscal politics have produced expenditure growth rates that not only outpace current year revenues, but also absorb the 'fiscal dividend' of economic growth up to a half decade in the future."[3]

The shrinking of appropriable resources, especially due to entitlement programs and mortgaged future revenues, exacerbated conflict within the Congress between junior members and their seniors; authorizing committees and appropriation committees; these committees and tax committees; and between leadership and rank and file. Moreover, the entire budget process, once seemingly cloaked in secrecy, complexity, and obscurity of documents, had gradually become unveiled. Outside interest groups and lobbies came to understand the process and were able to penetrate its workings. Born out of dozens of compromises, the new act and its procedures greatly enlarged conflict within the Congress because it both expanded the range of participation and moved the Congress in the direction of forced choices.[4]

Once considered a benchmark for establishing a President's professional reputation in the Washington community, the President's proposed budget serves less and less that purpose.[5] As Table 10.1 indicates, over the past twelve years, 1970–1981, only once (1979) did the President's proposed budget outlays come in under estimates. In nine of the past twelve years, deficits have run higher than forecasts, and in five cases, deficits ran more than double what the President and his advisors had originally forecasted. Such disparities stem from shortcomings in forecasting, economic fluctuations, and congressional demand for increased expenditures. More importantly, it tells us that what the President proposes in January has increasingly become further removed from what actually transpires in a fiscal year that does not end until 20 months later. Recent Presidents have contributed to the self-

Table 10.1. Presidents' Budgets: Proposed and Outcomes FY 1970– FY 1981 ($ billions)

Fiscal Year	Presidential Proposals		Actual Outcomes	
	Outlays	Surplus/ Deficit	Outlays	Surplus/ Deficit
1970	$195.3	$ 3.4	$196.6	$– 2.8
1971	200.8	1.3	211.4	–23.0
1972	229.2	–11.6	232.0	–23.4
1973	246.3	–25.5	247.1	–14.8
1974	268.7	–12.7	269.6	– 4.7
1975	304.4	– 9.4	326.2	–45.2
1976	349.4	–51.9	366.4	–66.4
1977	394.2	–43.0	402.7	–45.0
1978	440.0	–47.0	450.8	–48.8
1979	550.2	–60.6	493.7	–27.7
1980	531.6	–29.0	579.6	–59.6
1981 est.	615.8	–15.8	662.7	–55.2

Source: Office of Management and Budget, unpublished data. Excludes off-budget financing.

destruction of their own budgets as well. Responding to sudden changes in unemployment and inflation, Presidents have tried unsuccessfully to employ the budget as a fiscal tool to achieve short-term stabilization, only to incur longer term consequences.[6]

However, the new budget procedures do not appear to have been very successful in reducing deficits or in controlling expenditures. Consequently, additional reforms and changes have been proposed ranging from conceptual and definitional, procedural, statutory, to basic constitutional revisions. The Comptroller General, for one, has proposed a complete agenda of issues and problems that need to be dealt with: proliferation of accounts and programs; control and treatment of loans, loan guarantees, and credit activities; budget measurement; treatment of entitlements and multiyear programs; budget cycle timing and workload pressure.[7] Five years have passed since enactment of the Budget Reform Act and 13 years since the unified concept was set forth by the President's Commission on Budget Concepts. Re-examination of practices and concepts by outsiders may improve the functioning of the process.

Even more basic is whether the new congressional budget process will establish itself as an important, determinative force in shaping federal fiscal policy and spending priorities—or simply collapse, as did the Legislative Budgets of 1947 and 1948, as an unworkable reform. Hailed at first as being the most significant internal change in the postwar Congress, the Budget Act has received more critical reviews since. Due to lack of enforcement mechanisms, each successive budget has given way to new and more blatant methods of circumvention. For each of the law's ills, a vast array of prescriptions are being put forward. Some would tie spending levels to a measure of national income, while others would restrain revenues through indexation of income taxes. Constitutional measures include a mandatory balanced budget to changing terms of House members so as to reduce interest group pressures on spending.[8] Efforts will continue to develop sanctions such an enhancing budget committees' powers over the appropriations committees, converting resolutions into binding ceilings, and enforcing budget resolutions on all committees. These changes notwithstanding, new laws and procedures cannot compel the Congress to do what it simply does not want to do.

In contrast to those proposed changes internal to the Congress are ones intended to rectify what some perceive to be an imbalance between the President and the Congress in fiscal and economic policy: increasing presidential discretion on deferrals and recisions, including impoundment; curbing of budgetary bypass of executive agencies in budget submissions, and elimination of one-house vetoes; extra-constitutional mechanisms to provide a form of item-veto for the President to exercise on riders and nongermane amendments; and even a lengthening of the time between the President's budget submission and the federal fiscal year. In the program and regulatory area, suggestions abound to give Presidents greater program consolidation authority and discretion.

However, formal and informal remedies, either interbranch or intrabranch, may be insufficient to deal with growing problems of discipline, authority, and controllability that underpin the budget. Reformers underestimate what budgets are to politics and over-estimate the strength of new procedures or processes. The budget is the perennial battleground of American politics. Everybody fights —agencies and their constituencies for more money; budget offices for more control over spending; President and Congress over priorities; and one legislative institution with another. It could hardly be otherwise with tens of billions of dollars at stake and political fortunes and vital interests at issue. Still, we are the only democratically constituted government in which a President's proposed expenditures may be exceeded by the legislature; one of few where chief executives are not enpowered to alter tax policies to meet changing economic conditions; and one where the gulf between leaders and their own parties grows wider rather than narrower.

CAUSES OF BUDGETARY BLOAT

The means for achieving a balanced federal budget cannot be divorced from the underlying causes of government and expenditure growth. Some might argue that the budgetary bulge problem is worldwide. If measured by tax burdens, government spending as a percentage of GNP, government debt to total debt, growth of federal employment to private employment, real rates of expenditure increases in constant dollars, and the magnitude of deficits to overall GNP, the alleged problems may not be as great as rhetoric suggests. Overreaction could have profound institutional and economic consequences.

On the other hand, the trend lines are ominous. The Proposition 13 mood and 1980 election results have conveyed several messages to federal officials: tax burdens are too high, government spending is too much, and federal deficits are adding to inflationary pressures. We have created an environment in which expectations run high in voters and consumers, business and financial interests alike. To quote from the famous Kemp–Stockman memo to President Reagan, an economic policy package must contain "credible elements on matters of outlay control, future budget authority reduction, and a believable plan for curtailing... massive... credit absorption."[9]

The Advisory Commission on Intergovernmental Relations (ACIR), for one, has made a valuable contribution to research on governmental growth. Its interdisciplinary, case study approach to the dynamics of growth has focused on two broad types of policy (and spending) producing variables. The one set of variables includes both internal actors such as the President, the Congress, the courts, interest groups, and the bureaucracy and external actors and forces such as the media, political parties, public opinion, and elections. The other set is comprised of sociodemographic trends, wars, depressions, and the sweep of economic fluctuations and changes. The ACIR's case studies found that Congress played a critical role in each of the program areas studied, an increasing indication of how "hyperresponsive" it has become to its environment and outside pressures.[10]

The dynamic interaction of internal-external actors and their environment provides considerable insight into and understanding of how policies are developed, programs expand, and funding grows. Theories abound that tie government growth to congressional entrepreneurs, self-maximizing bureaucrats, judicial activists, presidential aggrandizement, interest group liberalism, iron triangles, or even Parkinson's law. Although elements of each may be present, the causes of growth are many and complex. It is surprising, however, to find out how much of the Leviathan State occurred accidentally or due to unintended consequences, more than by necessity, design, or choice. The examples are near limitless, whether in AFDC, food stamps, Medicaid, soil conservation, school impact aid, or trade adjustment assistance, to cite a few cases.

The ACIR's limited findings go a long way toward downplaying any particular theory of why government grows. They also suggest that limits to human intelligence and lack of foresight may be more at fault than governmental structure or procedure. Just as the causes are multifaceted and complex, so are the solutions. In the past we have tried to limit growth by unwinding the system, dismantling it, or better managing it. The histories of the Hoover and Kestnbaum commissions or the Ash Council do not warrant much faith in this approach. The twin deities of economy and efficiency as applied to reorganization have not had the curative features thought by one President who proclaimed, "the major cause of the ineffectiveness of government is principally a matter of machinery." Another saw in reorganization a panacea for restoring vigor and health to "a horrible bureaucratic mess."[11] Application of management techniques—PPB, MBO, and ZBB— also have had limited utility as gauged by their performance record on a government-wide basis.[12]

Thus, the problems associated with government growth and spending do not lend themselves to easy solutions. The traditional presidential resources for dealing with executive agencies and departments—staff agencies like OMB, appointment and removal powers, reorganizations, commissions, and introduction of management techniques—have not been very successful in controlling a confederation of sovereigns called the executive branch, and even less so with a Congress that has increasingly rejected presidential leadership. To some contemporary observers of the budget dilemma, the fundamental problems of our system transcend issues of administration, finance, and policies. Instead, they stem from the erosion of political legitimacy—the vital linkage between elected officials and the electorate, between interest groups and political parties, between congressional leaders and followers, between Congress and the President, and between state and local governments and the federal government.

Presidential counselor Lloyd Cutler, for example, thinks that the conglomeration of subgovernments in our system has gone beyond the control of Presidents, Congress, and even our Constitution, making coherent and consistent policy a near impossibility. Columnist David Broder sees in the great "openness reforms" of the late 1960s and early 1970s "a tyranny of so-called reform" in which reform beneficiaries have their own agenda to reconstruct the system.[13] One result is the severing of the links that once bound professional politicians whether congressmen, party leaders, governors, or mayors. Instead, these officials pursue individual survival strategies largely devoid of mutual stakes in policy or the fate of an incumbent administration. Brookings' James Sundquist laments the "Crisis of Competence in Government" which requires public attention to institutional and structural problems.[14] Finally, the ACIR finds the intergovernmental system to be "dangerously overloaded," devoid of much accountability, responsibility, direction, and purpose.[15] Each of these critics suggests various remedial measures, but all admit that more fundamental institutional and constitutional changes may be required in the long run.

Thus, balancing the federal budget has proved to be an elusive goal. Even under reasonably favorable economic assumptions, it is likely to remain so for the immediate future. Better managers, structures, and management techniques are insuffMMMicent alone to move government institutions toward the mark. It is equally unlikely that changes in the budget process itself, whether statutory or procedural, will of themselves close the gap. The budget process, above all else, is at base a political process. Until the time arises that a longer-term economic policy triumphs over shorter-term economic stabilization and political survival objectives, the drive for a balanced budget will continue to swing in many different directions, and, if coupled to wide economic fluctuations, will move as much away from as toward this goal.

THE INTERGOVERNMENTAL CASUALTY

Rather than forecasting how a balanced budget in FY 1985 might impact on state and local governments, a more fruitful exercise involves why federal grants will be a casualty of scarcer federal resources and increased budget conflict in the years ahead.

Dating from the use of national income accounts, a tripartite distinction of federal outlays has evolved that breaks down government expenditures by government purchases, transfer payments, and federal grants to state and local governments. These categories are neither mutually exclusive nor do they exhaust the range of government outlays in such areas as loans, loan guarantees, or interest on debt. Outlays in these categories are backed by varying degrees of mandatory to discretionary commitments. Outlays for each have different impacts on the economy as well as on state and local governments. Among the three, transfer payments have grown the fastest, more than quadrupling over the past decade. Grants in aid have grown slightly less rapidly, followed by government purchases, of which more than 60 percent are defense related.

The real demand pressures for future federal expenditures fall into the categories of transfer payments and defense-related purchases. From 1968 to 1981, national defense's share of budget outlays went from 43 percent to 24 percent, while benefit payments and grants moved from 31 percent to 58 percent. In terms of outlays by functions, national defense expenditures exceeded human resource expenditures by a 5-to-2 ratio in 1955, a 2-to-1 ratio in 1960, was equal to in 1970, and by 1980 was completely reversed with human resources over defense by a $2\frac{1}{2}$-to-1 ratio. It is reasonable to assume not only that national defense spending will increase as a share of federal expenditures, but also that it will exceed the rate of inflation over the next several years. So, too, the explosive growth in transfer payments will continue, propelled by demographic-induced outlays for older Americans, funding requirements for Social Security, inflation-driven health care and social services. More than 77 percent of the FY 1981 budget outlays are considered by OMB to be "relatively uncontrollable," an amount that has risen by nearly 2 percent per year since the late 1960s. About 50 percent of the total budget is tied to judicially enforceable entitlement programs, mostly transfer payments to individuals.

"Making decisions about the size and structure of the federal grant system when pressure for defense spending is rising at the national level and movements to limit taxes and expenditures are spreading at the state and local levels is not a task for the fainthearted," notes Brookings' George Break.[16] The inescapable conclusion from demand pressures and budget squeeze is that the major expenditure casualty will be federal aid to state and local governments. A future scenario involving the ratcheting down of grant programs is not necessary. It already has arrived. Following a twenty-year growth rate in federal grants that increased at a rate of 14.6 percent from 1958 to 1978, federal aid began its decline, whether measured by percentage of total outlays, GNP, or contribution to state and local expenditures.[17] The downward slope is steeper than most state and local public officials realize. Not only has it occurred in constant dollars, but excluding income support programs such as public assistance, Medicaid, housing assistance, and low income fuel support, it has occurred in current dollars as well for FY 1981–FY 1982. Federal grants as a percent of budget outlays peaked at 17.3 percent in FY 1978, and, in Carter's proposed FY 1982 budget, will be 13 percent. This would return us to the 1970, pre–Revenue Sharing era level.

Further erosion of federal aid for states and localities can be gleaned from the most recent revenue-sharing renewal battle in late 1980. The State and Local Fiscal Assistance Act of 1972 marked the high point of unified intergovernmental lobby: the short-lived alliance between the White House and state and local officials in their mutual quest to decentralize and to restructure federal aid programs. The General Revenue Sharing Program provided $30.2 billion over a five-year period, and upon 1976 renewal, another $25.6 billion over four years. The program expired on September 30, 1980 and the Carter administration requested a five-year renewal at $6.9 billion per year. Carter also asked Congress for a $1 billion standby countercyclical fiscal assistance program and a one-year targeted fiscal assistance program for localities of $250 million.

Instead, the Ninety-sixth Congress rejected targeted fiscal assistance and countercyclical programs and, next, eliminated the states from the three-year extension of general revenue sharing for FY 1981. However, the State and Local Fiscal Assistance Act Amendments of 1980 (H.R. 7122), reinstated the $2.3 billion annual state share on an appropriation rather than entitlement basis, provided that states returned to the U.S. Treasury categorical grant funds equal to their revenue-sharing allotments. The Congress took literally the National Governors Association position that its members would prefer continuation of GRS in exchange for 10 percent of their categorical funds. An era of intergovernmental relations ended when Congress seized the initiative by stemming the growth of the Treasury pipeline to cities and dismantling the state–local alliance surrounding revenue sharing. It rejected the use of state and local governments as agents of macroeconomic policy during a weakening of the economy and sent a strong message to governors and mayors concerning the need for multiyear financial planning.

The revenue-sharing shock wave has not fully set in for state governments nor have the consequences fully materialized for localities. Various estimates hold that 25 to 40 percent of the aggregate $2.3 billion states' share had been passed through to local governments. Several states, like Illinois, had earmarked the funds entirely for education. Although GRS had increased by 30 percent since 1972, in constant dollars it had decreased by almost 50 percent. So, too, it represented only 2 percent of state-generated resources, but its withdrawl occurred during a national recession when many states have experienced shortfalls on income and sales tax revenues. If the program is continued under annual appropriations and on a categorical trade-off basis, then the program may be unworkable due to existing requirements on categorical expenditures, unclear scope and coverage, and overall disruptive impacts on state budgeting.

On the other hand, a trade-off approach to intergovernmental grants has the potential for replacing monopoly with competition and overloading with decongestion. Indeed, a "buy-out" market approach to the categorical morass could open the entire system to a form of shadow pricing in which governments could bid categorical funds against one another in exchange for unrestricted aid. The enormous diversity in grant preferences among states and regions—social services in the East versus water projects in the West—could be balanced through a cash-out basis. Even with declining federal dollars, elected officials in Congress and in state and local governments could move toward a "win-win strategy." Congress could continue its support for separate programs, but leave to individual state and local officials the choice of what mix and priorities. Minimum service levels and civil rights requirements would be maintained, but in a far more flexible system of resource allocation. Dismissed by most, this approach deserves further consideration, if not experimentation.

A SYSTEM MORE IN BALANCE

The ACIR has observed that "the quadrennial battle over revenue sharing serves as the single best forum for periodically evaluating the state of fiscal federalism."[18] If this is so, then Congress rendered a judgment that the state–local fiscal system has made sufficient improvement over the past decade, relative to the condition of the federal government, that the state GRS entitlement could be discontinued. Admittedly, GRS began as an unpopular program in the Congress—separating tax collection from spending responsibility—while recent state surpluses, tax cuts, and cries for a balanced budget only further eroded whatever support the program had. Nevertheless, Congress did make a decision governing its assessment of the system's condition.

Evolutionary changes in the federal system have occurred that place general-sharing renewal in a far different light than the conditions that existed in the 1960s and the 1970s. The deterioration of the federal government's fiscal situation is the most prevasive factor. In the 1960s, some viewed revenue sharing as antidote to federal surpluses. Also, in FY 1972 and FY 1973, federal deficits were $23.4 billion and $14.8 billion, respectively, roughly in synchronization with the then full employment budget concept. Budget deterioration then followed. The severe 1975–1976 recession postponed a serious debate on GRS in the mid-1970s.

The leading rationale for the program turned on vertical imbalance in the intergovernmental system. The federal government had the elastic revenue sources responsive to growth, and state and local governments depended on less elastic and more regressive tax systems. As Nelson Rockefeller, the acclaimed father of revenue sharing, put it, "The federal government has the money; state-local governments have the problems." The fiscal position of the states has improved remarkably over the past two decades: thirty-seven use both the personal income and sales taxes; thirty shield property owners from property tax overloads; forty-five collect more tax revenue than their local governments; state share of state–local expenditures from own funds continue to increase; and state aid to local governments increased not quite as rapidly as federal aid to state and local governments. All are indicators of strength. As Table 10.2 indicates, twenty states raised less than half of state and local revenues in 1959, and by 1977, only five states fell below that mark.[19]

In terms of horizontal balance—the fiscal position between states and regions as measured by the differences in per-capita income—continues to narrow between the poorest and the wealthiest states. "Regional convergence" is often used to describe the greater balances between states and regions that have occurred over the past thirty years.[20] Many categorical grants were enacted simply to reduce fiscal disparities among states. Even revenue sharing sought to balance poverty, income, and tax effort factors.

However, the most glaring fiscal disparities have become intrastate rather than among states. The differences in expenditures and income levels among central cities and suburbs in the largest metropolitan areas have widened rather than narrowed over the past thirty years.[21] Federal programs during the 1970s sought to overcome this disparity by targeting funds to most-needy places.

Table 10.2. State Share of Total State–Local Tax Revenue (frequency distribution of states)

State Share	1977	1975	1971	1967	1963	1959
Less than 40%	1	1	0	3	3	4
40 to 50	4	6	15	11	16	16
50 to 60	17	17	13	17	15	14
60 to 70	17	15	11	9	10	8
Over 70	11	11	11	10	6	8
U.S. average percent	57.5%	56.7%	54.1%	52.1%	49.9%	48.9%

More than half of all nonwelfare federal grants to state and local governments is currently allocated to localities, bypassing state governments. It is some concern as to whether local governments, especially older cities, have become overly dependent on federal aid. But the political fact is that the federal government extricates itself from local aid at far greater risk over the short run than from state aid.

Admittedly, there are those five to six large states in the snow-belt, including Illinois, that suffer from high taxation, a high welfare burden, and low growth in jobs and per capita income. If one includes California in this group, these states bear 52 percent of combined state expenditures on AFDC and 60 percent of Medicaid costs.[22] Yet it has become increasingly difficult in an era of computerized formulas, of rising confrontations between the frost-belt and the snowbelt, and of demographically shifting political power, to provide substantial aid to six states at the expense of the other forty-four. If revenue-sharing and other major grant allocation programs have taught us anything, it is that modest redistribution may no longer be financially practical. If you want to get New York City one additional dollar, you had better be prepared to spend $10 elsewhere.

Finally, proponents of retaining the states in GRS argued passionately about maintaining a well-balanced federal aid system consisting of categorical grants, block grants, and general-support payments or unrestricted aid such as GRS; however, this balance already has been eroded by recategorization of and floundering support for most block grants. The unrestricted aid portion of total federal grant outlays has been cut by one-third since the early 1970s. How to best deal with the morass of 500 categorical aid programs and the 59 general policy and administrative requirements called "crosscutting" (since they apply to grant programs of more than one agency) involves a distinctive set of problems altogether.

THE STATE GOVERNMENT ERA HAS ARRIVED

The era of state government has arrived, whether by necessity or choice. The Washington "can do era" is coming to a close. Intergovernmental fiscal forces are converging on the states. Property tax pressures and lids are pushing responsibilites up, and the ratcheting down of federal aid is pushing responsibilities down. The demographics are working against the federal budget, yet are working for the states in their principal expenditure area—education. Although a diversity in financial functional responsibilities still exists among states and regions, nearly all states have moved into a senior fiscal partnership with their localities. This has occurred with the aid of more balanced revenue systems and the fastest-growing revenue instrument in our intergovernmental revenue system—the income tax. The New York City financial crisis established the principle that states have the primary responsibility for the financial well-being of their local governments.

The constellation of political forces also has moved in the direction of the states: Mr. Reagan's substantial electoral victory, Republican control of the Senate for the first time in more than twenty-five years, and an aggressive governor's constituency prepared for a serious debate on the roles, responsibilities, and revenue sources of different government levels.

If a sorting out and restructuring is to occur, as many predict it must, then what directions might it take? Briefly, there are at least four directions the federal system of relationships might lead and, conceivably, it could move in all four simultaneously.[23]

The first and least controversial is the administrative procedures direction. OMB circulars, presidential directives, and agency guidelines would seek to ameliorate major grant irritants, largely at the margin rather than extracting the fundamental causes of problems. The new procedures would aim at relaxing crosscutting requirements and mandates, simplifying funding and decentralizing more program decisions. Procedures would be developed to expedite disputes among assistant agencies and grant recipients as well as among grant-giving agencies. Regulatory burdens could be softened through a liberalized compliance process or blocked through fiscal impact statements. The Federal

Regional Councils may be reinvigorated. In short, this adminis-trative direction would not differ greatly from the approach employed by the Carter administration, although its implementa-tion might be more consistent and government-wide.

The second direction would be more controversial, involving a fundamental restructuring of federal grant assistance. It would represent a continuation of the Nixon–Ford New Federalism ef-forts in which Nixon proposed six special revenue-sharing pro-grams and Ford, the consolidation of fifty-nine categorical pro-grams into three major block grants. The common elements in these earlier efforts included consolidation of categorical grants into block grants, elimination of matching requirements, strength-ening of elected state-local government officials at the expense of functionalists, and decentralized administration.

Under this scenario, the President would gain congressional approval for grant consolidation and simplification authority, which, like most reorganization plans, would carry a single house veto. Tied to a budget control strategy, the Reagan administration would try to "buy out" the public interest group (mayors, gov-ernors, county officials) constituency through funds, flexibility, and authority. Intergovernmental battles among governors and mayors over pass-through arrangements and fair share would re-emerge, as would the protectionist devices of hold harmless, dual formulas, pockets of poverty, and discretionary funds to compen-sate losers. Even if new or additional funds are provided, each proposal would still run a gauntlet of state and local officials as well as program beneficiaries that may produce more fatalities than new structures and responsibilities.

A third alternative goes beyond consolidation and simplifica-tion, and instead begins to address a fundamental sorting out of financial and functional responsibilities among government levels. The new administration might frontally pursue a massive overhaul by articulating a philosophy and plan, mindful that the costs of federal assumption of health and welfare costs far exceeds the aggregate of minor categorical grants and aid to education. A less high-temperature, high-risk venture might be carried out through an intermediate. One option is to establish another Hoover-type commission that would include state and local offi-cials. The ACIR and the National Governors' Association have endorsed another proposal: a "Convocation on Federalism" led by governors and mayors who would seek a working consensus on which government levels should do more in a particular area, and which ones less. The trade-offs and programmatic decisions stemming from such a body would be the basis for recommendations to the President and to the Congress. Whatever the forum or plan, the sorting out of the basic administrative, programmatic, fiscal, and political dimensions of our contemporary federal system will not come easily.

Finally, the most significant changes in intergovernmental relations may continue to occur intrastate—the sorting out of functional and financial responsibilities between individual states and their local governments. In such areas as school finance, welfare, and health and hospitals, this process already is occurring. Patterns will differ by state and region. In some cases, voters have taken the initiative such as in California. Over the long run, these changes may better equip states to deal with their federal constituency on matters of federal versus state responsibilities than would the other directions.

CONCLUSIONS

The prospects for balancing the federal budget in the near future are not promising. The issue is not so much one of when, as it is one of control over future resource commitments. The issue is not the magnitude of this year's or next year's deficit, but rather a fiscal policy in the context of an overall economic policy that leads to less inflation and more moderate economic cycles. Our governmental system is being tested as perhaps never before under peacetime and nondepression circumstances. In many respects, the federal budget has become the bellwether of that test, and its importance transcends fiscal and economic policy.

If we are to pass this test, the ratcheting down of the federal grant system will be an inevitable consequence of budgetary control. Less resources mean greater conflict. Less federal aid may necessitate greater state efforts, and increased casualties among state and local elected officials. Governors will be caught between the upward pressures from local governments and downward pressures from Washington. Local officials, many of whom contend with static or shrinking tax bases as well as levy limits and full utilization of local revenue sources, will continue to be on the firing line between service demanders and revenue providers. These conditions are not new, but they now appear to be more durable and challenging than before.

The important task of restructuring our federal system, in many respects, has only just begun. We have passed through rather dramatic cycles and changes, evolutionary developments and trends. Contrary to those who proclaimed federalism to be dead or those who prophesized the end of state government, the most exciting era of intergovernmental relations is upon us.

NOTES

1. *The U.S. Budget in Brief—FY 1974* (Washington, D.C.: G.P.O., 1973), p. 8; ibid—FY 1978, (1977), p.5, and ibid—FY 1982 (1981), p. 4
2. Allen Schick, "The Battle of the Budget," in *Congress Against the President,* Harvey C. Mansfield (ed.) (New York: The Academy of Political Science, 1975), p. 65.
3. David A. Stockman, "The Social Pork Barrel," *The Public Interest* 39 (Spring 1975): 5.
4. Schick, "The Battle of the Budget," p. 69.
5. See Richard Neustadt, *Presidential Power* (New York: J. Wiley, 1960), Chap. 4.
6. See George P. Shultz and Kenneth W. Nam, *Economic Policy Behind the Headlines* (New York: W. W. Norton, 1977), Chap. 2.
7. Address by Elmer B. Staats, Comptroller General of the United States, George Washington University, Washington, D.C., November 21, 1980.
8. John Shannon and Bruce Wallin, "Restraining the Federal Budget: Alternative Policies and Strategies," *Intergovernmental Perspective* 5 (Spring 1979): 8-15.
9. "Avoiding a GOP Economic Dunkirk," *The Wall Street Journal* (December 12, 1980): 14.
10. Cynthia Colella, "The Creation, Care, and Feeding of Leviathan: Who and What Makes Government Grow," *Intergovernmental Perpective* 5 (Fall 1979): 6-11; ;and David R. Beame, "The Accidental Leviathan: Was the Growth of Government a Mistake?" ibid, 12-19.
11. Presidential Message to Congress on "The President's Departmental Reorganization Program," March 25, 1971; "Promises Book: A Compilation of Statements made by Presidential Candidate, Jimmy Carter," mimeograph, January, 1977.
12. Donald Haider, "Presidential Management Initiatives," *Public Administration Review* 30 (May/June, 1979): 248-259, and H. Helco, "Political Executives and the Washington Bureaucracy," *Political Science Quarterly* 92 (Fall 1977): 421.
13. David S. Broder, "Openness in our Political System," *Edited Proceedings from a National Forum on Emerging Issues,* Public Affairs Council, Washington, D.C., September 14-16, 1977, p. 34.
14. James L. Sundquist, "The Crisis of Competence in Government," in *Setting National Priorities: Agenda for the 1980s,* Joseph Peckman (ed.) (Washington, D.C.: The Brookings Institution, 1980), Chap. 16.
15. See ACIR, *The Federal Role in the Federal System—A Crisis of Confidence and Competence* (Washington, D.C., 1980).
16. George F. Break, "Intergovernmental Fiscal Relations," *Setting National Priorities, op. cit.* p. 276.
17. Richard P. Nathan, "Federal Grants—How Are They Working?" in *Cities Under Stress,* R. Burchell and D. Listokin (eds.) (New Brunswick, N.J.: Center for Urban Policy Research, 1980), pp. 529-530.

18. Will Myers and John Shannon, "Revenue Sharing for States: An Endangered Species," *Intergovernmental Perspective* 5 (Summer 1979): 10.
19. Ibid., p. 15.
20. Janet R. Pack, "Frostbelt and Sunbelt: Convergence Over Time," *Intergovernmental Perspective* 4 (Fall 1978): 8–15.
21. ACIR, *Central City-Suburban Fiscal Disparity and City Distress* (Washington, D.C., 1980), pp. 7–12.
22. See John Shannon, "Revenue Sharing and the Changing Federal System," in *Issues in Revenue Sharing*, George D. Brown (ed.) (Columbus, Ohio: Academy for Contemporary Problems, 1980), pp. 5–13.
23. See ACIR, *The Federal Role in the Federal System—Hearings on the Federal Role*, (Washington, D.C., 1980), Appendix A.

Chapter 11

The Slowdown in the Growth of State-Local Spending: Will It Last?

John Shannon *

The state-local sector has recently undergone a most re-markable change—the rapid transition from a fast-growth to a slow-growth industry. During most of the post-World War II era, state and local spending (including federal aid) grew at twice the rate of the economy, rising from about 7 percent of Gross National Product (GNP) in the late 1940s to a 14.5 percent of GNP in the late 1970s. Starting in 1977, there has been a remarkable decrease in its rate of growth. In fact, Figure 11.1 shows that state and local spending is not increasing as rapidly as the economy or the rise in the price level.

This great transformation raises three questions:

1. What has caused this remarkable slowdown?
2. Is this slowdown a temporary abberation or can it be ex-pected to continue for some time to come?
3. What are the intergovernmental and budgetary implications of this slowdown?

CAUSES OF THE SLOWDOWN

In retrospect, the combination of four external shocks and three major internal changes have transformed the state-local sector from a fast-growth to a slow-growth industry.

* Assistant Director, Advisory Commission on Intergovernmental Relations

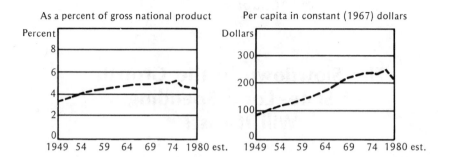

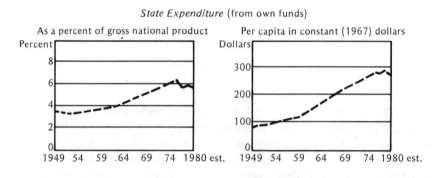

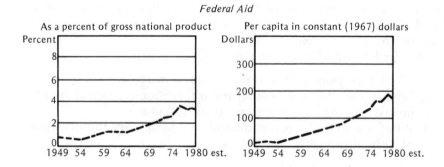

Figure 11.1. The slowdown in state-local spending: State and local government expenditures, and federal aid, selected fiscal years 1949–1980 local expenditure from own funds. (From ACIR, *Significant Features of Fiscal Federalism,* 1979–80 ed., p. 3.)

Four External Shocks

The 1974–1975 recession stands out as the first major jolt. The severity of that recession shocked state and local spenders, particularly in the Northeast and Midwest. For many the message was clear—"the days of wine and roses" were over. On a Richter-type scale the shock would probably fall in the 4 to 5 range.

The New York City fiscal crisis—starting in 1975—stands out as the second major external shock. It caused many state and local officials to make an agonizing reappraisal of their spending policies in general and of their short-term borrowing practices in particular. On a scale of 1 to 10, the New York City crisis probably had a shock value somewhere in the 5 to 6 range.

Proposition 13 and its aftermath (1978 to present) was far more severe than the two earlier shocks—probably a rating of 9 would be conservative. As pointed out later in this paper, Proposition 13 left in its wake a whole new set of restrictions on the power of state and local officials to tax and to spend.

The fourth and most recent external shock was the November 1980 election of President Reagan and a Republican Senate. Early indications suggest that its shock value will also be in the 9 category. This latest strengthening of conservative forces promises to severely constrict the influence of federal aid on the state-local system for some time to come. This is especially important because, until very recently, federal aid was the most dynamic force driving the state–local sector.

Three Major Internal Changes

Much of the recent change in state and local fiscal behavior is attributable to fundamental changes in our society.

Public opinion has changed from support, or at least toleration, of fast growth to a demand for slower growth. Many of the recent lids imposed on state and local spenders are designed to prevent state and local taxes from growing faster than taxpayers' income.

The economy has changed from significant real growth to slow or no real growth and high rates of inflation. Inflation injects high-octane fuel into the fires of local property-tax discontent. The recent explosion in California serves as the most dramatic case in point. It also shows portents of sparking an indexation fire among income-taxing governments.

Demographics have changed. During most of the post-World War II era, steadily rising school enrollments exerted enormous upward pressure on state and local fiscs. Now declining enrollments have stabilized pressure on this important expenditure front.

A PROGNOSIS

In my judgment, the great slowdown in state-local spending will be with us for the forseeable future—at least the next four years. Three developments underpin this judgment.

Uncle Sam Loses His Trump Cards

First, there is little likelihood that federal aid will soon regain its status as a driving force for growth. Why? Because federal policymakers can no longer play their fiscal trump cards—unique fiscal advantages that enabled federal policy makers during the 1954–1979 period to expand their control of the domestic public sector at little political risk.

Income Tax. The federal government came out of World War II and the Korean War with a highly responsive income-tax system. During most of the 1954–1979 period, the interaction of economic structure produced sufficient additional revenue growth to help finance repeated tax cuts and expanded domestic programs. *Now* there is clear evidence of growing opposition to the income tax—a development that can be traced in part to the fact that "taxflation" has automatically pushed taxpayers into higher marginal tax rates. The demand for tax cuts and indexation will become strident (See the following survey response and Figure 11.2).

Defense. Since Korea there has been a steady decline in our outlays for defense—falling from about 13 percent of GNP in 1954 to about 6.5 percent in 1979. This defense cut helped finance a sharp increase in domestic programs, as shown in Figure 11.3. *Now* there is growing recognition that we "underinvested" in defense during the 1970s. The generals will be claiming an increasing share of the federal budget for the next several years.

Social Security. For years Congress could increase Social Security tax rates with little opposition (Figure 11.4). *Now* with growing opposition to steadily rising Social Security taxes, it is becoming increasingly apparent that the Congress will have to

Percent

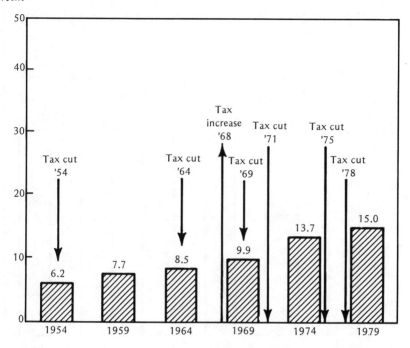

Source: ACIR, *Significant Features of Fiscal Federalism,* 1978–79 and 1979–80 eds.;
and staff computations.

Which Do You Think Is the Worst Tax—That Is, the Least Fair?

	Percent of U.S. Public		
	March 1972	May 1977	May 1980
Federal income tax	19%	28%	36%
State income tax	13	11	10
State sales tax	13	17	19
Local property tax	45	33	25
Don't know	11	11	10

Source: ACIR, *Changing Public Attitudes on Governments and Taxes,* 1980 (Washington, D.C.: Advisory Commission on Intergovernmental Relations), August 1980, S–9.

Figure 11.2. Federal domestic spending as a percent of GNP.

siphon off general tax revenue to help underwrite expanding Social Security commitments, thereby intensifying the financial crunch.

Federal Aid. Massive federal penetration in the domestic field can also be attributed to federal aid to states and localities.

Percent

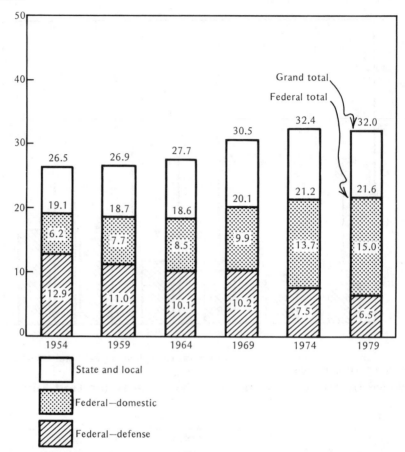

Figure 11.3. Government expenditures from own funds as a percent of gross national product, 1954–1979. (From ACIR, *Significant Features of Fiscal Federalism*, 1978–79 ed.; and staff computations.)

By means of conditional matching grants, the Congress developed a facile method for co-opting state and local policy makers and their resources. As a result, the federal aid system grew prodigiously from about 40 programs amounting to $3 billion in 1954 to approximately 500 programs distributing more than $80 billion by 1979—with over a thousand "strings" attached, as demonstrated in Figure 11.5. *Now* critics contend that the Congress has badly overplayed its federal aid trump card. Instead of bringing clear-cut federal control, it has resulted in a mishmash of federal–state –local authority with a resultant loss of efficiency, accountability, and public confidence. While basic reform of the federal aid

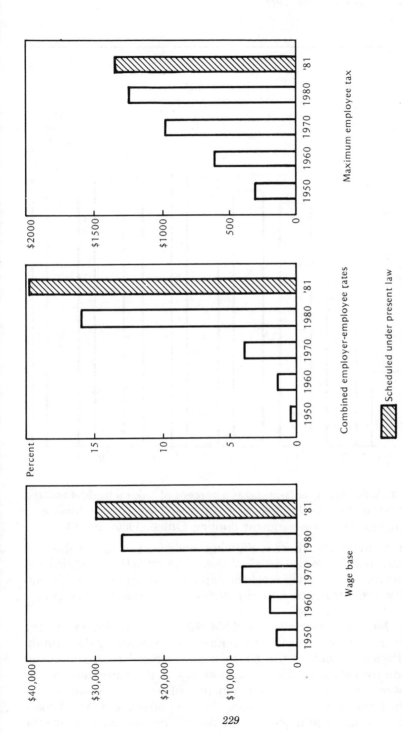

Figure 11.4. The dramatic growth of the Social Security tax. (From ACIR staff computations based on *The Social Security Bulletin, Annual Statistical Supplement.*)

229

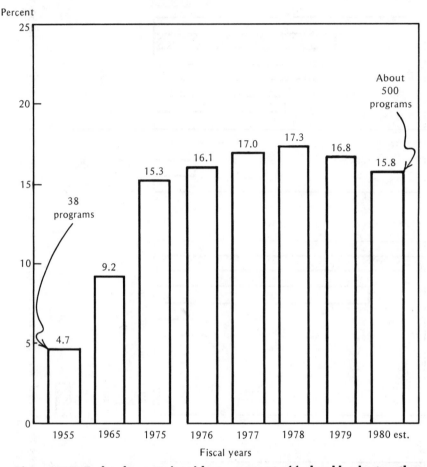

Figure 11.5. Federal grants-in-aid as a percent of federal budget outlays, 1955–1980. (From *The Budget for Fiscal Year 1981,* Special Analysis H (Washington, D.C.: Government Printing Office, 1980), p. 254.)

system is uncertain, there is growing evidence to suggest that the Congress will be forced to slow down the growth in federal aid flows as one way to help meet the expansion of defense and Social Security commitments and the strident demand for tax cuts.

The Deficit. During this 1954–1979 period, federal policy makers could also cover their revenue shortfalls with deficit financing, thereby avoiding the political pain caused by tax hikes or expenditure cutbacks. Figure 11.6 shows that in nineteen of the last twenty years, Congress spent more than it collected—these deficits total about $400 billion. *Now,* confronted with chronic inflation of major proportions, the deficit finesse can no longer be

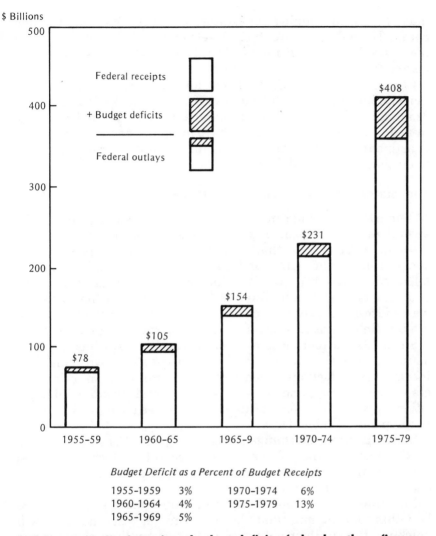

Figure 11.6. Federal receipts, budget deficits, federal outlays, five-year averages. 1955–1979. (From *Federal Budget for 1981* (Washington, D.C.: Government Printing Office, 1980), Table 8, and ACIR staff computations.

worked with the same ease of earlier years. The business community, and especially foreign investors, regard perennial deficits as convincing evidence of poor fiscal discipline and a major contributor to inflation—the nation's number one domestic problem.

Federal Aid Prognosis. The federal government appears to be entering a period of sustained fiscal stress. Once again, to use the card game analogy, federal policy makers are being forced to make higher and higher expenditure bids with fewer top revenue cards. To make the situation more binding, it is also becoming increasingly difficult to finesse these revenue shortfalls with heavy deficit financing.

Conceivably, Uncle Sam's fiscal fortunes could rebound fairly quickly, but this would take an extraordinary luck of the draw—a dramatic reduction in international tensions, a rapid and sustained economic recovery, a sharp drop in energy prices, the enactment of a "popular" new federal tax, and/or renewed public toleration of heavy deficits.

The States Have Lost Their Tax Drive

A remarkable change in state tax behavior stands out as the second reason for believing that the state–local sector will not grow at a faster rate than the economy over the next several years. During the 1960s and early 1970s, the public generally tolerated almost 600 state tax increases and about 40 new tax enactments as shown in Table 11.1. It is no wonder that, when he was addressing a conference of state governors in the late 1960s, Walter Heller hailed them as "the 50 tartars of taxation."

Since 1977, a moratorium on state tax increases has not been sufficient to satisfy the demand for a fiscal slowdown. Thirty-six income tax reductions, twenty-two sales tax cuts, nine indexed state income taxes, and eighteen state tax and spending-lid impositions give remarkable testimony to a "sea change" in state fiscal policy. (Table 11.2).

Why this dramatic change in state tax policy? The combination of the four external shocks and three internal changes cited earlier in this paper go a long way in explaining this sweeping change in fiscal behavior.

Now that the governors have broken their tax hike habit, there is nothing on the immediate horizon that suggests that they will quickly return to their old ways. In fact, everything points in the other direction. The pro-spending coalition, led by the public school lobby, can no longer run effective political interference for general tax increases.

Moreover, it is highly unlikely that most states will decide to raise their taxes to offset federal aid cuts. The mood of the country favors a somewhat diminished domestic public sector, and the governors are likely to move very slowly and cautiously into the relatively small tax area vacated by the federal government.

The point must be emphasized that most of the fifty state-local revenue systems require fairly frequent tax hikes in order to grow at a consistently faster rate than their economies. To put the issue more directly, without frequent tax increases, particularly in the sales and income-tax areas, total revenue increases will lag slightly the growth of the economy.

Local Authorities Lose Property Tax Autonomy

Inflation has caused residential values to rise at a faster rate than the income of the homeowners. Moreover, residential values have been rising at a faster clip than the values on commercial and industrial property.

In order to keep home owner discontent at tolerable levels, the states have taken over forty actions since 1970 designed to make it more difficult for localities to raise property taxes. Table 11.3 shows that these restrictive actions range from relatively mild full disclosure requirements to draconian Proposition 13-type remedies.

Of most significance, the concern for political tranquility— banking the fires of homeowner discontent—has emerged as the major operating principle. In many states, it has superceded the older doctrines of local fiscal autonomy and property tax uniformity. Preferential treatment for home owners and farmers and curbs on the tax and spending powers of local authorities have become the legacy of the inflationary 1970s.

The fiscal constraints created by this all-out effort to keep property taxes tolerable for homeowners will not be easily swept aside during the 1980s.

LIKELY BUDGETARY IMPLICATIONS

Prior to 1977, all our fifty state-local systems were doing "more with more," that is, they were providing an increasing number of services with an ever increasing "share" of the market —their revenues were increasing at a faster rate than the economy, as revealed in Table 11.4.

For at least the next five years, most state-local systems will probably be trying to do the "same with slightly less." By less, I mean that state and local revenues will tend to lag the growth in the economy due to the slowdown in federal aid flows and reluctance of state officials to raise taxes repeatedly. The decline in school enrollments supports the prediction that the same for somewhat less is not an impossible prescription. A few truly innovative states, aided by belt-tightening, may be able to stretch their budgets so as to do slightly more with slightly less—in real terms.

Table 11.1. The States Race Their Fiscal Motors: States Increasing Tax Rates and Enacting New Taxes, Selected Taxes, January 1, 1959–December 1, 1976

State	No. of legislative actions			General sales	Personal income	Corporation income	Motor fuel	Cigarette	Alcoholic beverage
	Total	Increasing rates	Enacting new taxes						
Alabama	7	7	—	x	...	x	...	xxxx	x
Alaska	5	5	—	...	x	....	xx	x	x
Arizona	18	18	—	xxx	xx	xxx[1]x	xxx	xxx	xxx
Arkansas	8	8	—	...	x	x	xx	xxx	x
California	14	13	1	xx	xxx	xxx	xx	Nx[2]	xx
Colorado	10	9	1	x	xxx	x	xx	Nxx	xx
Connecticut	21	20	1	xxxxx	N[3]	xxxx	xxxx	xxxxx	xx
Delaware	16	16	—	...	xxx	xx	xxxx	xxxx	xxx
Florida	11	10	1	x	...	N	x	xxx	xxxxx
Georgia	7	7	—	...	...	xx	x	xx	xx
Hawaii	6	6	—	x	x	x	x	x	x
Idaho	16	15	1	N	xx	xxx	xxx	xxx	xxx
Illinois	13	11	2	xxx	N	N	xx	xxxx	xx
Indiana	9	6	3	N[4]x	N[4]	N[4]x	x	xx	x
Iowa	18	18	—	x	xxxx	xxx[1]x	x	xxxxx	xxx
Kansas	12	12	—	x	x	xx	xx	xxx	xxx
Kentucky	5	4	1	Nx	...	....	x	x	x
Louisiana	6	6	—	x	x[5]	x[5]	x	x	x
Maine	18	16	2	xxx	Nx	Nx	xx	xxxxxxx	xx
Maryland	9	9	—	x	x	xx	xx	xx	x
Massachusetts	20	19	1	Nx	xxx[5]x	xxx	xxx	xxxx	xxxx
Michigan	11	9	2	x	Nxx	Nx	xx	xx	x
Minnesota	21	20	1	Nx	xxxx	xxxx	xxx	xxxxx	xxx
Mississippi	11	10	1	xx	x	x	x[6]xx	xxx	N
Missouri	11	11	—	x	xx	xx	xx	xx	xx

234

Montana	15	15	—	...	xxxxx	xxxx	xx	x	xxx
Nebraska	20	17	3	Nxx	Nxxxx	Nxxxx	xx	xxx	xx
Nevada	5	5	—	x	...	...	...	xx	xx
New Hampshire	10	8	2	...	N[7]	Nx	xx	xxxx	x
New Jersey	23	20	3	Nx	N[7]xxxN[8]	xxx[1]xx	xxx	xxxxxx	xxx
N. Mexico	12	12	—	xx	xx	xx	xx	xx	xx
New York	19	18	1	Nxx	xxx	xxx	xxx	xxxx	xxx
North Carolina	4	3	1	...	...	...	x	N	xx
North Dakota	12	12	—	xxx	xxx	xx	x	xx	x
Ohio	10	8	2	x	N	N	x	xxxx	xx
Oklahoma	7	6	1	...	x[5]	x[5]	...	xxx	Nx
Oregon	7	6	1	...	x	x	x	Nx	xx
Pennsylvania	16	15	1	xxxx	N	xx	xxx	xxxx	xx
Rhode Island	17	16	1	xxxx	N[9]x	xxx	xxx	xxxx	x
South Carolina	11	11	—	x	x	x	x	xx	xxxxx
South Dakota	11	11	—	xx	...	...	xx	xxxx	xxx
Tennessee	12	12	—	xx	...	xxx	x[6]	xxx	xxx
Texas	10	9	1	Nxxx	...	xxx	...	xxxx	xx
Utah	9	9	—	xxx	...	...	x	x	...
Vermont	12	11	1	N	xxx	x	xx	xxxx	xx
Virginia	10	8	2	N	x	x	xx	N	xxxx
Washington	13	13	—	xxxx	...	...	xxx	xxxx	xx
West Virginia	11	9	2	x	Nxx	N	xx	xxx	x
Wisconsin	17	16	1	Nx	xxxxx	x	x	xxxxx	x[10]
Wyoming	7	7	—	xx	...	...	xxx	xx	xxx
Dist. of Columbia	24	24	—	xxxxx	xxxx	xxxx	xxx	xxxxx	xxx
Rate increases	586	586	—	76	74	85	95	151	105
New tax enactments	41	—	41	12	13	9	—	5	2
Total	627	586	41	88	87	94	95	156	107

Source: ACIR, *Significant Features of Fiscal Federalism,* 1976–77 ed. (Washington, D.C.: Advisory Commission on Intergovernmental Relations, 1980), p. 105.

Note: Each x indicates a tax rate increase enactment, and each N indicates a new tax.

Table 11.2. The States Apply Their Fiscal Brakes, 1977–1980: Major State Tax Reductions, State Spending Lids, and Indexation Actions

State and Region	Ad Hoc Tax Reductions		Indexation of Individual Income Tax	Tax and Spending Lids
	Personal Income Tax	General Sales Tax		
Total	36	22	9	18
New England				
Connecticut		x ('77)		
Maine	x ('79)	x ('79)		
Massachusetts	x ('80)			
New Hampshire				
Rhode Island				S^a ('77)
Vermont	x ('78)	x ('78)		
Mideast				
Delaware				C^b ('80)
District of Columbia	x ('78, '79)			
Maryland	x ('77, '80)	x ('80)		
New Jersey		x ('78)		S ('76)
New York	x ('78, '79)	x ('77, '79, '80)		
Pennsylvania				
Great Lakes				
Illinois				
Indiana				
Michigan				C ('78)
Ohio	x ('79)			
Wisconsin	x ('79, '80)	x ('79, '80)	1979	
Plains				
Iowa	x ('80)		1979	
Kansas				
Minnesota	x ('79, '80)		1979	
Missouri				C ('80)
Nebraska	x ('79)	x ('79)		
North Dakota	x ('79)			
South Dakota				
Southeast				
Alabama				
Arkansas		x ('80)		
Florida				
Georgia				
Kentucky		x ('80)		
Louisiana	x ('80)	x ('80)		S ('79)
Mississippi	x ('80)			
North Carolina	x ('78, '80)			
South Carolina			1980	S ('80)
Tennessee				C ('78)
Virginia				
West Virginia		x ('80)		

Table 11.2. *(continued)*

State and Region	Ad Hoc Tax Reductions		Indexation of Individual Income Tax	Tax and Spending Lids
	Personal Income Tax	General Sales Tax		
Southwest				
Arizona	x ('79, '80)		1978	C ('78)
New Mexico	x ('77, '80)			
Oklahoma				
Texas		x ('79)		C ('78)
Rocky Mountain				
Colorado	x ('78, '79, '80)	x ('78, '80)	1978	S ('77)
Idaho				S ('80)
Montana	x ('78, '80)		1980	
Utah		x ('80)		S ('79)
Wyoming				
Far West				
California	x ('79)		1978	C ('79)
Nevada		x ('80)		S ('79)
Oregon	x ('80)		1979	S ('80)
Washington		x ('79, '80)		S ('79)
Alaska	x ('79, '80)			
Hawaii	x ('77, '78)			C ('78)

Source: ACIR staff.

x = a major tax decrease, i.e., a decrease in excess of 10 percent of the economic growth of the tax.

[a]S-Statutory.

[b]C-Constitutional.

There are two major exceptions to this "same with slightly less" prediction:

1. At least a few of the energy-rich states will definitely continue to provide "more with more." In fact, they will be in an eviable position (such as Alaska) of expanding services while cutting taxes on the home folks, thanks to massive increases in oil and gas revenues.
2. At the other end of the spectrum will be a few frostbelt states (such as New York and Massachusetts) that will be forced to cut their overgrown public sectors on both the tax and expenditure sides. For these states the message is grim, less with less—in real terms.

It is not likely that the southeastern states, marked by below-average tax burdens and above-average national economic growth rates, will abandon their conservative fiscal traditions. Many southern states will probably try to keep their effective tax rates

Table 11.3. State Limitations on Local Government Taxing and Spending Powers Imposed Since 1970

	Full Disclosure Laws[a]	Property Tax Levy Limits	Expenditure Lids	Assessment Constraint[b]	Exhibit: Property Classification[c]
	Arizona	Alaska	Arizona (Prior '70)	California	Minnesota (1913)
	Florida	Arizona (Prior '70)	California	Idaho	Montana (1917)
	Hawaii	Arkansas	Iowa	Iowa	West Virginia (1934)
	Kentucky	Colorado (Prior '70)	Kansas	Maryland	Oregon (1961)
	Maryland	Delaware	Massachusetts	Minnesota	Arizona (1968)
	Montana	Florida	Nebraska	Oregon	Illinois (1971)
	Rhode Island	Indiana	Nevada		Alabama (1972)
	Tennessee	Iowa	New Jersey		Tennessee (1973)
	Texas	Kansas			South Carolina (1976)
	Virginia	Kentucky			Iowa (1977)
		Louisiana			Louisiana (1978)
		Massachusetts			Massachusetts (1979)
		Minnesota			Ohio (1980)
		New Mexico			
		Ohio			
		Oregon (Prior '70)			
		South Carolina			
		Utah			
		Washington			
		Wisconsin			
No. of States	10	20	8	6	13

Source: ACIR staff compilation based on data prepared by IAAO, CCH, and ACIR.

Note: Due to rapidly rising property values, tax rate limitations have lost most of their effectiveness as a tax control mechanism. As a result, states are now adopting other forms of tax and expenditure controls.

[a]Includes only those states that require automatic property tax rate rollback to offset most or all of annual increases in the assessment base in the absence of a rigorous full disclosure procedure, i.e., paid announcement of proposed tax increase and public hearings.

[b]Includes those states placing a limitation on annual assessment increases.

[c]Generally to provide lower assessments for residential property.

238

well below that of their northern neighbors in order to retain what many of them regard as an important competitive advantage.

Most of the states west of the Mississippi—be they energy rich or poor—will probably continue to pursue cautious spending policies for some time to come. Their state constitutions permit the citizenry to bypass the state legislature and, by means of direct initiative and referendum, impose constitutional lids on state and local spenders. In view of the very conservative mood of the West, this populist shotgun behind the legislative door provides added incentive for their policy makers to maintain low fiscal profiles. Most of the energy-rich states in the West, therefore, are more apt to cut taxes on the home folks rather than to go on a spending spree.

LIKELY INTERGOVERNMENTAL IMPLICATIONS

There are at least four likely implications to flow from this transformation from a fast-growth to a slow-growth state-local sector.

1. The "feds" will play a somewhat diminished role as their aid to states and localities lags the growth in the economy, and the states will play a stronger role because most of them now have two fairly powerful revenue producers—an income tax and a sales tax.

2. Local governments will pay more attention to states and less to Washington, thereby lessening certain schizophrenic tendencies. Until a few years ago, professional "city watchers" were becoming increasingly concerned about the growing dependency of local governments on direct federal aid. They claimed that the cities were developing split personalities—legally the creatures of the state but financially the wards of the federal government.

3. Both state and local officials will become increasingly strident in their demand that a slowdown in federal categorical aid flows be compensated by federal reimbursement for all new expenditure mandates and that federal grants come with fewer strings and with a greater degree of certainty.

4. There will be considerable attention given to the problem of "decongesting" an overloaded federal aid system, especially as President Reagan's proposal for turning back programs and resources competes with the more traditional ways of reforming the federal aid system—the "sorting out" and the block grant alternatives, shown in Table 11.5.

Table 11.4. State and Local Direct General Expenditure in Relation to State Personal Income, by State and Region, Selected Years, 1942-1979: Direct General Expenditure as a Percent of Personal Income

State and Region	1979	1976	1971	1966	1957	1942
United States	19.08%	20.32%	18.86%	15.57%	11.60%	7.51%
New England						
Connecticut	15.90	15.77	16.46	12.78	11.31	5.91
Maine	21.02	21.35	20.04	15.15	12.14	7.90
Massachusetts	21.16	20.55	18.14	14.16	12.42	7.78
New Hampshire	16.82	19.68	17.63	14.98	12.83	9.46
Rhode Island	21.06	20.57	17.78	15.38	10.59	6.29
Vermont	23.28	25.44	24.91	20.16	14.34	9.07
Mideast						
Delaware	18.56	20.48	21.57	17.36	8.64	5.42
Dist. of Col..	26.80	26.38	22.47	14.06	8.90	5.08
Maryland	20.04	21.03	18.57	14.11	11.15	5.25
New Jersey	17.96	17.90	15.70	11.82	9.36	7.17
New York	23.88	26.38	22.71	16.31	11.73	8.63
Pennsylvania	17.48	18.78	17.45	13.13	9.18	7.64
Great Lakes						
Illinois	16.14	17.45	15.88	11.72	9.17	6.87
Indiana	14.63	16.00	15.56	13.56	10.07	6.88
Michigan	19.74	21.06	18.85	14.96	11.97	7.09
Ohio	16.44	17.64	14.86	13.01	9.83	6.49
Wisconsin	21.64	21.82	20.91	17.24	12.34	8.69
Plains						
Iowa	18.52	18.89	18.90	16.13	12.75	8.52
Kansas	17.91	18.42	16.96	15.28	14.80	7.46
Minnesota	21.14	23.70	21.45	17.93	14.04	9.80
Missouri	15.46	16.47	16.60	13.53	9.70	6.57
Nebraska	18.73	17.50	17.60	14.83	11.02	7.71
North Dakota	22.07	20.76	24.55	20.84	17.69	12.34
South Dakota	20.88	23.11	23.02	19.59	15.43	10.58
Southeast						
Alabama	19.54	20.28	19.97	18.04	13.38	6.86
Arkansas	18.53	18.59	18.37	17.63	12.77	6.35
Florida	17.58	18.01	17.32	16.05	12.77	8.12
Georgia	19.66	19.26	18.71	15.67	12.97	6.28
Kentucky	20.44	19.42	19.12	16.75	11.17	6.96
Louisiana	20.60	23.00	22.42	20.36	17.43	9.84
Mississippi	22.77	23.82	23.19	20.44	15.49	7.59
North Carolina	19.04	18.75	16.62	14.93	12.14	6.84
South Carolina	19.18	21.13	17.30	14.71	12.89	8.70
Tennessee	18.00	19.22	18.74	16.79	11.43	7.21
Virginia	17.81	17.91	16.61	14.64	10.84	5.13
West Virginia	21.28	21.45	21.14	17.43	9.86	9.52

Table 11.4. *(continued)*

State and Region	1979	1976	1971	1966	1957	1942
Southwest						
Arizona	21.34	21.92	20.28	20.16	14.57	8.85
New Mexico	24.46	23.81	23.18	23.45	16.20	10.13
Oklahoma	17.64	18.48	19.16	18.48	14.98	9.14
Texas	16.52	17.39	16.28	14.88	11.44	6.71
Rocky Mountain						
Colorado	19.19	21.53	19.64	19.24	13.90	9.51
Idaho	18.85	21.56	20.26	17.65	14.06	9.16
Montana	23.68	23.41	22.72	20.15	14.86	10.36
Utah	22.69	23.13	21.79	21.36	13.37	8.64
Wyoming	24.37	27.56	27.05	27.18	16.11	9.64
Far West						
California	18.83	22.06	20.86	18.41	12.67	7.21
Nevada	19.89	22.05	21.39	20.90	14.86	7.25
Oregon	22.16	23.90	20.99	18.32	13.79	8.76
Washington	20.04	19.76	22.19	16.86	13.72	8.49
Alaska	42.09	35.38	40.86	29.49	(9.05)	n.a.
Hawaii	23.09	27.62	25.79	19.95	(15.61)	n.a.

Source: ACIR, *Significant Features of Fiscal Federalism*, 1979–80 ed. (Washington, D.C.: Advisory Commission on Intergovernmental Relations, 1980), p. 13.

SUMMARY

The recent and fairly dramatic slowdown in public spending clearly reflects a significant change in public thinking. Prior to 1978, the public either tolerated or actively supported various liberal policies that caused the domestic public sector to grow at a consistently faster rate than did the private sector (Table 11.6). Now there appears to be broad support for a moderately conservative policy that would have the growth in domestic public spending either parallel or lag slightly the growth in the private economy. Prior to 1978, we were moving slowly toward this new conservative consensus. The California taxpayers' revolt and the 1980 election simply hurried history along.

The critical issue will be the effect of this slowdown on social welfare programs. A rising public sector tide carried up all the ships—even those of the poor and the powerless. The liberals contend that once the public sector reaches high tide and begins to recede, the disadvantaged groups will be the first to be stranded on the rocky shores of fiscal austerity.

Thus, the great slowdown in state-local spending will underscore the need to strike a new balance between the resurgent conservative demand for fiscal discipline and the traditional liberal concern for social compassion.

Table 11.5. Decongesting an Overloaded Federal Aid System: An Analysis of Three Alternative Strategies for Accomplishing This Decongestion Objective[a]

1.	2.	3.	4.
Decongestion Strategy	*Sorting Out*—Assigns to the federal government complete financial and administrative responsibility for all major income maintenance (including unemployment benefit) programs; freed of this financial responsibility, states would be completely responsible in other areas for which federal grants would be eliminated.	*Block Grants*—Many narrow categorical grants would be consolidated into broad functional "block" grants with most strings untied.	*Turnbacks*—Federal government eliminates selected programs and turns back not only program responsibility but also financing resources.
5. **Leading Protagonist**	6. ACIR	7. Senator Baker	8. President-Elect Reagan
9. **Instrument of Choice When...**	10. Primary objectives are also to provide more uniform benefits and fairer financing of welfare-type programs and more discretion and possible variation in areas of state-local program responsibility.	11. Primary objective is to build greater flexibility into the federal aid system while still maintaining a congressional presence in multiple program areas.	12. Primary objective is decentralization—to return both overall taxing and spending responsibilities to the states in our federal system.

	13.	14.	15.	16.
Other Advantages		If the federal government assumes complete responsibility for taking care of poor people, the states will be in a far better position to take care of their poor local governments, especially the central cities.	At least everyone's second choice.	It becomes easier to contain the growth of the domestic public sector in general and the domestic federal sector in particular.
	17.	18.	19.	20.
Sources of Opposition		Strongly opposed because (a) centralization of welfare policy in Washington, (b) the higher costs associated with leveling up of benefits, and (c) disproportionate fiscal relief to frostbelt states and California.	Block grants criticized for lacking clarity of purpose and therefore being very vulnerable to re-categorization.	Difficult to secure agreement on programs to be turned back and to solve the fiscal mismatch problem.

Source: Al Davis and John Shannon—ACIR staff (January 13, 1981).
[a]These strategies are not mutually exclusive, especially if only limited progress can be made on any one front.

Table 11.6. Government Expenditure, from Own Funds, Selected Years 1929–1980: The Dominant Federal Role in the Public Sector

Calendar Year	Total Public Sector	Federal Total	Defense	Domestic	State	Local	Exhibit: Gross National Product, Population, and Personal Income
							Amount (Billions of Current Dollars) / **GNP (In Billions)**
1929	$ 10.2	$ 2.6	$ 1.1	$ 1.5	$ 2.1	$ 5.5	$ 103.4
1939	17.4	8.9	1.5	7.4	3.7	4.8	90.8
1949	59.3	41.3	22.0	19.3	8.9	9.1	258.0
1954	97.0	69.8	47.1	22.7	12.7	14.5	366.3
1959	131.0	91.0	53.6	37.4	18.7	21.3	486.5
1964	176.3	118.2	64.0	54.2	27.3	30.8	635.7
1969	285.6	188.4	95.5	92.9	49.6	47.6	935.5
1974	458.2	299.3	105.3	194.0	85.2	73.7	1,412.9
1975	532.8	356.8	114.5	242.3	95.7	80.3	1,528.8
1976	573.9	385.0	119.7	265.3	103.4	85.5	1,702.2
1977	626.1	421.7	129.3	292.4	111.0	93.4	1,899.5
1978	686.0	459.8	139.1	320.7	124.4	101.8	2,127.6
1979 P	758.8	509.0	154.5	354.5	139.3	110.5	2,368.8
1980 est.	848.0	580.0	181.0	399.0	150.8	117.2	2,621.0
							As a Percent of GNP / **Population (000)**
1929	9.9	2.5	1.1	1.5	2.0	5.3	121,767
1939	19.2	9.8	1.7	8.1	4.1	5.3	130,880
1949	23.0	16.0	8.5	7.5	3.4	3.5	149,767
1954	26.5	19.1	12.9	6.2	3.5	4.0	163,026
1959	26.9	18.7	11.0	7.7	3.8	4.4	177,830
1964	27.7	18.6	10.1	8.5	4.3	4.8	191,889
1969	30.5	20.1	10.2	9.9	5.3	5.1	202,677
1974	32.4	21.2	7.5	13.7	6.0	5.2	211,901
1975	34.9	23.3	7.5	15.8	6.3	5.3	213,540
1976	33.7	22.6	7.0	15.6	6.1	5.0	215,152
1977	33.0	22.2	6.8	15.4	5.8	4.9	216,880
1978	32.2	21.6	6.5	15.1	5.8	4.8	218,717
1979 P	32.0	21.5	6.5	15.0	5.9	4.7	220,584
1980 est.	32.4	22.1	6.9	15.2	5.8	4.5	222,100
							Per Capita in Constant Dollars (1967 Dollars) / **Personal Income**
1929	$ 163	$ 42	$ 18	$ 24	$ 34	$ 88	$1,359
1939	320	163	28	136	68	88	1,330
1949	555	386	206	180	83	85	1,923
1954	739	532	359	173	97	110	2,196
1959	844	586	345	241	120	137	2,461
1964	989	663	359	304	153	173	2,781
1969	1,283	847	429	417	223	214	3,351

Table 11.6. *(continued)*

Calendar Year	Total Public Sector	Federal			State	Local	Exhibit: Gross National Product, Population, and Personal Income
		Total	Defense	Domestic			
1974	1,464	956	336	620	272	235	3,690
1975	1,548	1,037	333	704	278	233	3,647
1976	1,564	1,050	326	723	282	233	3,766
1977	1,591	1,071	328	743	282	237	3,891
1978	1,605	1,076	325	750	291	238	4.019
1979 P	1,580	1,060	322	738	290	230	4,007
1980 est.	1,540	1,053	329	725	274	213	3,870

Source: ACIR, *Significant Features of Fiscal Federalism,* 1979–1980 ed. (Washington, D.C.: Advisory Commission on Intergovernmental Relations, 1980), p. 4.

Chapter 12

Growing Disparity Among States in Revenues from Nonrenewable Energy Sources

Tom Cochran* and J. R. Prestidge**

National resource policy problems will continue to be among the pivotal issues facing our nation during the 1980s and 1990s. Over the past eight years the United States has attempted to come to grips with the world liquid-fuel crisis with a variety of policy responses. For example, just recently, President Reagan removed all price controls on oil, ending the phased decontrol of domestic crude oil prices and producing substantial adverse domestic economic shock effects. Decisions such as this have been forced by a world energy market monopolized by a political entity, the Organization of Petroleum Exporting Countries (OPEC). The new energy economics confronting the nation requires that the market price of energy approximate the replacement value of the consumed product. This painful short-term path is necessary both to avoid a more difficult transition to world prices as domestic sources are exhausted, and to encourage domestic production of energy.

The domestic economic repercussions of energy price decontrol are difficult to predict with precision, but it is apparent that regional effects will be profound. Energy-consuming regions of the nation will be faced with the negative consequences of energy decontrol. Individuals and firms in these regions will pay higher

*Executive Director, Northeast-Midwest Institute, Washington, D.C.
**Policy Analyst, Northeast-Midwest Institute

costs for energy without directly receiving the benefits of production-related economic activity. In a paper published in April 1980, the Northeast-Midwest Institute introduced a second and largely unanticipated result of energy decontrol: the "windfall" of vastly increased revenues flowing to major oil-producing states as a result of ad valorem energy severance taxes, royalties, and other fees applied by these states, which will produce state government surpluses in energy-producing states and an outflow of capital from the energy-consuming regions. The economies of energy-poor states, faced with escalating energy prices and unable to benefit directly from the energy production-related benefits of decontrol, will also find some of their tax revenues declining. This unanticipated result of energy decontrol will increase the regional disparity in economic growth rates that are currently "unbalancing" our national economy.

BACKGROUND

One has only to look north from the "lower forty-eight" and east from Alaska to witness a set of serious energy-related tensions threatening the Canadian federal system. These tensions are rapidly developing in our own country also. The parallels are too strong to ignore. For example:

In both countries, a small number of states (or provinces), with a relatively small share of the nation's population, control most of the nation's domestic energy resources or production, as shown in Table 12.1.

In both countries, the major producing states or provinces are endeavoring to reap the greatest possible economic or fiscal advantage from their positions as net energy exporters, although by somewhat different methods.

In both countries, the energy consuming states or provinces are more heavily industrialized and older than the energy-producing areas—and in both countries the older manufacturing regions are suffering problems of economic stagnation.

In both countries polarization between what the *National Journal* has called the energy "winners" and "losers" has been growing rapidly.

The U.S. Situation

In the United States, a strong contributing factor to new energy tensions will be the extraordinary increase in severance tax and royalty revenues derived from the extraction of oil, gas, and coal during the era of domestic price decontrol.

Table 12.1 shows that in the United States nine states are major exporters of conventional energy commodities. This table ranks states by their exporting position and reveals that there is no "generally accepted" level of severance taxation. Oil is taxed at rates ranging from 12.5 percent to 1.5 percent, gas at rates ranging from 10 percent to zero, and coal at rates ranging from 30 percent to zero.

The revenues derived from the taxation of nonrenewable energy resource extraction vary dramatically from state to state, as shown in Table 12.2. In several of these states, energy-related royalties and other fees are also very substantial, and adding these revenues to severance revenues produces even higher rates of dependence on nonrenewable energy for the support of state government expenses. The reliance upon revenues from energy nonrenewables by these states enables them to use other taxes less intensely or not at all (e.g., no personal or corporate income taxation in Texas). Oil and gas severance tax revenues had already grown substantially since the Arab oil embargo; there was an almost three-fold increase in these revenues from $710 million in 1972 to over $2 billion in 1978.[1]

However, the increases expected between 1980 and 1990—the era of domestic decontrol—will dwarf anything we have seen so far. The Treasury Department estimated in 1979 that all state and local revenue increases in this decade as the result of oil price

Table 12.1.   Energy Surplus States By Rank[a] and Tax Rates (percent of value),[b] 1978

Exporting Rank[a]	Oil Percent	Gas Percent	Coal Percent
1. Louisiana	12.5%	3.5%[b]	0.2%
2. Wyoming	4.0	4.0	10.5
3. New Mexico	7.0	5.8	8.4
4. Kentucky	1.5	n/a	4.5
5. Alaska	12.25	10.0	n/a
6. Oklahoma	7.0	7.0	0.3
7. West Virginia	4.35	8.63	3.5
8. Montana	2.1–2.65	2.65	30.5
9. Texas	4.6	7.5	n/a

Sources: [a]Chase Econometrics, cited by *National Journal*, March 22, 1980, no. 12, p. 469.
[b]Calculated by Harley T. Duncan, Staff Associate, National Governors Association, March 6, 1980. From *State Tax Collections 1978*, U.S. Bureau of Census.

Table 12.2. Severance Taxes as a Percent of State Revenues, 1978

State	Percent
Louisiana	23.55%
Wyoming	22.81
New Mexico	19.16
Kentucky	6.96
Alaska	19.13
Oklahoma	17.51
West Virginia	13.99[a]
Montana	11.95
Texas	17.68

Source: Calculated from U.S. Bureau of Census, State Tax Collections 1978[a] and state-supplied data.

decontrol alone will add up to more than $127 billion.[2] According to this estimate 90 percent of these enormous new sums of revenue will be concentrated in the eight major oil-producing states. The oil price assumptions underlying these estimates are now seen as quite conservative. No reliable estimates have yet been made concerning revenue increases resulting from the phased decontrol of natural gas. However, an estimate by one reliable analyst is that the figure will be about $50 billion—and this amount would be in addition to the $127 billion increase resulting from oil price decontrol. It must be emphasized that these are unsophisticated estimates made more than a year ago with econometric modeling techniques that did not distinguish between severance, royalty, and other forms of revenue. The Institute is now in the process of completing a more accurate projection exercise—preliminary results suggest that the Treasury estimates are of the correct order of magnitude, but may be low.

Information newly available from one major producing state certainly supports this conclusion. Alaska is the only state that has rigorously projected oil severance and royalty revenues into the future. Table 12.3 shows that estimates for oil revenues made by Alaska's Petroleum Revenue Division approach $200 billion in the next twenty years. It should be noted that these estimates relate only to proved reserves at Prudhoe Bay—yet a strong possibility exists that further fields will be opened during this period in such areas as the Beaufort Sea. Alaska currently has a population of approximately 400,000—less than the average individual U.S. Congressional District.

State revenues such as these are only a part of the extraordinary economic rent that OPEC monopoly power has created

Table 12.3.   Alaska Petroleum Revenue Estimates, by Source (Millions)

Fiscal Year	Royalties	Severance	Property Tax	Income Tax	Revenue
1981	$1,502.4	$1,183.5	$170.0	$ 770.0	$ 200.0
1982	2,354.9	1,753.3	170.0	882.9	222.2
1983	2,924.4	2,140.4	198.2	1,013.8	246.9
1984	3,431.1	2,416.8	225.3	1,165.7	274.7
1985	4,003.4	2,816.2	248.9	1,333.1	304.7
1986	4,451.8	3,130.8	271.3	1,469.1	338.5
1987	4,955.5	3,483.9	271.8	1,635.3	376.1
1988	5,482.7	3,856.7	271.4	1,809.3	417.9
1989	5,969.5	4,238.9	270.2	1,969.9	464.2
1990	6,208.5	4,418.4	267.8	2,048.8	515.8
1991	6,264.1	4,446.7	259.1	2,067.2	573.0
1992	5,976.9	4,189.0	249.5	1,972.4	636.6
1993	5,713.6	3,954.4	239.3	1,885.5	707.3
1994	5,281.5	3,581.0	228.1	1,742.9	785.8
1995	4,905.9	3,252.7	216.3	1,618.9	873.0
1996	4,595.6	2,981.0	203.7	1,516.5	969.9
1997	4,302.7	2,731.5	190.3	1,419.9	1,077.6
1998	4,029.0	2,503.6	175.9	1,329.6	1,197.2
1999	3,773.3	2,295.0	160.8	1,245.2	1,330.1
2000	3,534.2	2,104.3	144.8	1,166.3	1,477.7

Source: Alaska, Department of Revenue, Petroleum Revenue Division, *Revenue Forecast Quarterly Report* (September 1980).

These estimates also do not include any natural gas or coal revenues.

in the oil industry. With OPEC control over prices and supplies, the "market" in oil is destroyed, with resulting "windfalls" flowing to all parties engaged in oil production, or in the taxation of that production.

Canadian Comparison

In Canada, Alberta is the producer of 85 percent of the nation's oil and 90 percent of its natural gas. This province has received large increases in energy-related taxes and royalty revenues since the 1973 OPEC embargo. The Alberta Heritage Savings Trust fund, with a current balance of $6 billion, is projected to grow to $25 billion by the end of the decade.[3] This will occur despite the retention by Canada's central government of price controls on domestic oil sales.

The Canadian response to the OPEC monopoly has been markedly different from that of the United States. The National Energy

Plan (NEP) proposed by the Trudeau regime is a dramatic, controversial, and nationalistic program. It proposes a Canadianization of the domestic oil and gas industry, a large increase in federal revenues from oil and gas production, several new institutional programs to govern development and control the regional impacts of higher energy prices, and a decrease in provincial revenues and control over natural resources.

Albertan opposition of the Trudeau plan has been equally dramatic. Premier Peter Lougheed recently announced a 15 percent reduction in oil production over the next nine months as a means of retaliating for the NEP. He has also stated that Alberta will fight the NEP in the courts. Alberta is not alone in opposing portions of the NEP. Newfoundland has laid claim to the outer continential shelf areas in defiance of Ottawa. British Columbia has expressed extreme displeasure at the proposed natural gas tax contained within the NEP.

These issues in Canada and the United States deal with revenue increases resulting from energy taxation in producing states or provinces. However, there is an opposite effect of energy price decontrol as well.

Impact of Decontrol on Energy-Poor Regions

No reliable estimates have been made concerning the various revenue decreases the energy-importing states will suffer as the result of energy price decontrol, except in the area of motor fuel taxes. For example, how will the corporate income taxes of energy-importing states be affected by the higher costs of energy? Our guess is that there will likely be substantial reductions with respect to firms that buy a significant amount of energy. Already enormous cash outflows from such firms to energy-producing firms are developing, but the state revenue effects of this shift have not been projected. However, it is reasonable to assume that state government budgets in energy-consuming states will be eroded.

One organization, the Energy Action Educational Foundation, has focused on natural gas decontrol and its regional impact in the American economy. A February 1981 report by the Foundation stated that "natural gas decontrol alone will accelerate the decline of the Northeast and the Midwest, and will overwhelm any action by either the federal government or the states to prevent the erosion of the country's northern industrial base."[4]

The Foundation estimates that immediate decontrol of natural gas would drain $275 billion from the economies of 16 Northern states between 1981 and 1985, and goes on to estimate that the Texas, Louisiana, Oklahoma, and New Mexico economies will receive $493 billion in private and public benefits between 1981 and 1985 if gas decontrol is immediate. The implications of such projections for public, gas-related revenues in these states are clear.

Pending Legislation

Considerable attention is being paid by federal lawmakers to coal severance taxes. This attention is due in part to the well-organized lobbying efforts of some of the nation's electric utilities. Several members of the Ninety-sixth Congress introduced bills with many cosponsors to limit such taxes to 12.5 percent, and one of these bills was actually ready for floor action in the House when the session closed. The identical S. 178 has been introduced in the current Congress. This bill would limit severance taxation of coal production from federal and Indian land to 12.5 percent. As was noted in Table 12.1, there is enormous variation in coal severance tax rates around the country, with western coal generally taxed at high rates—with Montana being at the top of the scale—and eastern coal taxed at low rates or not taxed at all.

Pending Litigation

Two cases now pending in the U.S. Supreme Court regarding state severance taxation bear significant implications for energy-producing states' financial systems and may alter the regional economic disparities that we project if no legal or legislative interventions are made. A decision in *Commonwealth Edison, et al.* v. *The State of Montana, et al.*, Supreme Court 80–581, could either require a "testing" of existing severance taxes to determine whether or not they are valid under the Commerce Clause, or alternatively could allow existing severance tax rates to be dramatically increased without recourse for consuming states. The *State of Maryland, et al.* v. *State of Louisiana* Original No. 83, could either reduce the tax burden applied to natural gas produced from the Outer Continental Shelf (OCS), or alternatively, could allow other states to tax this resource production without fear of federal intervention.

Commonwealth Edison, et al. has challenged the imposition by Montana of a 30 percent coal severance tax on coal produced from federal leases. The intergovernmental and the interstate commerce implications of a 30 percent tax are highly significant when the "natural resource lands" are concerned. This case has produced substantial questions of law and numerous interests have filed briefs. The major points of law at issue are:

whether or not a state severance tax that burdens interstate commerce is subject to Commerce Clause scrutiny,

whether or not the rate and amount of a tax can justify its being ruled invalid under the Supremacy Clause, because it is inconsistent with the Mineral Lands Leasing Act of 1920,

whether or not the rate and amount of a tax can justify its being ruled invalid under the Supremacy Clause, because it frustrates "national energy policy" designed by the Congress, and

whether or not a state tax substantially paid by out-of-state interests violates the U.S. Constitution's Commerce Clause because the revenues exceed the financial requirements of the state to mitigate the impacts of the industry.

This case—and the numerous arguments advanced by the opposing parties—raise serious questions regarding the nation's nonrenewable-energy taxation policies. The plaintiffs and their supporters argue that the wealth gap created by OPEC monopoly power, decontrol, state energy levies, and the uneven geographic distribution of nonrenewable energy reserves have ominous implications for energy-importing regions. With domestic oil prices the same as OPEC-determined world prices, market-value–related state severance taxation reaps monopoly level revenues. This extraordinary tax burden may produce divisive and recriminatory state actions that would severely threaten interstate commerce. For example, recently enacted and under litigation at the present time are gross receipts taxes applied by New York and Connecticut to oil companies.

Neither party disputes the fact that Montana "exports" approximately 86 percent of its coal severance tax burdens and under federal law receives 90 percent of the economic rent demanded by the federal government in the form of royalty sharing and reclamation fund transfers. The central question at issue in the case is whether or not a 30 percent severance tax on production, including that from federal land, is justified or constitutes a burden on interstate commerce.

Available precedent appears at first blush to support the defendents. *Heisler* v. *Thomas Colliery*, 260 U.S. 245 (1922), a case whose foundation was laid in the 1880s in *Coe* v. *Errol*, 116 U.S.

(1886), forms the basis for the lower-court decisions currently under appeal. Relying on this case, which found that mining was a purely local concern and that the existence of a "natural monopoly" had no effect on interstate commerce, the lower courts denied the motions of the plantiffs for a trial. The narrow reliance on this 60 year-old precedent would allow energy-exporting states to impose monopoly-type taxation policies that could threaten the economic and social systems of financially strained energy-importing regions.

There is little doubt that the Commerce Clause powers can easily reach state severance taxation and regulate the application or existence of this taxation. Nonetheless, it may be that the Supreme Court will find for the defendants and throw the ball into the national legislative court by claiming that no existing statute requires court intervention.

The other energy taxation case with somewhat narrower legal implications but large dollar values at stake, Supreme Court Original No. 83, *State of Maryland et al.* v. *State of Louisiana*, challenges the imposition of a "first-use" tax on natural gas extracted from Outer Continental Shelf (OSC) land as it moves through the state on its way north by pipeline. This taxation by Louisiana of production from land owned by the federal government is under legal attack by states in the Northeast because it appears to be an attempt by Louisiana to extract revenue from a discriminatory tax. The Court's validation of this tax would add $255 million annually to natural gas prices in the Northeast and could allow other states with energy resources located on federal enclaves or OCS property to extract billions from energy consumers.

ANALYSIS

Despite all the attention paid to state coal taxes, it is important to keep in mind that the net economic impact of coal severance taxes is much smaller than the impact of either oil or gas taxes and fees. The rates on oil and gas imposed by the states are somewhat more uniform from state to state—and might appear to be more reasonable (see Table 12.1). However, because of the massive volumes of oil and gas purchased now and likely to be purchased in the future on the domestic market, together with the decontrol of domestic prices and monopoly control of world prices, the impact of oil and gas severance taxes and royalties is much greater than the impact of coal taxes.

A general concern is that the creation of a kind of "United American Emirates," a group of "superstates" with unprecedented power to beggar their neighbors in the federal system in economic and fiscal terms, will accelerate the decline of energy-poor regions and thwart efforts to revitalize the troubled economic structure of the older industrial regions.

At least three separate problem areas of a more specific nature can be identified:

1. These enormous new revenues will almost inevitably lead to powerful new location incentives for people and businesses — accelerating the massive shifts of population to these areas already taking place. In the next several years, one can expect other states to follow Alaska's lead and cut or eliminate more traditional taxes, making them even more attractive places in which to relocate. States that do not have the natural resources to tax will not be able to compete with such tactics, and will lose out.
2. Several major federal funding formulas will be distorted. Under these formulas, the energy-rich states could actually receive larger shares of federal funds — or continue receiving the same favorable shares now received — even though the actual need for these funds will be much smaller because of the new-found wealth which can be tapped by these states.
3. There is a strong possibility that a dangerously divisive tax warfare will break out, with each state striving to tax a precious commodity just to preserve its competitive position. In fact, this warfare may already have begun — Montana's state legislature passed its huge coal tax increase after a strong debate including language about the need to keep up with Texas in the severance tax business. In the mid-1970s, Pennsylvania contemplated a severance tax on electricity to be generated at mine-mouth plants and exported to other states. Connecticut and New York have passed special taxes on oil companies, although these taxes are under question in the courts. New Jersey, Pennsylvania, and other states are now looking into a tax on oil refineries. Oregon has a tax on trees — there is nothing preventing the imposition of state taxes on other crops. It should not be a surprise if agricultural states retaliated against other severance taxes by putting their own taxes on grains used in alcohol fuel production, or perhaps all grains.

In any tax warfare, the Northeast and Midwest region will be heavy losers—and so, ultimately will the whole nation, as its states and perhaps its local governments impose heavy new tax burdens on certain sectors, and become dangerously reliant on these narrow and probably regressive tax bases.

The perception in energy-consuming states is that tax burdens of severance taxes and royalties are fully "forward-shifted" to consumers and, thus, "exported" beyond the borders of the state imposing the tax. Actually, this is a more complicated question than most observers in the consuming states have acknowledged. The answer to the issue of forward-shifting lies in understanding that OPEC monopoly pricing and domestic decontrol combine to provide windfall revenue to *all* parties engaged in oil production. There is no effective supply and demand mechanism in the world oil market; OPEC controls enough incremental supply capacity to enforce its general price decisions on the entire market. Under decontrol these inflated prices will provide a layer of monopoly revenue returns from which jurisdictions imposing ad valorem taxes will reap corresponding windfalls. This economic rent does not affect price any more than any other cost of production because of the layer of monopoly revenue return already provided by OPEC pricing. However, a capital transfer does occur between energy consumers' pocketbooks and energy-producing states' treasuries, as the oil and related products are transferred domestically.[5]

The Congressional Research Service (CRS) has calculated that major oil-producing states siphon off a substantial share of the rent stream paid by consumers in importing states to energy-producing firms, as shown in Table 12.4. These calculations deal only with crude oil disposition and do not include the severance tax liability found in final oil-based products. The transfer of refined products ready for consumer use from producer states will carry the severance tax burden applied to the domestic crude from which the final product was made.

Table 12.4. Oil Severance Taxes

State	Oil Severance Tax Revenue 1979	Percentage of Oil Severance Tax Exported
Texas	$1,009,174	64%
Louisiana	453,708	79
Oklahoma	244,791	57
Alaska	173,491	85

Source: Congressional Research Service—calculations prepared at congressional request.

The exported portion of a severance tax burden carried by these final products has not been estimated; however, it would add substantially to the amounts extracted through crude oil transfers. In the absence of state severance taxation, royalties, and other fees, the price would remain the same but the windfall revenues would all flow to the producer where the Windfall Profit Tax (WPT) and corporate income taxation might reduce the capital accumulation in the oil industry in a regionally equitable fashion because they are national taxes, unlike state-applied severance taxes. Although the Northeast and Midwest regions are in a deficit position with respect to the federal revenue inflow and federal expenditure outflow relationships,[6] corporate income tax and WPT revenues are still spent in a more regionally equitable fashion than state severance tax revenues can ever be. However, partly as a result of the WPT's special treatment of state lands and severance taxes, and the existence of state-by-state severance taxation, royalty, and other policies, a significant interregional capital transfer will occur.

Related Concerns

The current policy of energy price decontrol assures that consumers will pay the approximate replacement cost for liquid fuels in the near future. However, the Congress, through the enactment of the WPT, has effectively stated that the "price floor" imposed by OPEC will distort the replacement value of energy to such a degree that a WPT and the equitable distribution of its revenues are justified. The federal government allocates its energy nonrenewable revenues to production of other nonrenewable energy commodities—coal synfuels, shale oil, etc.—and to the general fund. The same is true of federal mineral leasing revenues, which are spent on parks, recreation, historical preservation land, and water conservation and general services. Although these items may deserve support, the use of revenues from an irreplaceable energy resource to provide it seems myopic at best. The federal policy is this regard also contrasts sharply with one investment strategy of an energy-producing state, as shown in the discussion of the Alaskan experience.

One should also recognize that resource depletion in various other strategic minerals is approaching, with no consistent national policy in place. The nation as a whole faces a bewildering array of resources scarcities in the coming decades, from minerals like silver and bauxate, to foodstuffs like fish, to the resource taken for granted too long, water. The economic and national security implications of these scarcity problems demand that we develop institutions or procedures that effectively address these concerns.[7] These considerations will compel Congress to take action during the next few years despite obvious constitutional objections that any federal intervention in state taxing powers may encounter.

Policy Alternatives for the Congress

There are several possible federal policies to deal with these effects. In addition to doing nothing, the alternatives include the following options, taken singly or in any combination:

reforming the current royalty arrangements set out in federal law. The current allocation of the economic rent demanded by the federal government would be one question addressed in such an evaluation. Another should be the appropriate level of economic rent. Additionally, the question of how the present leasing of production rights affects the susceptibility of federal resource production to state taxation needs consideration;
correcting for distribution formula distortions, either through some form of omnibus legislation or through amendments to specific authorization bills;
limiting state severance taxes, royalty fees, and other rates and/ or total revenues in some fashion, or outlawing the state levies on energy nonrenewables altogether;
replacing state severance taxes and royalties with a uniform system of national severance taxes and fees, the revenues from which could be shared in some equitable fashion around the nation.

The last option deserves further elaboration, and a useful starting point may be a look at the Alaskan experience. The state government of Alaska has chosen to invest some of its energy revenues in the Alaska Renewable Resources Corporation (ARRC), a large-scale, flexible public development entity charged with taking debt and equity positions in private venture projects designed to reduce the state's dependence on energy nonrenewables and other nonrenewable natural resources. This bold experiment could be the single brightest hope for a stable, diverse Alaskan economy of the future, an economy that need not be dependent on finite supplies of fossil fuels.

Other domestic energy-producing states should also be concerned about their overdependence on revenues derived from energy nonrenewables as a fiscal tool. A recent GAO report stated:

> ...continued reliance on decreasing resources (oil) has caused little concern for diversification planning, perhaps largely because rising energy prices are stimulating the region's economy and generating increased public sector revenues.... Through appropriate oversight, the Congress can help assure that potentially severe economic dislocations in the Southwest's basic industry are anticipated in time to take mitigating actions, and thus, to preclude the need for huge federal aid expenditures in what could become a distressed area.[8]

These conclusions must have ominous implications for those states that import the oil and gas produced by Texas, Louisiana, and Oklahoma.

As noted earlier, present individual state severance taxation, under market conditions, results in a large capital transfer from energy-consuming states to energy-exporting states. These effects vastly increase the likelihood of congressional action during the 1980s. But how should the revenues of an equitable, uniform national severance tax be spent?

As a nation, perhaps we should follow Alaska's lead and give consideration to setting up a National Resources and Economic Recovery Corporation that would incorporate the current Synfuels Corporation but go far beyond its all-too-narrow charter. A National Resources Corporation could be charged with investing in the development of a wide range of renewable energy production and conservation technologies, designed to deal with a wide range of other natural resource scarcities as well. In addition, such a corporation could provide the capital necessary to revitalize basic industrial sectors and assist in the development of world-competitive new industries.

The source of capital for such a corporation could be the national uniform severance tax suggested in the final federal policy option noted earlier. There are those who will say that it is not necessary to replace state severance taxes with a national severance tax in order to finance the investments and reindustrialization. The windfall profits tax, estimated to bring in $227 billion over the next ten years, could be the source of the needed revenue. However, while that tax is in place, it seems increasingly clear that its revenues are not going to be reinvested exclusively in making the United States energy independent. The Synfuels Corporation—an enterprise about which there are an increasing number of doubts in Washington—may be the only significant use of windfall profits tax revenue for that purpose. Instead, other fiscal pressures are going to determine that WPT revenues be used for general purposes and to balance the budget. President Reagan's new-found willingness to retain the tax is perhaps the clearest signal of this fact. Also, the WPT is only temporary—its statute will end it within 10 years. Yet, a permanent, predictable method is needed of ensuring that capital created from the sale of OPEC-priced, nonrenewable energy is reinvested in ways that can preserve and enhance our independence from increasingly uncertain world resource markets.

Revenues from a permanent national severance tax could also be used in the form of general revenue sharing, with two "pots" of money. One pot could be used exclusively to hold the energy-producing states "harmless" in real dollar terms from the fiscal effects of replacing their severance taxes with a national severance tax. Thus, their tax base as of the year in which the change was made could be fully preserved. The second "pot" could be distributed under any fair formula. Since the economic rent probably is extracted from consumers, consumption patterns might be used with other data elements in this formula. This proposal is offered because it illustrates the need to find some solution that is not only fair to all parties concerned, but that at the same time seizes an opportunity to address some of the difficult problems that confront our nation. The failure to address the regional inequities created by the combination of federal energy policies and state energy severance taxation will in the words of Felix Rohatyn lead to: "Half the country nearly bankrupt, many of its major cities pools of unemployment and unrest and the other half swimming in oil, industry, and wealth. This is not the stuff of a stable democracy. It is not the stuff of a union of States."[9]

NOTES

1. National Governors' Association, Harly Duncan, Center for Policy Research, *Tables on State Oil, Natural Gas and Coal Severance Taxation,* Table V (March 6, 1980).
2. U.S. Treasury, unpublished report.
3. *Business Week* (May 26, 1980): 87.
4. *The Decontrol of Natural Gas Prices—A Price Americans Can't Afford,* Energy Action Educational Foundation (February 19, 1981), pp. V–VI.
5. Anthony Scott, *Natural Resource Revenue* (Vancouver, British Columbia, University of British Columbia Press, 1976).
6. *The Federal Balance of Payments, Regional Implications of Government Spending,* Northeast-Midwest Institute (August 1980).

7. *The Global 2000 Report to the President—Entering the Twenty-First Century* (Washington, D.C.: U.S. Government Printing Office, 1980).
8. General Accounting Office, PAD 81-09 *Long Term Planning Needed in Oil and Gas Producing States* (December 10, 1981), p. i.
9. Felix Rohatyn, *Address to the Federal City Council,* Washington, D.C., April 29, 1980.

Index

A

Advisory Commission on Intergovernmental Relations (ACIR), 48, 95; block
grants proposals of, 106, 107; governmental growth research of, 210–211; on
intergovernmental relations, 212;
revenue-sharing programs and,
215–218, 219; revenue studies of, 158,
161, 167
AFDC programs, 97–98, 99, 217
Agricultural property taxes, 51, 256
Aid programs. *See* Federal aid system;
Intergovernmental aid; *and specific
programs*
Aid to Families with Dependent
Children (AFDC), 97–98, 99, 217
Alaska: energy investment strategy of,
258, 259; energy revenues of, 249, 250;
income tax in, 158, 256; oil severance
tax in, 257-258; petroleum revenue
estimates for, 250, 251; spending in,
237
Alaska Renewable Resources
Corporation (ARRC), 259
Alberta, energy revenues in, 251
Alberta Heritage Savings Trust fund,
251

B

Birch, D. L., 180, 189
Block grants: consolidation of, 105-106,
219; constraints in use of, 13-14; costs
of projects in, 14; federal aid distribution in, 217-218; fiscal strain for cities
and, 4. *See also* Community Development Block Grants (CDBGs)
Bonds, municipal. *See* Municipal bonds

Arizona: migration to, 168; tax
limitation movement in, 23, 28, 29
Arkansas: income tax in, 122, 123;
property tax revenue in, 118; sales tax
in, 125, 126
Aronson, J. Richard, 126
Ash Council, 211
Assessment, property tax, 41–42;
complexity of, 85; historical perspective on, 41-42; homestead credits in, 71,
73; inflation and, 82-83; informal rules
developed in, 44–45; reform in, 82;
shift in tax burden to residential property and, 83; tax limitation movement
and, 50; use-value, 51, 82
Atlanta, fiscal strain in, 10

Boskin, Michael, 21
Boston: manufacturing in, 191; taxpayer revolt in, 166
Bowen, H.R., 20
Brazer, Harvey E., 19-34
Break, George, 213
Brennan, Geoffrey, 20, 30
British Columbia, 252
Brodner, David, 212
Buchanan, James, 20, 30
Budget, 205-222; Budget Reform Act of 1974 on, 206-207; causes of bloat in, 210-212; changing financial base for, 226-231; defense spending and, 226, 230; deficit policies for, 230-231, 232; federal grants as percent of, 228, 230; imbalance between Congress and President in, 209; means and ends in balancing, 206-209; presidential proposals and outcomes for, 205, 207-208; Social Security program demands on, 226-227, 229; transfer payments in, 212, 213; tripartite distinction of outlays in, 212-213
Budget Reform Act of 1974, 206-207, 208, 209
Buffalo, federal aid to, 150
Bureau of the Census: local revenue statistics from, 111, 112, 113; property tax statistics from, 48, 63
Business property: property tax on, 51; shift in tax burden from, 80-81, 83; tax exemptions for, 74, 83, 163
Butler, Stuart, 177, 178-179

C

California: financing education in, 154; income tax amendment referendum in, 28, 30; intergovernmental aid to, 217, 220; property tax levels in, 24; property values in, 158; public surveys on spending policies in, 23; residential tax base increase in, 83; revenue diversification in, 118; state surplus in, 25, 26; taxpayer revolt in, 23, 157, 170, 241 (*see also* Proposition 13); water and transportation charges in, 116
Canada: energy revenues in, 248, 251-252; National Energy Plan (NEP) of, 251-252
Capital gains: California tax limits

movement and, 26; in enterprise zones, 196-197
Capital spending: changing function of public borrowing and, 132-134, 139; fiscal strain in cities and, 14, 15
Carter administration: antirecession programs of, 92-93; budget balancing attempts of, 205, 214; intergovernmental aid during, 91, 94-95, 97, 102; General Revenue Sharing and, 99-100; targeting during, 94, 107
Census Bureau. *See* Bureau of the Census
CETA funds program, 97, 150
Circuit breakers, 66-69, 163, 170; definition of, 66; eligibility for, 66; expansion over time of benefits from, 84; as percentage of tax collections, 63; progressivity of, 85; renters under, 73; versatility of, 66-69
Cities: aid to (*see* Federal aid system; Intergovernmental aid); capital spending in, 14, 15; collective bargaining and, 14, 15; comparative indicators for management of, 15; enterprise zone revitalization of, 178; fiscal differences between suburbs and, 216-217; fiscal management in, 14, 15-16; fiscal strain in (*see* Fiscal strain); mayoral level decisions and policy of, 16; productivity improvements in, 14, 15
Citrin, Jack, 23
Clark, Terry Nichols, 3-18
Classification, 238; court rulings on, 82; definition of, 75; expansion over time of benefits from, 84; local tax yields and, 148; property tax relief with, 75-76
Cleveland, manufacturing in, 189
Coal taxes, 249, 253-254, 255
Cochran, Tom, 247-262
Coe v. *Errol*, 254-255
Collective bargaining, and fiscal strain, 14, 15, 155
Colorado: migration to, 168; tax limitation movement in, 29
Commerce Clause, and energy litigation, 253, 254, 255
Commonwealth Edison, et al. v. *The State of Montana, et al.*, 253-254
Community Development Block Grants (CDBG): cuts in federal aid to, 99, 100,

Local government revenue: administrative qualities of, 121; alternative sources of, 89-141; balancing budget in, 147-153; block grant consolidation and, 106; cash management practices in, 117; changing function of public borrowing in, 132-134; changing legal environment for financing in, 154-155; criteria in choosing new sources of, 120-122; deregulation of federal programs and, 105; diversification of, 117-118; federal aid to (see Federal aid system; Intergovernmental aid); general revenue of, 111; historical perspective on, 40-47; increase in fees and charges used by, 149-150; legal limitations in, 120-121; miscellaneous revenue in, 116-117; neutrality of revenue sources in, 121; new revenue sources for, 110-111; nonproperty tax revenue in, 112-116; property taxes in, 52-53, 62-63, 66, 76-78, 112; revenue base in, 110-126; revenue elasticity in, 121; sales tax revenue in, 113; sources of, 111, 112; stability of revenue sources in, 121; state aid to, 78, 150-151; strategies for, 110; tax-exempt borrowing purposes of, 134-135; taxpayer revolts and limits in, 164-165; total public spending as percent of, 145-146; user fees in, 116

Local taxes: income tax in, 45, 120, 122-124; increasing yield in, 147-148; indexation issues for, 166-167; limits on, 79-82, 148, 233, 238; personal property exemptions in, 75; property tax administration in, 43; property tax authority in, 42-43, 233; property tax relief in, 79-82; sales taxes in, 45, 120, 124-126, 147-148; state authority and, 42-43, 232-233, 238; tax base erosion in, 161-164; uneven impacts of tax limits in, 31

Location decision: central city manufacturing growth and, 188-190; factors affecting, 186-192; federal programs for, 176; intrametropolitan decisions on, 186-188; property taxation and, 50

Lougheed, Peter, 252

Louisiana: energy revenues in, 249, 250, 260; natural gas price decontrol and, 253; oil severance tax in, 257-258;

pending energy litigation and, 253-255; sales tax in, 126

Low-income groups: circuit breakers and, 85; equity effects of tax limits on, 32

M

Maine, tax limits in, 120

Management techniques, in budget, 211

Manufacturing, in enterprise zones, 188-190, 192

Maryland, income tax in, 122, 124

Massachusetts: future fiscal directions of, 237; municipal fiscal management in, 15; property tax levels in, 24, 166; tax limitation movement in, 23, 28-29, 157, 165

Mass transit programs, federal aid to, 98-99, 100

Maxwell, James E., 126

Mayors, and fiscal policy, 16

Measure 6 (Oregon), 27-28

Medicaid, and federal aid, 97-98, 99 103, 217

Meltzer, A., 30

Michigan, 22; circuit breakers in, 63, 66, 69, 73, 163; farm tax relief programs in, 73, 74; income tax in, 122; local nonproperty taxes in, 78; Milliken's tax proposals for, 32-33; personal income taken by property tax in, 63; personal property tax exemptions in, 75; property tax levels in, 67, 77, 78; property tax limits in, 79; property tax relief in, 68; proportion of state–local taxes collected by, 76, 77; shift in tax burden to residential property in, 80, 83; state aid distribution in, 78; tax limitation movement in, 23, 25, 28, 29, 30; voter dissatisfaction with public spending in, 22-23

Midwest: energy tax warfare in, 256, 258; natural gas price decontrol and, 252; property tax relief in, 61-87; recession and state spending in, 225; relocation of population and jobs from, 4

Migration, and fiscal pressures, 168-169

Mill, John Stuart, 21

Milliken, William G., 32-33

Milwaukee, location choices in, 188

Mineral Lands Leasing Act of 1920, 254

About the Editors

Norman Walzer earned a B.S. in business administration from Illinois State University and a Ph.D. in economics from the University of Illinois at Urbana-Champaign. Since then, he has actively researched urban poverty, housing, and public finance. For the past seven years, Professor Walzer has served as a consultant to state and local governments and as research director for a state government commission studying problems facing cities. Currently professor of economics at Western Illinois University, he has published articles in *Review of Economics and Statistics*, *Land Economics*, and *National Tax Journal*, among others.

David L. Chicoine is an assistant professor of agricultural economics at the University of Illinois at Urbana-Champaign. Prior to joining the university's faculty (on a research and Cooperative Extension Service appointment), he spent several years with the field staff of the Illinois Cooperative Extension Service and with the Northeastern Illinois Planning Commission. Professor Chicoine, who received an undergraduate degree from the South Dakota State University and advanced degrees from the University of Delaware and Western Illinois University, received a Ph.D. in agricultural economics from the University of Illinois. His current research involves taxation, local government finance, land economics, and public policy.